13.37

Other Telecom Titles From Aegis Publishing Group:

Telecom Business Opportunities
The Entrepreneur's Guide to Making Money in the Telecommunications Revolution
by Steve Rosenbush
$24.95   1-890154-04-0

How to Buy the Best Phone System
Getting Maximum Value Without Spending a Fortune
by Sondra Liburd Jordan
$9.95   1-890154-06-7

Telecom Made Easy
Money-Saving, Profit-Building Solutions for Home Businesses,
Telecommuters and Small Organizations
by June Langhoff
$19.95   0-9632790-7-6

The Business Traveler's Survival Guide
How to Get Work Done While on the Road
by June Langhoff
$9.95   1-890154-03-2

Getting the Most From Your Yellow Pages Advertising
Maximum Profits at Minimum Cost
by Barry Maher
$19.95   1-890154-05-9

1-800-Courtesy
Connecting With a Winning Telephone Image
by Terry Wildemann
$9.95   1-890154-07-5

Telecom & Networking Glossary
Understanding Communications Technology
$9.95   1-890154-09-1

Strategic Marketing in Telecommunications
How to Win Customers, Eliminate Churn, and Increase Profits in the Telecom Marketplace
by Maureen Rhemann
$39.95   1-890154-17-2

Digital Convergence
How the Merging of Computers, Communications, and Multimedia Is Transforming Our Lives
by Andy Covell
$14.95   1-890154-16-4

The Telecommuter's Advisor
Real World Solutions for Remote Workers
by June Langhoff
$14.95   1-890154-10-5

The Cell Phone Handbook
Everything You Wanted to Know About Wireless Telephony
(But Didn't Know Who or What to Ask)
by Penelope Stetz
$14.95   1-890154-12-1

Data Networking
Made Easy

The Small Business Guide to Getting Wired for Success

by

Karen Patten

Aegis Publishing Group, Ltd.
796 Aquidneck Avenue
Newport, Rhode Island
401-849-4200
www.aegisbooks.com

Library of Congress Catalog Card Number: 00-36233

Aegis Publishing Group, Ltd.
796 Aquidneck Avenue
Newport, RI 02842

International Standard Book Number: 1-890154-15-6

Printed in the United States of America.

10 9 8 7 6 5 4 3 2 1

Library of Congress Cataloging-In-Publication Data:

Patten, Karen, 1947-
    Data networking made easy: the small business guide to getting wired for success/by Karen Patten
        p. cm.
    Includes index.
    ISBN 1-890154-15-6
    1. Data transmission systems. 2. Business enterprises—Computer networks.
    I. Title.

TK5105.P385   2000
650'.0285'46—dc21   00-36233
                                                                            CIP

Acknowledgements

Writing a book is not a solo effort, especially when it's not your full-time work, and writing this book has impacted every part of my ordinary life. I'd like to thank everyone who encouraged me, and I have special thanks for some important people:

Bob Mastin, my editor and publisher—ours was truly a collaborative effort—and Dee Lanoue, for her careful editing and gentle prodding;

Jim Terracino and Jerry Fjermestad, professors, for being my mentors and creating opportunities to learn more;

My students at New Jersey Institute of Technology and the workshop participants at Bell Atlantic, whose questions forced me to find simpler explanations;

My colleagues at Bell Laboratories, for sharing years of telecommunications networking experiences as we built the telecom business within a business;

June Langhoff, my colleague at the International Telework Association and Council (ITAC), who suggested that I write this book;

Nancy Wilcox, Bud Prast, and John Prast and their families, and my sister and brothers, all of whom have always supported whatever I do;

And, finally, my patient and loving husband, Bill, who was there every day, encouraged my work, and did the extra things to keep our life on track.

Contents

Chapter 3
Real World Applications 61

Chapter 4
Planning, Installing, and Maintaining a Network 75

Chapter 7

Chapter 8

Chapter 9

Chapter 13

Part
I

Introduction

THIS BOOK IS WRITTEN PRIMARILY for those people who own, operate, or manage small businesses and organizations not yet big enough to have information technology (IT) staff or managers. You make all the technology decisions yourself, whether you want to or not. This book is written for you.

More than likely you purchased this book because you feel that your business will benefit from some sort of networking technology. Whether upgrading your current system or starting from scratch with your first local area network (LAN), use this book as your personal IT consultant. By helping you assess your needs for your specific situation, it will assist you in making the right technology choices.

This is not a do-it-yourself book for those of you who want to physically install their own LANs. (That's probably not the best use of your time and talents.) Instead, this book teaches you the language of networking vendors. A basic understanding of data networking technology will help you to weigh the merits and shortcomings of the many network options available. Then you can confidently choose the vendor that will install and support the best system for your business.

This book is also written for people who are new to the telecom/networking industry, whether newly hired employees or students in telecom or data networking courses. I have attempted to offer an overview of the many issues faced by organizations involved with designing, planning, and implementing their data networks.

In addition, readers will get a good basic understanding of tele-communications and data networking fundamentals.

I have divided this book into two parts. Part I discusses why you need to get networked and how to go about getting accomplishing this task. Part II examines the underlying technology that makes it all work. A busy manager may want to read all of Part I, but only refer to certain sections in Part II for background. A student, on the other hand, may be more interested in the fundamentals discussed in Part II.

Data networking is a relatively new technology. Although it is only a couple of decades old, it is transforming the way we work and play. The Internet, which is a huge, global network of data networks, is a good example. But there's more to it than just the Internet. The pace of technological advances has been nothing short of amazing. It wasn't all that long ago that the 300 bit-per-second modem reigned supreme. Now, network scientists are trans-mitting a trillion bits per second through one strand of fiber by using light waves. Soon, that kind of bandwidth will go directly to your desktop!

You want to be ready when that happens. In fact, you want to be ready well before that happens. Prepare now, because today's tech-nology is the foremost business tool for improving competitive-ness and efficiency—in ways you could only dream about a few years ago.

Chapter

1

Network Basics

· ·

THIS CHAPTER STARTS WITH a big-picture overview of what networks are all about. It will not go into the nitty-gritty detail of the underlying technology. Part II will do that, but in this chapter you will learn about the evolution of data networks and the general characteristics of these networks. You will become familiar with some of the terminology used to describe networks.

A network is an easy concept to grasp. Typically, it is the interconnection of several elements (known as nodes) to provide some sort of added benefit. The interstate highway system is a good example of a network that benefits us all. We use it ourselves for a variety of reasons, and we rely on it to deliver most of the goods we purchase every day.

The interstate highways are the high-speed backbones that connect the smaller networks together, ending with the local streets lined with houses or businesses—the ultimate end users (nodes) of the network. You start a journey from your driveway, which feeds into a two-lane avenue, which feeds into a four-lane highway, which might feed into a beltway that surrounds the city, which feeds into the interstate highway. If one of the routes is blocked, you can find a way around it because there are many alternate paths to your destination.

A data communications network is very similar to the highway system. Instead of transporting cars and trucks, however, a data network transports digital bits, which represent text, images, audio, video, or any combination of these. Just like the highway system, where the wider freeways and expressways can transport more vehicles at higher speeds, data networks also have high-speed "roads." These are the network backbones consisting of fiber-optic cable.

Also similar to the highway system are the bottlenecks that can occur in a network—invariably at choke points where many routes intersect. Yes, data networks also get traffic jams. Some roads are in much better shape than others, and many of the antiquated rural routes are slow and full of potholes.

Because networks are categorized in many ways, discussing them can get quite confusing. Everything has a different name based on what we're talking about: the size of the network, its purpose, the underlying technology, its physical configuration, the relationship among its parts, and the rules governing its operation. This chapter will organize this material so you can easily see how it all fits together and makes sense.

After giving you some general background about the telephone network and the evolution of data networks, much of the chapter describes these basic characteristics of the network:

> **Network size and function**—LANs, WANs, intranets, extranets
> **Direction and destination of data flow**—broadcast, multicast, simplex, duplex
> **Geometry of the network**—star, bus, mesh, ring, etc.
> **Network relationships**—client-server, peer-to-peer

Then we'll wrap up the chapter by discussing, in very general terms, the building blocks of the network and the methods used to communicate among nodes and other networks.

THE TELEPHONE NETWORK AND CIRCUIT SWITCHING

The telephone network comprises an important part of larger data networks that extend beyond the confines of the office—it's the way many data networks get linked together. Its precursor, the telegraph network, was a true data network. The telegraph simply used a different signaling system (Morse Code) than the binary digits in use today.

The telephone network has been in existence since the 1880s. Many advances were made over the years, but real improvements in performance, features, and capabilities didn't come until the network went digital. Up until the 1970s, the entire network was still mostly analog. We'll get into a detailed description of analog in Part II, but, for now, let's just remember that analog is the old-fashioned way of doing things, like using vacuum tubes instead of transistors in your stereo system.

Do you recall how bad long-distance calls were in the early 1980s? And how expensive? They were full of noise and static, broke up often, and were generally quite unreliable. The reason for these problems is that it is hard to maintain the integrity of an analog signal over any kind of distance. All kinds of heroic efforts were made by the phone companies to make the transmission as clean as possible, but the inherent limitations of analog technology were impossible to overcome.

When you talk, your voice creates sound waves that travel through the air. An analog telephone converts these sound waves into analogous electrical waves and transmits them through a wire. At the other end, another phone converts the electrical waves back into sound through a little speaker. Along the way, amplifiers are used to keep boosting the signal. However, an analog amplifier can't distinguish a good signal from noise, so it amplifies everything! Any noise on the line—atmospheric disturbances, electric motors, or faulty connections—keeps getting amplified, and the cumulative effect over a long distance will degrade the signal quite a bit.

Then along came digital. It's as though someone suddenly built the interstate highway system to replace the rutted dirt roads everyone used to travel on. Digital signals can be transmitted around the world—several times, if you like—and they do not lose their integrity. At its destination, the signal is reproduced exactly the same as when initially created. The noise found on an analog line is virtually eliminated.

Most of the backbone of the public switched telephone network (PSTN) has been changed to digital. That's why long-distance calls are so much better now. A call from Los Angeles to New York sounds the same as if you were calling the house across the street. Distance no longer matters.

However, unless you have recently upgraded to one of the new digital services, such as ISDN or DSL, the local connection between your home or office and the telephone company's backbone network is still analog. You, and everyone else, connect to the phone company's network at the central office. Each house or business has its own pair of copper wires that connect directly to the central office. A small town might have one central office, while a big city will have dozens.

The connection between you and the central office is called the local loop. The local loop is the only part of the telephone network that is still analog. We're still using slow, bumpy roads for local transportation, but from the central office on, everything is digital and very fast. This includes connections from one central office to another or from the central office to a long-distance phone company facility.

CIRCUIT SWITCHING

The public switched telephone network is a circuit-switched network. Each time you make a phone call, one dedicated circuit is reserved for the duration of the call. This is not very efficient.

To go back to our highway analogy, this would be the same as traveling from Boston to New York with an entire lane to yourself for the whole trip (conversation). For the four hours you're on the road, nobody else can use your dedicated lane, and you will never have to pass anyone because the lane has been cleared just for you.

Imagine what this would do to real traffic between two cities. At any given time, the total capacity of the "circuit-switched" highway would be only three or four cars each way! Not only would this create a traffic jam of monumental proportions, but imagine how much it would cost to reserve that dedicated lane. One solution might be to pave over everything in sight to make as many lanes as possible, but there wouldn't be enough room left to do anything else. Although the PSTN is mostly digital and very reliable, it is not very efficient in the way it uses its resources, or its "lanes."

DATA NETWORKS AND PACKET SWITCHING

Is there a better solution? Yes. It's called packet switching, and it is the method used to transmit data in digital form. It does this by splitting the data up into packets (each with its own address), which are then sent through the network to their destination.

Again, think of how our highway system operates. Each car is hauling its own load of data and knows exactly where it's going. It can share lanes with other cars, so thousands of cars can be traveling on the route between Boston and New York, all at the same time. Each car knows where it's going, and each can take a different route if the need arises, such as avoiding congestion around New Haven. Also, cars are merging onto the highway from different points along its length, and then departing the highway on hundreds of different off-ramps.

It becomes obvious that packet switching is more efficient than the circuit-switched model, and virtually all data networks are now packet switched. The Internet is the big granddaddy of packet-switched data networks, which partially explains the pricing difference between Internet services and phone services. Internet connections are inexpensive because they are so efficient.

Can voice be broken down into packets and transported over a packet-switched network? Yes, and it's being done all the time. In fact, many international calls are now sent over the Internet or over private data networks. As long as all the packets arrive at their destination in a reasonable amount of time and are reassembled in their correct sequence, there is no problem. However, problems sometimes do occur.

Out-of-sequence packets cause what is known as "jitter," while the time delay in packet delivery is called "latency." Jitter and latency are two of the big issues surrounding the transmission of voice and live video—both time-sensitive communications—over packet-switched networks. Nonetheless, it's likely that you have already spoken over a packet-switched network and didn't even know it.

Keep in mind that every form of communication—text, images, photos, voice, music, video, and multimedia—can be converted into a digital format and transmitted over a data network. Data networks have become so important precisely because they allow us to communicate anything to any location. Digital information can be manipulated, combined, transmitted, and stored in all kinds of imaginative new ways.

We are becoming a digital world. All you have to do is look at the Internet to see what's being done and where we are heading. The inexorable trend is to route all digital bits over one extremely fast and robust packet-switched data network. Though it's still a long way off, we are steadily heading in this direction.

In 1999, for the first time ever, the amount of data traffic over the PSTN surpassed the amount of voice traffic due to the vast number of people using data networks and interconnecting through the phone network. In the same year, more than 100 million people were connected to the Internet. Data is fast becoming much more important than voice. Voice is a limited communications device, requiring both parties to be present at the same time to carry on a conversation. Certainly, it has its advantages, but think about how much more you can do with data. You can transmit not only voice, but also a video of yourself speaking and an accompanying multimedia presentation of the project you're working on. The possibilities are endless and limited only by your imagination.

Depending upon whose figures you use, telecommunications is a $600 to $800 billion dollar global industry. U.S. long distance accounts for $84 billion annually, broken down as follows:

❏ $63 billion for voice, growing at 3 percent yearly
❏ $21 billion for data, growing at 30 percent yearly

Although more data passes through the network than voice, the phone companies make more money on voice, mostly due to tariffs approved by regulators in a system still based on the monopolistic foundation of the telephone industry. However, the day will come when voice too is essentially free. Carriers will make their money on value-added services, such as voice mail, enterprise messaging, caller ID, e-commerce, and services not yet invented. Note the relative growth rates for voice and data in the above figures. Data is growing ten times faster than voice.

	Telecom	Internet
Suppliers	monopolistic/oligarchic	wide open free-for-all
Growth	5%-10% per year	100% per year
Regulation	extensive	none
Innovation lead time	years	months
Type of connections	one-to-one	any-to-any
Applications	voice, fax, intra-company data	Web, email, voice, fax, video, intra- and inter-company data, multimedia, e-commerce

Table 1-1

HISTORY OF DATA COMMUNICATIONS

Data communications systems came into existence shortly after the computer became widely used in organizations. Initially, users obtained the services of the computer by walking to the computer room and submitting jobs. In those days, the computer accepted the user's job, performed its operations, and returned the results on hard copy printouts. This process was called a batch run, and it is still widely used on big mainframe computers.

As the computer became more widely adopted and relied upon in the workplace, it became inefficient for all users to walk to the computer room, submit their jobs, and return later to get the results. Consequently, computer-based terminals were built and placed in user work spaces within a building. This approach allowed the users to submit their jobs remotely from each building. Typically, the terminals were each connected to the computer by private communications lines. This concept is known as time-sharing, and it was a big step in making computer operations much more efficient.

As organizations grew, it became necessary to share the computer with other users in different buildings. However, an organization might not have the means to place wire between buildings. Perhaps they didn't own the land in between the buildings, or perhaps local building codes and zoning regulations would not permit it. The solution was to utilize the widely used telephone system to transport this traffic. Though the telephone system was designed for voice traffic, various techniques were employed to send data through the telephone system. Known as remote time-sharing, this system is a prevalent form of data communications today.

THE NEED FOR SPEED

The massive increase in the availability of inexpensive, high-speed personal computers has led to the deployment of large-scale computing networks capable of serving thousands of users spread out across the globe. Such systems permit the users to share software and databases to accomplish tasks that were once the sole province of mainframe time-share computers.

They are characterized by centrally located file servers that store the main programs and back up the PC systems. Direct communications between computers is now necessary in many wiring environments, resulting in greatly expanded requirements for high-speed digital communication channels. Many applications require extremely high-speed interconnections, and a few of them are discussed below.

Rapid access to very large databases
This application is one of the primary reasons for the presence of high-speed PCs in many offices today. Processor

speeds of 100 MHz and up are certainly not required for word-processing applications.

High-definition image transmission
These transmissions include medical images, such as X-rays, magnetic resonant images (MRIs), and computerized axial tomography (CAT) scans for intercity medical teleconferencing; high-definition TV; and three-dimensional (3D) images for robotics and next-generation surveillance and tracking systems.

Computer-to-computer communications and **internal communication within supercomputers**
In particular, there has been interest in employing optical communications within massively parallel machines.

World Wide Web communications and e-commerce
This graphics-rich environment demands speed in order to grow and progress.

Cable TV to support an increasing number of channels.

At the present time, fiber optics is the strongest candidate for achieving the communications speeds required for the above-mentioned tasks. Data rates of a trillion bits per second have been achieved in the laboratory, and practical systems with data rates in excess of one billion bits per second are being deployed by major communications carriers throughout the world. We'll talk more about this in Part II.

NETWORK CHARACTERISTICS

As I mentioned earlier, networks can be categorized in a variety of ways, and a number of different characteristics can be applied to any single network. For instance, a LAN (local area network) may have the geometrical form of a star, use a peer-to-peer relationship, and employ simplex transmission—all at the same time.

This section will attempt to present the various network characteristics in a straightforward, coherent manner. Networks may also be characterized by the transmission technologies and protocols used (such as Ethernet, token ring, SONET, or WDM) or by its switching and routing schemes (such as frame relay, SMDS, x.25, or ATM). We will save the discussion of these topics for Part II.

NETWORK SIZE AND FUNCTION

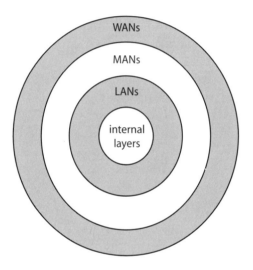

Figure 1-1

Local area networks

The first fundamental way to characterize a network is by size. Local area networks (LANs) are the smallest networks, essentially the building blocks of larger networks. A LAN will often serve a handful of users in a single location. Six people in the accounting department of a small business, for example, might share a LAN that connects their PCs to a bigger computer, called a server, which stores all the financial records of the company.

The technology that makes LANs work also limits the number of users on a single LAN and the distance between them. Nonetheless, the use of a device, such as a bridge or a router, can connect LANs to one another without any effective limitation. Each department in a company might have its own LAN, but it would also be interconnected to the LANs of all other departments. This way, someone in production can communicate with someone in personnel, and company-wide services, such as email, are provided.

	LANs	WANs
Examples	enterprise owned networks	public telephone networks
Geographical area	small areas	wide areas
Ownership	private/individual	third party/multiparty
Transmission capacity	high speed (Mbps)	low speed (kbps)
Error rate	relatively error free (environmentally controlled area)	error prone (many interconnected networks, technologies)

Table 1-2

Campus area networks

The next step in size would be a campus area network (CAN). As the name implies, a CAN would serve a group of buildings, perhaps in a college campus or in an office park. It is nothing more than a collection of LANs in various buildings. Because all the real estate is usually owned by one entity, the connection between buildings can be privately owned too. Thus, there is no need to rely on telephone company wires traveling along public roads and rights-of-way to interconnect the buildings. Many people lump CANs together with either LANs or MANs, depending on their size. We will do the same for the rest of this book.

Metropolitan area networks

The next step is the metropolitan area network (MAN). This is a network of LANs spread out over a city or a metropolitan area, connected by lines leased from the telephone company. MANs can also be connected by the PSTN's regular dial-up lines as needed. The interconnection method depends on the varying needs of the organization, such as heavy data movement or occasional use. A MAN might connect the local bank with all its branches and ATM machines located in its territory.

Wide area network

Once we decide to connect locations over long distances, we need a wide area network (WAN). A WAN can cover a region, a country, or even multiple countries. The connections are usually via leased lines from one or several long-distance telephone companies. If usage is intermittent, they can also be dial-up lines. A WAN can be a collection of its smaller cousins in any combination: LANs, CANs, or MANs.

Global networks

The largest network is a global network, such as the public switched telephone network (PSTN) or the Internet. LANs, CANs, MANs, and WANs are usually privately owned and serve specific organizations or groups. The PSTN and the Internet are also privately owned by hundreds of different telecommunications companies all over the world, but the difference is that anyone can get access by paying the required fee. Each network is interconnected, so a conversation or a data packet can traverse several different networks on its way from Denver to Dakar.

Intranets and extranets

Two other network terms relate to network size: intranets and extranets. In addition to size, however, these terms also describe the function of these networks. An intranet is usually a private, company-wide network. Whether a LAN, CAN, MAN, or WAN, it usually incorporates security measures, such as passwords and firewalls, to keep unauthorized people out. The function of an intranet is to facilitate intra-enterprise communications, such as access to databases and intra-enterprise email.

An extranet works the same as an intranet, except its a little bigger (if not in size, then in scope). It might include a group of related companies, such as a manufacturer and its suppliers and its customers. It is in their common interest to be able to communicate efficiently when conducting commerce with one another. Purchase orders, invoicing, inventory management, and many other functions are performed electronically over the network. Like the intranet, this network is protected by firewalls, passwords, and other security measures to prevent unauthorized access.

As the names imply, these networks function like the Internet, but they are much smaller. They often use off-the-shelf browsers, such as Netscape Navigator or Microsoft Explorer, and they use the same technologies as the Internet for transmitting data. Essentially, they are private, specialized versions of the Internet.

DIRECTION AND DESTINATION OF DATA FLOW

Another basic way to characterize a network is the direction and the destination of the data flow. A telephone network provides a two-way connection between two points. A television station, on the other hand, broadcasts one way in all directions from its antenna to anyone who chooses to tune in. A typical LAN can transmit in only one direction at a time. This is because a data collision will occur if two computers try to send data to each other on the same wire.

Broadcasting, multicasting, and unicasting

We have already discussed an example of broadcasting, where a TV transmitter broadcasts in all directions for anyone who tunes in the signal. Cable TV and radio also send out a one-way broadcast signal to anyone who wishes to receive the information.

Multicasting is a little different. It's still one-way, from a central source, but only to a preselected group of recipients. For example, an email newsletter is multicast once a week to the list of subscribers.

Unicast is also one way, but to only one recipient. An example would be custom news over the Internet. You can sign up for such a service and specify your interests. News bits from a variety of sources are collected accordingly and then unicast to you. You are the only recipient to get that specific transmission.

Simplex and duplex transmission

A simplex circuit is designed so that data can flow in only one direction. This is not necessarily a bad thing. Many LANs operate this way, and the data speed is very fast. For example, in a network configured in a circular shape, the data might flow in a clockwise direction only, thus preventing collisions.

A duplex circuit allows information to flow in two directions. It is further categorized as full duplex or half duplex. A full-duplex circuit allows simultaneous two-way communication. A telephone conversation is full duplex, because you can interrupt the person you're talking to. Full duplex simulates an actual face-to-face conversation.

On the other hand, half duplex allows information to flow in only one direction at a time. When talking on a CB radio, for example, you have to say "over" or "go ahead" after you finish speaking so the other party will know it's okay to speak. Many speakerphones are also half duplex, especially the ones built into inexpensive phones. Expensive teleconferencing systems, though, use full duplex to better simulate a live, interactive conversation.

GEOMETRY OF THE NETWORK

This is a really simple network characteristic—the basic shape or physical configuration of the network. Many in the industry refer to this as the topology of the network. There are several options:

Bus (or linear) topology—All nodes, or stations, are connected by a single bus. Some LANs are designed this way.

Fully connected (or mesh) topology—A network topology featuring a direct path between any two nodes. The backbone of the PSTN looks like this, where most major cities have a direct connection to most other major cities. There's plenty of redundancy and alternative routes to go around trouble spots.

Hybrid topology—A combination of any two or more network topologies. The PSTN is ultimately a hybrid network. Although the backbone is mostly a mesh network, each local loop is a star network with the central office at each hub.

Ring topology—Every node has exactly two branches connected to it, usually forming a circular shape. Some LANs are configured this way.

Star topology—All peripheral nodes are connected to a central node. Transmissions received from any peripheral node are re-broadcast to all other peripheral nodes on the network. Thus, peripheral nodes may communicate with one another by transmitting to, and receiving from, the central node only. The telephone company central office is the hub of a star network.

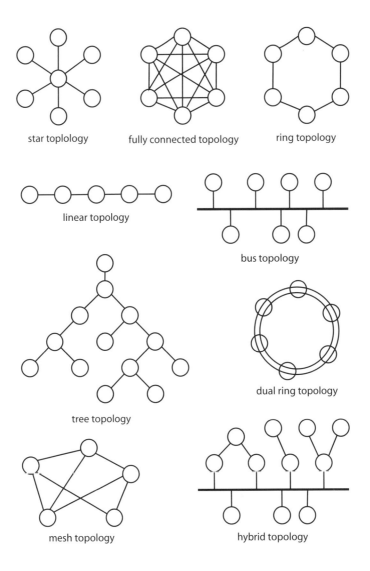

star toplology   fully connected topology   ring topology

linear topology

bus topology

tree topology

dual ring topology

mesh topology   hybrid topology

Figure 1-2

Tree topology—From a purely topological viewpoint, this network resembles an interconnection of star networks. Individual peripheral nodes must transmit to and receive from one other node only, toward a central node.

NETWORK RELATIONSHIPS

Another basic characteristic of networks is how the various nodes, or users, relate to one another. An arrangement where a powerful central computer serves many less-powerful terminals or PCs is called a client-server network. A collection of equal computers is called a peer-to-peer network.

Client-server networks

Many communications processes today are organized around a client-server model. We talked earlier about the central computer and its remote terminals that used time-sharing to get tasks done. This was an early client-server model.

A server isn't necessarily a big mainframe computer (although it can be). It is often a specialized PC with a bigger hard drive, and it is designated to perform a specific role in the organization. The server usually acts as a central storage facility for any organization files that need to be accessed, worked on, or updated by multiple clients on the network. In this way, everyone has access to the same up-to-date data.

The server can also hold software application programs, such as word processing programs, so that updates to the software can be made more easily. Only one computer needs updating rather than all the client computers. Because only one central computer is involved, this arrangement also makes backups and security easier to implement.

Personal computers and workstations (actually, any type of machine) operate as clients. These clients communicate over a network to a server. The client's responsibility is to formulate a simple request for the server to perform. In turn, the server performs the operation and sends a reply back to the client.

This request/reply concept is imbedded into most client-server networks that provide functions such as file services, database services, electronic mail services, terminal services, and the like. The client-server approach is widely used in local area networks, where diskless workstations access servers to obtain application software, files, and electronic mail. A request/reply dialogue is always used, and the request is always initiated by the client.

Peer-to-peer networks

Many LANs are peer-to-peer networks, meaning every node, or computer, has equal status. Thus, each node can transmit or receive data at any time without first getting clearance from a central control node. If your small business does not require database access for many different people, you may get away with a peer-to-peer network. In fact, some attributes of a client-server network can even be emulated in a peer-to-peer network.

For example, one of the computers in a peer-to-peer network can be designated as the file server, and all accounting files, say, would be stored on that computer only. Several computers on the network may have the QuickBooks accounting software installed, and they all can work on the same accounting files located on the designated "server." In this manner, the one computer storing the files is the only one that needs to be backed up periodically. This yields some of the benefits of a formal client-server network without its complexity.

NETWORK ELEMENTS

Network elements is the catchall term used for everything that makes up the network. Included are all the components for network operatiion: the hardware, the software, and the signaling methods used to transmit the data. Most of this book is about these network elements. This is the nitty gritty, nuts-and-bolts part of the network.

HARDWARE

The hardware involved in a network is potentially quite extensive, ranging from computers, network interface cards, and modems to switches, hubs, and routers to fiber-optic cables, microwave transmitters, and even satellites. And everything else in between. A lot of very expensive hardware goes into a large network. We'll talk a lot more about all the hardware components that make up a data network in Part II of this book.

SOFTWARE

Most of the devices in a network are fairly "intelligent," meaning they have their own processors and electronics, but they need software to tell them what to do. There is software for LANs, for routers, for client-server networks, and for virtually everything the network does to transmit data. You have probably heard of two of the more popular LAN software packages: Novell's NetWare and Microsoft's Windows NT.

SIGNALING METHODS

This is one of the more complicated subjects concerning networks. It refers to the technology used to encode, transmit, and then decode the data on its way through the network.

Although a data network is all digital, it doesn't use the same signaling methods from end to end. Signaling starts with the computer, which uses a constant stream of bits to communicate internally among its processor, RAM, and hard drive. The computer doesn't have to coordinate its communication with any outside sources, so it isn't too concerned about conforming to any rigid communication rules.

Once the data leaves the computer, however, it needs to be in a form capable of being transmitted to another computer and subsequently deciphered into an understandable format. Communication protocols are used for this purpose. Protocols are the rules for communication or the agreed-upon language that will be employed. There are often several options to choose from, in the same way that English, German, or French can be used between two people who speak these languages.

At the smallest network level, LANs have their own protocols, such as Ethernet and token ring. These are simple, fast protocols that are ideal for small networks covering short distances. If the data needs to move across country, however, other protocols must be used once the data departs the LAN. These come in many shapes and flavors, and they are designed to cram a lot of data into one pipe for long-distance transmission.

Many private networks are built around a specific signaling protocol, such as frame relay. For example, the Internet uses Internet protocol (IP), and the PSTN uses asynchronous transfer mode (ATM) in its backbone. A given packet of data can undergo several "protocol conversions" on its way through the network. This is because the data may go through several networks built by different companies using different signaling protocols. In the United States alone, we have long-distance networks owned by AT&T, MCI WordCom, Sprint, Williams Communications, Qwest, Frontier, IXC Communications, and Level 3, to name just a few. Though all the networks don't operate the same way, they are smart enough to convert the protocols as data passes from the edge of one network to another.

Chapter

2

Why Do You Need a Data Network?

YOU ARE READING THIS BOOK BECAUSE you recognize how important it is to get your business networked. Whether you are starting from scratch or improving on what you already have, you must get networked just to stay in the game. The very survival of your business is at stake. Because your competitors are networked, you cannot afford to be left behind.

In your imagination, go back to the 1880s when telephones were just being introduced. It didn't take long for them to become a standard business tool. Now imagine what happened to those companies that were reluctant to embrace this newfangled technology. Their competitors—those that installed the first business phones— got a big head start and snatched business away from the laggards.

Technology offers businesses the same scenario today. Laggards will get trampled in the stampede as virtually the entire business world rushes to adopt this networking technology. It will happen. The only question is how fast.

Data networking is such an important technology because it changes the entire basis of how we work and interact with one another. Our society is physically designed around geographic constraints. We work in office buildings so we can be near our supervisors, coworkers, and subordinates. We live in a nearby apartment complex, townhouse, or suburban house so that the daily commute is manageable. The physical evolution of our cities and surrounding suburbs is almost entirely based on how we work. Indeed, the design of rapid transit systems, roads, transportation hubs, and product distribution facilities are all based on the need for geographic proximity.

The automobile certainly spread us out a bit. We moved from dense urban centers to live a bit further out in the countryside, but beltways, commuter trains, cookie-cutter housing developments, shopping malls, and traffic gridlock were the inevitable result. Still, most of us "went to work" every day, and most of us still do. All that may very well change.

Networks allow us to redesign—from the ground up—the way we work and interact. They unshackle us from the need for physical proximity, and we no longer need face-to-face contact. Of course, we have been able to talk to others remotely via telephone for more than a century, but only recently has long-distance communication become clear and inexpensive.

But, networks allow us to do so much more. We can see the other person via videoconferencing, and it won't be too long before every PC is equipped with a little video camera and videoconferencing software. Two people on opposite coasts can work simultaneously on the same document by using groupware. Other special remote-access software allows us to work on our office PC while on the road or telecommuting from home.

All kinds of files can be transferred as email attachments—text, spreadsheets, drawings, X-rays, music, voice recordings, and video clips—and offices can now get along with fewer pieces of hardware

Keep in mind that when we talk about networks, it's not always the Internet. Yes, the Internet is the granddaddy of data networks, but many businesses have their own private networks, too. These networks operate in much the same way as the Internet—only smaller and more secure. Companies use them to help run their business in ways we'll talk about later in this book.

because networks allow multiple workers to share printers, fax machines, and scanners. In addition, we can make purchases from our suppliers or process orders from customers over a network. It's called e-commerce, and we all know what a huge trend it is becoming.

The removal of geographic constraints has created a fundamental change in the way we can do business. A company in Seattle can hire talented workers living in Miami. A small company based in Phoenix can sell to customers scattered around the globe. You can communicate with key suppliers located in Munich, Manchuria, or Monrovia. Geographic proximity is no longer an issue. Now, connectivity to the network is the overriding concern.

Instead of worrying about your proximity to downtown or to the nearest interstate, the issue is one of bandwidth accessibility—what kind of telecommunications services are available at your work location. This will be a critical issue over the next decade, as fiber-optic, high-speed wireless, and enhanced copper cable networks are built, all competing for your business. Urban areas and their surrounding suburbs will be the first to benefit simply because they are the most cost effective to serve—they have a higher concentration of people per mile of cable.

Don't despair, however, if you want to run your business from a ski resort in New Hampshire. The Telecommunications Act of 1996 deregulated all telecommunications services, including local service, which is the most common way to connect to any off-premises network, such as the Internet or a private WAN. The telecommunications industry is not yet truly competitive, but progress is being made. Larger service providers might bypass rural areas for now, but there are scores of small entrepreneurial start-ups that are happy to do business in rural areas. These businesses are not encumbered with ponderous bureaucracies and antiquated equipment. They are lean and mean, and they are installing all the latest technology. That's a direct benefit for you.

We are in a new world of competitive networking. The unrelenting introduction of ever newer networking technologies is helping to drive the trend. The results are faster data speeds and more powerful business tools than we could possibly have imagined a decade ago. Data networking has helped to unleash the collective imaginations of millions of entrepreneurs who are all designing new ways to innovate and do business over the network. Much of this movement has been spurred by the deregulation of the telephone industry and the evolution of the Internet.

Companies large and small need telecommunications to perform such basic functions as:

✓ Sharing information with customers, fellow employees, and vendors
✓ Marketing your company's products and services
✓ Maintaining control of dispersed operations (as if everyone was in one location)
✓ Sharing limited resources, including everything from large mainframe computer systems to fax machines, printers, and other peripherals

Any company already using various telecommunications tools also needs a network to integrate voice, data, and video, whether within their buildings on LANs or between their buildings over WANs. They need to expand their networks to reach more customers, build critical relationships with different vendors, and keep in touch with technological changes and new business tools. Think of how electronic commerce can revolutionize business by offering new ways to reach customers, mine markets, improve customer support, and lower costs.

All this raises important issues, however. What about security? Customer privacy? Fraud? Businesses and consumers will not fully embrace e-commerce until these issues are adequately addressed to their satisfaction. I believe, though, that the same new technology that came up with e-commerce opportunities will also find workable solutions to its problems. There are more talented people working on solutions than there are hackers and crooks trying to take advantage of weaknesses. Billions of dollars are at stake, and

I'm sure the people with the money have no intention of losing these battles.

The more we update networks and add new capabilities, the harder these networks are to manage. Can we enhance the networks and, at the same time, make them easier to manage, more flexible, and less expensive? Or it this a pipe dream? One thing is certain today. Whether you are the largest corporation in the world or a mom-and-pop shop based in your garage, every business is facing these same challenges.

The small business market numbers millions worldwide, and there are tremendous opportunities available for these companies to interconnect and share knowledge. Small businesses will benefit by forming alliances for the purpose of pooling resources in areas such as training, market research, or sales support.

COMPETITIVE ADVANTAGES

This chapter describes ways to use your existing telecommunications tools plus emerging data communication and Internet tools to provide your company with a competitive advantage. However, that competitive advantage must be built on your own business strategy. Not every business needs every new technology tool, bell, or whistle that comes along, but you do need at least some of the basic telecommunications technology tools to survive, grow your business, and increase your profits. Data networks in some form will surely be among those core tools, just as the basic telephone has been for over a century.

Many small businesses have been successful because they concentrated on a small piece of the business: providing excellent customer service; offering the lowest prices on products and services; offering specialized products and services to a narrow customer base; or providing convenient and easy-to-use products and services.

You may be one of these successful businesses or you may be just starting out. Either way, most of you are familiar with the basic telecommunications tools of business—telephones, fax machines, answering machines, pagers, and even cellular phones. Imagine try-ing to conduct your business without any of these tools.

Most of you have also ventured into the computer market and are using computers for numerous purposes. Many of you already use computer communications tools, such as email and electronic file transfers. By coordinating all the various telecommunications tools of your business and connecting them together, you can form a comprehensive tool that is much more powerful than the sum of its parts. Networks will do this for you and make your business more successful in the process.

GLOBAL REACH

We have seen how the Internet has made distance immaterial. As recently as ten years ago, how often would you communicate with someone in a foreign country? If you're with a small domestic com-pany, maybe never. Now, assuming you have email, how often do you hear from foreign companies offering their services? If you haven't yet, you will soon. The Internet has compressed the world into one cyber community. International commerce is blossoming as a result. My publisher gets email all the time from typesetters, translators, distributors, and even administrative assistants from places like India, Hungary, Russia, and Argentina. He reports that the prices are very competitive.

Size doesn't matter anymore. Everyone can look equally impres-sive on the Internet. Your Web page can be your virtual storefront in the world, and anyone with an Internet connection can shop in your store. You can describe your products, publish your sales terms, give up-to-the-minute inventory levels, and even show a video clip of how to use your product.

Tens of millions of people worldwide are going online every year. It's a market that's growing incredibly fast. Courier services, such as Federal Express, Airborne Express, UPS, and DHL, have also proliferated, making it easy for companies to ship or receive prod-ucts to or from anywhere in the world. The world is getting a lot smaller.

Strategic planning involves determining how a new technology or new product will help your business be more competitive. There are four separate business strategies that use telecommunications technologies to gain a competitive advantage:

Low-cost leadership—Low-cost leadership refers to your making products and services as price-competitive as possible, while maintaining quality and added value for the customer. For example, technology can be used to reduce customer transaction time during order processing. Savings the business may realize could be passed along to the customer. Another example is just-in-time delivery, which reduces inventory costs.

Focusing on a market niche—This strategy involves selecting a special submarket that may be overlooked or underserved by the competition. Telecommunications technology can help you identify unique customer needs or changes in the marketplace via surveys or data mining.

Developing product or service differentiation—Differentiating products and services from your competitors can be achieved with telecommunications technology. For example, you can improve customer service through the use of toll-free numbers or computer telephony integration (CTI) systems.

Making critical links with partners—Getting connected to vendors and customers can create strategic competitive advantages by streamlining your communications and interaction with such key organizations.

No longer does a company have to be a multinational conglomerate in order to have a presence overseas. Anyone with a Web site automatically has a global presence. That's a potential market of six billion people! Here in the U.S. we have an added advantage due to the fact that English has become the de facto language of international commerce. Most people using the Internet expect to use English. Nonetheless, if you have a big potential market in Latin America, by all means offer a Spanish version of your Web site. (Now you can even hire a translator based in Ecuador to do the work.) The Internet makes it easy to conduct business globally.

One of the most powerful uses of the Internet is email. Its primary advantages is that it's asynchronous in nature. In other words, the two parties do not have to communicate back and forth simultaneously as in a telephone conversation. Schedules need not be coordinated, and the time need not be mutually convenient. It's much like sending a letter or leaving voice mail messages. You perform your end of the communication on your schedule, at your convenience.

However, it's so much faster than a letter (nearly instantaneous), and it's much more powerful than voice mail. You can attach files containing text, graphics, photographs, audio, video, and anything else that can be digitized, which now includes virtually all media. You can even simulate voice mail by attaching a recording of your voice, or better yet, a video clip of yourself talking. I guess we'd call it video messaging, and it won't be long before it becomes as common as voice mail.

Think about what all this means. There isn't any type of information that cannot be digitized and then transmitted, instantly, to any place in the world. For the cost of an Internet connection, you are now able to have close working relationships with people or companies anywhere on the globe. Unbridled, spontaneous communication is now a given, not a luxury. All geographic barriers have been eliminated, and technological barriers are falling fast as networks get more powerful and more connected. There are thousands of very smart, imaginative people out there coming up with new applications for this network, from unified messaging to database management to business tools we can't yet envision.

LEVEL THE PLAYING FIELD

The Internet takes away many of the advantages of being big. With nothing more than a Web site, a tiny one-person company can have a global presence. Using email, he or she can communicate with anyone, anywhere, at any time. In fact, being small can be a decided advantage in many fast-moving industries where adapting to technological change can make or break a company. Small businesses are nimble. They are capable of both adapting quickly to changes and seizing opportunities in the marketplace.

Data networks are already being used extensively by big businesses. They understand the importance of networks, and they have the staff and resources to plan, build, and manage them. Up to now, networks have been complicated and required highly trained people to manage them. Now, however, a small business can manage its various locations by piggybacking onto the Internet to create a wide area network. Even private networks are simpler and less expensive today, and these trends will continue as more competitors enter the fray. Many of the new, start-up network service providers are small businesses themselves, and they understand your needs in ways that big service providers cannot.

This is a boon to small business. Tiny companies can now compete with their gargantuan rivals. Empowered by networks, virtual companies can be formed through strategic alliances, outsourcing, and a dispersed workforce. Many of the sophisticated, expensive business tools that heretofore were previously available only to big business are now off-the-shelf computer peripherals or software that anyone can purchase at Radio Shack or Office Max. The small business doesn't need an information technology department or a telecommunications manager. This book, plus the help desk at your ISP or network service provider, could very well be enough, though I recommend taking advantage of the many seminars currently offered.

The bottom line is that networks and the applications that ride on them are extremely powerful business tools. Regardless of financial resources or technical know-how, these tools are now available to any business.

ATTRACT BETTER EMPLOYEES

A networked business can attract employees from a much larger pool of qualified people. You can post job openings on the Internet and potentially hire people who live anywhere in the world. Many people now tap into the company's network from a home-based office and telecommute to work several days a week. This may be an acceptable trade-off for an occasional longer driving commute.

Being able to telecommute may be the only way some people would accept a position, particularly working parents with children at home. Highly qualified, desirable job prospects increasingly dictate many of the terms of their employment, and being able to work from locations away from the main office may be one of them. Companies lacking the networking technology to accommodate the best people will lose them to competitors. This is a serious disadvantage in a tight job market, such as the one we experienced through the late 1990s.

GAIN NEW CAPABILITIES

Networks give us tools we didn't have before. We can teleconference with a geographically dispersed group of people, saving travel time and expense. We can telecommute from home or work remotely from virtually anywhere, tethered by the network to the main office and all of its databases, information, and support. We can collaborate and conduct research with people on other continents—in real time. We can be much more responsive to our customers, giving them access to information and support services that would be impossible otherwise.

We can embrace e-commerce and customize products for markets consisting of only one person. The term coined for this concept is mass customization. Dell Computer is a good example of a company that has leveraged this technique. Nearly every PC sold through its Web site is customized to order. The individual gets exactly the product he or she wants. There is no need to spend extra for unnecessary features and no need to sacrifice any of the features you really need. The Web and e-commerce have empowered the individual. In today's highly competitive market, the vendor who best satisfies the customer's needs will win.

The advent of computer-aided manufacturing equipment has enabled small manufacturing plants to customize their products and deliver them as efficiently as their larger rivals. In addition, the Internet provides a wealth of information to service-based businesses. Examples include Lexis-Nexis, Dunn & Bradstreet, Electric Library, and Commerce Clearing House's Business Owner's Toolkit. Doctors, accountants, writers, and consultants no longer need to purchase their own reference books or resources, as much of this information is now available online.

Technology makes it easier to work from home, saving both a commute as well as office rent. Although no one knows with certainty how many people are running businesses from their homes, estimates range from 5.6 million to 30.7 million. Some predict that as much as half of the work force may be involved in full- or part-time home-based businesses by 2003. Some 44 percent of new businesses started in the U.S. in 1996 were home based. They included:

Construction	19,194
Cleaning services	4,238
Retail store	3,707
Consultant	11,078
Designer	9,279
Computer services & repair	7,899
Real estate	7,749
Painter	6,600
Lawn maintenance	6,320
Arts & crafts	6,139
Landscape contractor	6,136
Automotive services & repair	5,173
Building contractor	5,167
Management & business consulting	5,117
Marketing programs and services	5,090
Trucking	5,043
Wholesale trade, nondurable goods	4,956
Communications consultant	4,949
Restaurant	4,801
Audio-visual production services	4,792

In 1998, the Internet was involved with an estimated $1.7 billion in sales according to a PricewaterhouseCoopers Consumer Technology Survey. However, 78 percent of all the online sales were business-to-business transactions between small and medium-sized companies. Clearly, the early adopters of e-commerce are those companies most likely to sell their own products and services online, and it makes sense that they would buy and sell to other like-minded companies.

Nonetheless, the Internet can be an effective sales and marketing tool. Not even half the population has easy access to PCs, let alone fast Internet connections, but the rate of adoption has been faster than any other earlier technology. It took decades for TV and VCRs to reach every home. In comparison, the Internet is being tapped into at a breakneck pace that is measured in months, not years.

• •

The Web is unique and needs its own marketing strategy. The rules that work for other marketing channels are not likely to work here. As you develop an Internet marketing strategy, some things to keep in mind are:

Online customers are comparison shoppers who will change vendors based on the best price or the newest features. Customer loyalty is not a given.

The Internet is not a "broadcast-to-many" medium, such as newspapers, television commercials, or direct mail. The Web offers a degree of customer intimacy and interaction that is profoundly unique, allowing for mass customization. Customers can create their own product or service packages.

This interaction yields valuable information about your customers—their habits, their preferences, and their demographic profiles. Such information can be put to use in developing strategies to increase business from existing customers or to win back business from former customers.

• •

IMPROVE PRODUCTIVITY AND EFFICIENCY

We have already discussed some of the ways networks improve productivity. Indeed, virtually all of the advantages of networks eventually boil down to better productivity. More is accomplished using fewer resources. Networks make workers more efficient, so the company doesn't need to employ as many. Computers, databases, printers, fax machines, and software can be shared, so less equipment needs to be purchased. Travel can be cut down, saving time and money, and repetitive processes can be automated, thereby minimizing duplication.

Companies use networks and the information systems that ride over them to:

- ✓ Increase sales by meeting customer's demands and knowing exactly what the customers want and when
- ✓ Reduce costs by maintaining low inventory levels and knowing what the customers want and when. Inventories are also kept low through electronic communications with suppliers resulting in "just-in-time" inventories
- ✓ Increase the quality of products through better research, planning, design, and quality control
- ✓ Create alliances with suppliers to design special products and deliver them quickly
- ✓ Reduce costs by optimizing production flow, thereby knowing when and where products are needed at every point in the process
- ✓ Increase productivity by electronically tracking employee performance

Surveys by Datamation over the past several years have determined that the most important role of information systems is to support organizations in their attempt to:

- ❐ Increase productivity (reduce cost, increase effectiveness)

❏ Improve quality
❏ Create competitive advantage
❏ Attain the company's strategy
❏ Reorganize and reengineer
❏ Make better and more effective decisions
❏ Respond quickly to both customer needs and
   changes in the business or its environment
❏ Access a wealth of information
❏ Improve creativity and innovation

DATA MINING

Data mining is a relatively new business tool that has been made possible by data networks. All customer information can be kept in one central database, or data warehouse, which is accessible to everyone on the network. Such demographic information as address, education, and family would be included as well as the customer's order history or calls to the help desk (plus the problem's resolution). You would know how he found out about you in the first place because you would know which advertisement or mailing initially pulled him, and you would know his preferences and buying habits.

Although this information is entered only once, different people on the network do the actual data entry. Accounting updates payment and credit status, while sales updates orders and address changes. When a customer calls in with a problem, the service rep has ready access to all the necessary information and further updates the record with the results of the current interaction. Every department updates the master record in the same way, so there is little duplication of effort and everyone benefits from the resulting efficiency.

In addition to keeping all customer information centralized in one place, it is now possible to manipulate this information by using sophisticated statistical analysis techniques. You can learn a great deal about your customers and their behavior in this way.

For example, a cellular telephone company can identify those customers who are most likely to switch to a competitor within a given period of time, and then target them with a special marketing effort to retain them. You can find out who the best prospects are for an upgraded service offering, ascertain exactly what they want, and then design a product and a marketing campaign tailored precisely for this group. The result is a lot more sales for the marketing dollar.

Data mining would be impossible without networks, especially in companies with multiple buildings or geographic locations. The beauty of this tool is that no matter where the data originated, it can be accessed by many different dispersed users. Each of these users then applies their own methods to analyze and interpret the data for their own specific purposes.

DO MORE WITH FEWER EMPLOYEES

Technology is driving productivity. The booming economy of the 1990s (essentially free of inflation) was a direct result of productivity increases made possible by technology. Computers and robots can perform mundane and repetitive tasks that were formerly done by two or three people. Thus, humans are freed to do the more creative and critical work.

In addition to keeping wages down, having machines perform the drudgery allows people to do more interesting and challenging work. This improves morale, motivation, and hopefully retention. Furthermore, the shortage of skilled labor makes it imperative that companies large and small make do with fewer employees. They have little choice in the matter.

The Bureau of Labor Statistics reports that 26 percent of the civilian labor force is now working flexible hours, compared to only 15 percent in 1991. Another 20 million or so telecommute one or more days a week. The key is not so much where or when an employee does his work, but that it gets done. The small business owner can benefit from better-quality work being done by better-quality employees, but she also needs to learn how to direct and manage a workforce that works anywhere, anytime.

This flexible work style means that there is no fixed time or place when employees are dedicated to the job. New methods for measuring performance need to be developed. Such methods will be based on results rather than time spent in a particular place. The old familiar workplace model—the 9-to-5 job in an urban office tower—is being displaced by a more fluid, flexible model, unhindered by time or place.

Share Resources and Peripherals

The ability to share resources is one of the more obvious benefits of networks. A half dozen workers can connect their PCs to a LAN and share one printer, one scanner, one tape backup system, and one outside connection, whether to the Internet or to another LAN in a building across town.

Networked computers do not need to be as powerful as stand-alone computers that perform all business functions. Hard drives can be smaller, and there is no need for a modem or a tape backup system. Expensive software can reside on the server for the use of everyone on the network. In addition, software fixes and upgrades are much easier to install because the task is only done once.

Save Money

Sharing peripherals is an obvious money saver, but there are additional benefits to having a network. The installation and maintenance of shared devices and software is easier because it's centralized in one place. From the perspective of the overall enterprise, a network is simpler to manage than a bunch of independent PCs. Redundancy of effort can be minimized because there is one network management environment and uniform communications procedures and resources.

Encourage Innovation

Networks permit people to interact more readily and informally. Dispersed workgroups can be quickly assembled for specific projects and then disbanded when the goals are achieved. Networks allow people to simulate a small-business environment of informality and spontaneity. This is a good model for big organizations to follow.

Smaller companies can make decisions quickly, partly because company owners are more accessible and partly because these companies offer more opportunity for individual expression. Putting an idea into action in big companies means filing formal proposals, preparing research reports, and attending too many meetings. A good idea could die before it has a chance to take off.

According to one expert, the attitude in big companies is to say "no" more often than "yes," whereas the attitude in smaller companies tends to be "let's try it." This innovative spirit frequently gives small businesses a competitive advantage.

Consequently, big companies are now trying to stimulate innovation by acting like smaller firms. Some are dividing their companies into smaller work units, while others, such as AT&T, DuPont, Motorola, and Hewlett-Packard, are nurturing *intrapreneurs*— people who create innovation within a large organization. Of course, corporate intrapreneurs often face giant stumbling blocks within these large organizations. Burdened by traditional corporate cultures, their innovative spirit can be smothered by strict reporting requirements and formal procedures.

Small businesses already have an inherent entrepreneurial advantage over their behemoth counterparts. Getting networked only furthers this advantage. Maybe we can liken the advent of networks and information technology to the ice age. It killed off the dinosaurs, but the furry little mammals were quick to adapt and came through just fine.

WHY YOU NEED TO KNOW ABOUT NETWORKS

Why should you be proactive and learn about your own networks? What if the person who planned or installed what you currently have leaves tomorrow? Such an event would be more than just a nuisance—your business could grind to a halt. Think of your network as the circulation system that keeps your company alive. Cutting off a segment of the network is similar to an amputation—you may survive, but you'll be seriously impaired. Here's a list of things you need to know:

❐ If the system crashes, what should be done first?
❐ Who do I call if a piece of equipment stops working?
❐ How do all the pieces of equipment (servers, PCs, printers, etc.) get connected?
❐ What passwords do I need for what systems?
❐ Where are the tutorials for all the software systems?

Here's what you can do to keep things from falling apart:

✓ Draw up a freelance contract and write it down
✓ Make a preemptive strike and draft a disaster plan
✓ Refine employment contracts and define specific responsibilities
✓ Use well-known systems with plenty of support
✓ Train a backup person
✓ Build a talent list
✓ Buy through an established, reputable VAR (value-added reseller)
✓ Create an apprentice system

You need to learn everything you can about networks—what they can do, what configurations are available, and how they work. They're too important to your business to have only superficial knowledge of their capabilities. Networks are one of the most important and useful business tools available to you, and you need to get the most out of yours. You are likely quite conversant about the specifications and features of your business computers, vehicles, telephones, and other critical assets. Networks are just as important, if not more so.

You will talk to many networking vendors as you plan to upgrade or install your network. You need to speak their language, so you can evaluate the relative merits of a 100BaseT Ethernet LAN versus a 16 Mbps token ring LAN. You must understand the capabilities and limitations of all the options available to you.

Six months after reading this book, when the time comes to actually start making selections and decisions, you may not remember all the facts. But you *will* remember reading about the technologies being discussed, and you'll know where to go for answers.

• •

OVERCOMING TECH ANXIETY
Learn one new software tool, such as a new communications tool, each week.

Read one article each week that discusses the various aspects of communications technology.

Read one book per month relating to technology.

Find out what your clients and customers are doing with technology. Can you link in with them? Can they link with you? Also, find out what your competition is doing. Focus on what seems to work especially well.

Consider subscribing to technical publications, such as *Home Office Computing*, *Computer Reseller News*, *PC Magazine*, or *InformationWeek*.

Pay attention to what is going on locally, especially technology trade shows and exhibitions.

Designate one night per week to spend two hours learning about technology.

Always remember that there are many people who were once less comfortable with technology than you are, and they have all been able to master communications technologies.

• •

Chapter

3

Real World Applications

BUSINESSES ARE NOT ALL THE SAME, nor do they have the same need for business networking. Different industries have very different needs for communications networking. This chapter describes how small businesses are using data and communications networking. Some of the applications are unique to the individual industries, while others can be applied across industries. Some may even give you ideas that can be adapted to fit your own business needs.

New technology should be implemented only if it enables the company to achieve critical business solutions. Every company can take advantage of the experience of other companies that have already deployed common industry applications, such as computer telephony integration (CTI), electronic data interexchange (EDI), teleworking, teleconferencing, and intranet applications.

To develop competitive applications, managers need to understand the unique business needs within individual industries. These applications end up changing the way companies do business. Examples include ATMs and online banking services, or advances in distance learning and electronic courses. Another example involves the shortage of diagnosticians in the medical field and their need to share critical resources. Medical alliances can now be formed by interconnecting through the newest networking technologies. Once the applications are understood, managers can begin to plan the proper implementation of a technology.

Retrieving and distributing information is critical to most businesses. In the past, telecommunications managers used proprietary solutions, unique applications, and single vendors. Today, however, the backbone telecommunications infrastructure must support a broad range of applications. This means that telecommunications networks must support the interconnection of data networks, efficient telephone communications, and computer telephony integration, as well as the integration of voice, data, video, and multimedia services.

Choosing the right network solution is not easy. The first step is to understand the customer's use of the technology—their business applications. If the right relationships are established, the customer defines his needs and the telecommunications manager turns those needs into technical requirements. Thus, the right technologies can be designed and implemented for the right applications.

The best applications must be business solutions. Don't acquire technology—acquire business solutions. Businesses are always finding new ways to solve problems or exploit opportunities through technology. Sometimes, to get the best results, we must consider reengineering processes. New technologies, such as the World Wide Web, allow us to reach and interact with customers in entirely new ways. We must adapt to a totally new customer relationship.

Alternative technologies require managers to be aware of choices available to them, analyze trade-offs between those choices, and, finally, understand the long-term impact of any possible solutions. The value of a technology is measured by its contribution to the firm's business objectives. For example, consider the control of dispersed operations:

Scenario 1—Mail out sales data tapes once a week to headquarters.
Scenario 2—Transmit all data as batch files each night over a dial-up connection.
Scenario 3—Capture and transmit data to headquarters in real time over a dedicated leased line.

There is no correct choice here. Your decision will depend on how important and time sensitive the information is to the particular company. A fast-moving technology company in a highly competitive industry, such as a cell phone manufacturer, will need scenario three, while a stodgy manufacturer of lamp posts can get by with scenario one.

TWO LANs ARE BETTER THAN ONE

Data Reproductions Corporation, a printing company in Auburn Hills, Michigan, has 130 employees and two LANs. Both networks use a protocol known as 100BaseT, or Fast Ethernet, which operates at 100 Mbps. They need this speed to transfer big graphics files without bogging down the network. In fact, that is the reason they use two networks: one for production and graphics and one for everything else, including accounting, sales, purchasing, estimating, and all other general business activities. The huge graphics files stay on the production network and do not interfere with the data flow on the general business network.

There are about 40 computers on the general network, mostly IBM-compatible PCs, and one dual-processor server. The graphics network consists of six Macintosh computers, two PCs, and one server (IBM compatible). It also has various peripheral devices such as scanners, printers, and imagesetters. The film used in the printing process is output from the networked imagesetter.

Although the technology exists to connect the newer printing presses to the network, it is rarely done when graphics files are not generated in-house. Data Reproductions specializes in printing books and must deal with computer files from hundreds of customers. According to the general manager, Doug Beauvais, it's too risky to directly network the printing presses. There are still too many inconsistencies among different desktop publishing programs. On the other hand, magazine publishers often network the printing presses because they have in-house control of the entire process.

NETWORK APPLICATIONS COMMON TO ALL INDUSTRIES

Certain data networking applications are common to most businesses, and they are continually evolving as new technologies become available. Some of the more common applications enabled by data networks include:

- ❐ Service bureaus
- ❐ Computer telephony integration (CTI)
- ❐ Electronic data interexchange (EDI)
- ❐ Teleworking
- ❐ Audio, video, and multimedia teleconferencing
- ❐ Intranets and extranets
- ❐ Electronic commerce

SERVICE BUREAUS

Service bureaus were an early example of how companies outsourced management information services (MIS). By sharing pooled access with other firms, smaller companies got access to large IBM or Control Data mainframes. Initially, the procedures were fairly low-tech, and the customer had to physically visit the service bureau to bring in data forms and then collect the printouts. Later, the customer could use dial-up and leased telephone lines to access these services. Data networking streamlined the process and allowed companies to access service bureaus in remote cities.

Service providers include Boeing Computer Services (BCS) and Computer Services Corporation (CSC). The cost of this type of service includes a fixed monthly fee plus variable charges for processing, storage, and program use. This is a good way for a small company to get access to the power of a mainframe computer without incurring the considerable expense of buying and maintaining one. Basically, it's a cost-effective pay-as-you-go system.

COMPUTER TELEPHONY INTEGRATION

CTI combines the switching of the telephone network with the data storage and decision-making ability of the computer. Using a

COUNTING BEANS OVER A T1 LINE

Rooney, Plotkin & Willey LLP is a regional accounting and management consulting firm with offices in Providence and Newport, Rhode Island. A staff of about forty people is divided between the two offices. Each office has its own LAN, using Ethernet protocol and Novell NetWare, and they are connected through a T1 line leased from Bell Atlantic.

The T1 line is divided into 18 voice channels and the equivalent of six channels, or 384 kbps, for data. According to MIS manager, Ron Torio, they are planning to reconfigure the T1 for 768 Kbps (12 channels) of data and 12 voice channels. The reason for this change is that the Providence office is getting a high-speed DSL connection to the Internet. Therefore, the Internet access of the Newport office will be limited to the speed of the connection between the two offices, soon to be doubled to 768 Kbps.

Although the company does not have an intranet, it does have an internal email system. Because so much work must be done in the field, often from the offices of clients, all accounting staff are equipped with powerful notebook computers. When they're back in the office, they connect to the LAN by using a PCMCIA card and an RJ-45 modular jack.

Each office has its own file server that is backed up daily. Staff in the Providence office can access files stored in the Newport office, and vice versa. Each office also has a CD-ROM tower, which holds the Commerce Clearing House (CCH) tax library, tax forms, and tax laws and regulations. Anyone on the network can access this information when conducting tax research.

One of the principals, Dave Rooney, telecommutes for part of the year from his home office in Florida. He uses Symantec's pcAnywhere software to access the computer located in his office. He gets around the firewall by using encryption and the software's callback security feature. This technology allows him to spend some of the cold, New England winter weeks in warmer surroundings.

All of the computers on the network use Windows 95/98, and users simply navigate the network by using Windows Explorer and Network Neighborhood. Anyone familiar with Windows can quickly learn their way around the network.

telephone network feature, such as caller ID or automatic number identification (ANI) to identify the telephone number of the caller, the computer matches the incoming call with the customer record in the database. If the record is available, it is displayed on the customer service representative's (CSR) computer screen at the same time he or she answers the call. This is also called a "screen pop."

Screen pops save a lot of time. In addition to having a complete record of the customer's history with the company, the need to enter routine information, such as name and address, is eliminated. The earliest adopters of CTI were catalog companies and travel agencies for use in their telemarketing services and call centers. Initially, managers cost-justified the service because of the time saved when agents did not have to retype information to access the customer's records.

Over the years CTI has become ever more sophisticated, and it is now becoming a sales and marketing tool as well. For example, based on the customer's demographics and order history, recommended upgrades or new purchases will automatically appear on the screen for the CSR to suggest to the customer.

ELECTRONIC DOCUMENT INTEREXCHANGE
Electronic document interexchange (EDI) standards, as specified by the American National Standards Institute (ANSI 12.31), provide rules for the creation, sending, and reception of standardized business communications messages. EDI is used for customs forms,

commercial invoices, insurance forms, purchase orders, bills of lading, banking forms, and other documents commonly used in commerce. It offers several benefits to companies that put it into effect:

- ❏ Better service to customers
- ❏ Greater accuracy, fewer errors
- ❏ Faster access to electronically stored data
- ❏ Lower costs from reduced overhead
- ❏ Faster delivery of products
- ❏ Better cash flow from faster billing/payment cycles

EDI "documents" are transmitted via an extranet that links a company with its suppliers and customers. Repetitive information relating to ordering, invoicing, shipping, and receiving are all essentially automatic and very efficient.

TELEWORKING

In 1997, more than 14 million employees were using telecommunications to work away from the office at least one day a week. Some were mobile workers who had full-time offices away from the traditional workplace. At the end of 1999, this number had grown to more than 20 million.

Improving technology has accelerated the trend. The need to telework existed years ago, but only in the last five years has technology evolved to the point where companies are able to successfully implement formal teleworking programs.

In our information age, knowledge workers do not always have to be in the same place as their colleagues. Most of the time they're sitting in front of a monitor working on a PC. This setup can be located virtually anywhere, as long as it's properly linked to the main office.

Teleworking has evolved over the years. According to June Langhoff, author of *The Telecommuter's Advisor*, the first telecommuter was the president of a Boston bank. It was only

1877 when he strung a phone line from his downtown office to his Somerville, Massachusetts home. After that, the technology didn't really improve significantly until the early 1980s when the telephone network started going digital. However, it is deregulation and competition that are now driving technological advances at a rapid clip.

The way people work has changed in other ways, too. Flextime was the first stage of transition. It referred to varying the hours when employees were expected to come into the workplace. The next stage was flexplace, where workers can choose their work environment.

Not all workers are able to work away from the traditional workplace, though. Nor can all work be done away from the traditional workplace. (You can't very well assemble automobiles outside of the factory.) The goal, however, should be "the right work by the right employee in the right place."

The advantages of teleworking extend to the organization, the individual employee, and the community. Benefits to the organization include:

✓ Better employee morale and retention
✓ Wider pool of potential employees
✓ More talented employees available
✓ Less brick-and-mortar space needed (lower rent)
✓ Better productivity

Employees enjoy the following advantages and benefits:

✓ Less distractions from coworkers
✓ Less time commuting and traveling
✓ More time for family, friends, and recreation
✓ Less money spent on transportation
✓ Less money spent on clothes
✓ More options on where to live

The community is also benefitted in the following ways:

✓ Less traffic congestion
✓ Less air pollution
✓ Less new investment in transportation infrastructure (such as roads, bridges, mass transit)
✓ Better conservation of limited resources (fuel, asphalt, concrete, steel)
✓ Better community design and development (less auto-centric, more pedestrian-friendly)

Remote access speeds

The key to successful teleworking lies in the employee's ability to remotely access the corporate telecommunications and data networks. The ultimate goal is to have the exact same capabilities remotely that are available in the employee's workplace. Current reality, however, falls somewhat short of this goal because different telecommunications technologies have different capabilities.

Also, the technology needs to be available. Newer technologies, such as digital subscriber line (DSL) and cable modems, have greater access speeds, but they are either not universally available or not yet standardized.

The table below illustrates the amount of time it takes to transfer a 10 Megabyte (80,000,000 bits) file using different access technologies.

10 Megabyte File Transfer

Technology	modem	ISDN	T1	ADSL	cable modem
Speed	28.8 kbps	128 kbps	1.54 Mbps	2.0* Mbps	8.0* Mbps
Time	46 min.	10 min.	52 sec.	40 sec.	10 sec.
* Although the technology is capable of this speed, and even higher, typical service offerings will vary, with higher prices for higher speeds.					

Table 3-1

TELECONFERENCING, VIDEOCONFERENCING, AND BEYOND

Interactive meetings among two or more people can be conducted over a distance via teleconferencing or videoconferencing systems or services. Teleconferencing is an audio-only technology that allows the group to talk to one another as if they were in the same room. The better systems are full duplex and allow for simultaneous two-way conversation (including interruptions).

Videoconferencing adds video to the teleconference, so the parties can see the people they are talking to. These can be simple PC-based systems with miniature cameras mounted on the computer monitor or sophisticated conference room systems costing tens of thousands of dollars.

Five Stages of Videoconferencing		
	Number of People	Bandwidth Required
Broadcast	1 to many (unlimited)	45 Mbps
Executive (top quality)	5-20/room	1.54 Mbps
Group	10-15/room	384 kbps
Huddle	2-4/room	384 kbps
Desktop	1/room	128 kbps

Table 3-2

As telecommunications technology improves, telecommunications managers can begin to offer a family of services that uses different technology. For example, videoconferencing is becoming a common application in the legal industry for remote arraignments, depositions, and testimony.

Multimedia collaboration adds even more capabilities. Two or more people can now not only talk to one another and see one another, but they can also work on the same project together by sharing the computer software. For example, while collaborating on a paper, employees can all work on the same word processing document, one writing while the others edit particular passages. It's like having everyone huddled around the same monitor, but each has his own keyboard.

INTRANETS AND EXTRANETS

An intranet is like a mini, private Internet—it looks the same and works the same. The main difference is that it's private, centered around the company's LANs, and protected from outsiders by a firewall, passwords, or other security measures. An extranet works the same way, except it includes outside companies, such as suppliers or customers. Because it is in everyone's interest to facilitate unhindered electronic communications, these companies are allowed past the firewall.

An intranet, whether well-planned or poorly planned, affects a company's operation, efficiency, development, and culture. An intranet greatly impacts the distribution of the company's internal information throughout the enterprise. It is also key when planning for remote access by teleworkers or outsiders.

The key benefit of an intranet is universal communications: anyone can communicate with anyone else, anywhere within the company. These communications include much more than text-based email. Also included are audio clips, videos, images, photos, and multimedia.

Employees can access information about their 401K retirement accounts or find out how much vacation time they have accumulated. A salesperson can find out how much inventory is available for a hot-selling item, and the personnel department can post internal job openings. All of the information resources of the company are instantly available to those who need them in a universal format that everyone can understand and use.

Intranets are very reliable. The public Internet uses proven technology that is robust and dependable. It also uses standard, universally adopted protocols that work with off-the-shelf equipment. Intranets use the same equipment and the same protocols. There is no need to reinvent the wheel here, and costs are kept down, especially when compared to proprietary networks.

Unified messaging

Unified messaging is an important feature of many intranets and extranets. The goal of unified messaging is to give any communications device (phone, fax, pager, PC) access to a single "in-box," which contains all your email, voice mail, fax mail, and pager messages. An increasingly mobile workforce needs to be able to access this in-box through wireless devices, as well as through standard retrieval means.

A new service from some Internet companies allows callers to dial a toll-free or local number and leave messages or fax documents. The voice messages are then converted into audio files, and the fax messages are converted into graphical images. Both types of messages are transmitted to subscribers as email attachments.

For example, a company in New York can have a local number in Los Angeles and avoid paying long-distance phone bills by emailing all messages to New York. A few Web companies are offering these services for free in exchange for the advertising they expect to receive. Telephone companies are also starting to offer these services as part of their wired and wireless phone services.

ELECTRONIC COMMERCE

We are all witnessing the phenomenal growth of e-commerce. It is finding its way into every type of business and industry. From home-based, mom-and-pop operations to multinational conglomerates, nearly everyone is dabbling in e-commerce. Some firms, such as Amazon.com, eBay, and eToys, started out as Web-based businesses with no physical storefronts. However, thousands and thousands of more conventional retailers have taken note and are catching up fast. Pretty soon everyone will have a Web page and a virtual storefront.

Today you can purchase virtually anything on the Internet: cars, vacations, plane tickets, CDs, medicine, toys, wine, clothing, furniture, TVs, or anything else you might need. E-commerce changes everything. Not only do shoppers get unparalleled choice, variety, and convenience, but they also get the best bargains available.

When you're selling over the Web, you're competing with everyone else in your industry. Competition really heats up, and you can no longer command high prices simply because you have a superior location in the mall. The Web levels the playing field so that all vendors have equal footing. You must differentiate your company and its products in other ways besides price.

Another fundamental change is the elimination of the middleman. The entire product distribution system is changing. We no longer need intermediaries, such as jobbers, distributors, agents, wholesalers, or even retailers, to help get goods and services from manufacturers to consumers. Manufacturers can now sell directly to their end users.

By using an interactive format that facilitates a seamless transaction, the Internet puts the manufacturer or the supplier in direct contact with the customer. This money saved is passed along to the consumers. You can buy custom computers directly from Dell, or you can book your bed-and-breakfast getaway weekend on the Web (at www.bedandbreakfast.com), without using a travel agent.

If you are a middleman, it's time to rethink your business plan and adjust to the new realities of the e-marketplace. If you don't adapt and add value to your role in the transaction, you just may become superfluous.

Chapter

4

Planning, Installing, and Maintaining a Network

. . . .

IMPLEMENTING A NEW COMMUNICATIONS plan may be as simple as calling a service provider or as complex as instituting a multiple-stage program using a variety of vendors. It all depends on your specific needs and the time frame required for installation. A small business installing or upgrading a LAN will not go through an involved, formal process. You figure out what you need and you buy it. But it's not always that simple.

First, you must figure out what your needs are, at least in a general way. How many computers and peripherals will be connected, and where are they located? What kind of speed is required? Is a central server—one that can be centrally managed and backed up—necessary? Should the telephone system be upgraded and integrated into the network as well?

Before you start trying to answer these questions, you will want to get an idea of what is possible. There may be technologies and capabilities out there that you're not even aware of. Hopefully, that's one of the reasons you're reading this book. Find out what can be done and then fine tune your wish list.

Next, talk to vendors and get an idea of the costs involved. Do this before you establish a budget, because budgeting cannot be done in a vacuum. Every technology decision is a trade-off and requires its own cost-benefit analysis. If you come across a new technology that will cost $50,000 to implement but will likely earn an extra $100,000 in the first year, it doesn't take a financial genius to conclude that this investment should be budgeted into the mix.

The planning is truly an iterative process. It goes from needs assessment to evaluating options (discovering new technology) to cost-benefit analysis (what makes money?) and back to needs assessment again. However, each time around, the needs will have been restated based on what you've learned in the previous phases. You may discover that you want to buy a lot more, or a lot less, technology than you first thought.

For those of you who want to pursue a more formal approach to your planning, you can try something that worked for me at Bell Labs. Based on my experiences as a telecommunications manager, I've developed a few simple assessment techniques that ensure everything is considered (and nothing is forgotten) when planning and installing new technology.

The method I developed makes sure that decisions affecting one aspect of telecommunications management do not adversely affect other parts. It also acts as a guide for weighing the impact of critical issues prior to the installation of new or emerging technologies. This chapter shows you how to use this simple method to choose the right solutions for your business needs.

When planning for the implementation of new technology, most project managers do very well managing the design and installation. But they often forget to consider how the new systems will affect ongoing operations: Who will manage the technology? Are new personnel needed and, if so, is additional training required? How will the end customer make changes once the new technology is operational? Are new processes needed? How will the new services or products be financed? Will the new service be able to support itself financially as part of the family of telecommunications products and services, or will it need to be subsidized by other products and services?

The best examples come from real life, so I'll share one of my experiences that involved the planning and implementing of ISDN technology. In the late 1980s, I was the manager of Strategic Technology Planning at Bell Labs, which was the research and development arm of AT&T. The basic function of my department was to support the equipment side of AT&T's business (now Lucent), which was involved in designing switches and transmission equipment for both the long-distance and local network service providers, our ultimate customers.

However, because I was the overall project manager for deploying ISDN throughout Bell Labs, my "customers" were the Bell Labs employees themselves, primarily the scientists and the engineers. As inventors of all this new technology, it made sense for us at Bell Labs to "practice what we preach," and implement it ourselves first. Therefore, ours was one of the first major ISDN deployments in the country.

At that time, Bell Labs employed approximately 22,000 people in 14 different locations, mostly in central New Jersey and Illinois. Additional facilities were located in Massachusetts, Colorado, Georgia, California, and a few other places. Because we operated in several different states, I had to coordinate with various local telephone companies. (Yes, even AT&T has to go through the local service provider for phone service.) Some of them had to be dragged kicking and screaming into ISDN deployment, but they were eventually convinced that it would be best to use Bell Labs as a guinea pig before offering ISDN to others.

The main reason for adopting ISDN, however, was to move the entire organization from its analog world to the new digital world. By bringing digital voice and data to every desktop, emloyees were given a valuable tool that enabled them do their jobs more effectively. The digital data capability was particularly valuable for engineers and scientists.

Although this example uses ISDN deployment, the planning model I developed can be used for implementing any type of technology—a new LAN, an intranet with a new enterprise messaging system, or computer telephony integration (CTI) in your call center. In fact, this planning model was subsequently adopted for the implementation of all new technologies within Bell Labs. It also doesn't matter what size business you have. Admittedly, Bell Labs is a large organization, but this approach works equally well for any small business.

TECHNOLOGY PLANNING AND IMPLEMENTATION TECHNIQUES

The analysis of the initial impact of ISDN implementation on Bell Labs can be described by using my telecommunications implementation model (see Table 4-1 below).

Telecommunications Implementation Model

Impact on Management Functions:	Technology Implementation Phase		
	Planning	Design & Installation	Operations
Organization			
Customer			
Financial			

Table 4-1

Evaluating the impact of ISDN on our existing management functions fell into three broad categories:

Organization—We considered the organization of the business to include personnel and physical facilities, products and services, and our company's internal business processes.

Customer—In Bell Labs' case, customer service initiatives included interactions with our customers (Bell Labs scientists and engineers) and the changing nature of their needs. This function included both improving customer satisfaction and marketing the products and services of the Telecommunications Services Center.

Financial—The financial management function referred to the economic analysis and business case processes we used to demonstrate the soundness of our technical decisions. Financial management also includes forecasting, budgeting, and spending activities. At the very least, everyone involved in the process needed to consider the business impact of the change.

A small business also needs to address the impact in these areas to anticipate what will happen when new technology is added to its network. What changes will be necessary in your organization its strategy, structure, and management processes? How will the migration to a new technology affect interactions with your customer or delivery of service? And, finally, how will such a change affect the financial strategy and well-being of the company?

The implementation activities for any technology project are divided into the three traditional project management phases: (1) planning, (2) design and installation, and (3) operations, administration, and maintenance phases (OA&M). Typically, project management specialists concentrate on the design and installation activities, while site operations personnel concentrate on the day-to-day OA&M activities.

My telecommunications implementation model is designed to make sure the technology project manager also considers the organizational concerns and financial strategies of the business, plus the changing nature of customer needs. It also helps managers to integrate the management functions with the design, installation, and day-to-day operations of the new technology.

PLANNING FOR ISDN DEPLOYMENT

The planning phase for the migration to ISDN technology included evaluating the impact of ISDN on the internal business, on customer service initiatives, and on the initial cost-benefit justification for deploying ISDN. In general, during the planning phase for ISDN, customer interaction was significantly affected, while organizational and financial functions were only marginally affected.

ORGANIZATIONAL IMPACT

ISDN planning affected three components of our organization: (1) strategic business planning, (2) the technical networks and services evolution plan, and (3) our internal organizational structure (personnel and facilities). The first part of this planning process required an understanding of ISDN and its technical capabilities. Next, ISDN's effect on existing and planned telecommunications products and services was determined, and then this analysis was shared with key employees and managers. The ISDN implementation strategy considered long-range technology planning as well.

The decision to migrate to ISDN was based on a traditional ISDN business case process that defined the scope of the project, its cost effectiveness, and its justification. Key objectives included:

- ✓ Applying integrated voice, data, and imaging services
- ✓ Enhancing telecommunications voice services
- ✓ Making ISDN services cost effective
- ✓ Positioning customers for future transparent telecommunications

Our annual business plan specified requirements for obtaining the necessary resources for ISDN and presented an action plan for all products and services within the Telecommunications Services Center, including ISDN services. Capital and expense dollars for the ongoing ISDN implementation were budgeted each year as part of the annual business planning process. In addition, we developed an ISDN service delivery plan that identified the project management, customer account management, and operations processes that were impacted by the ISDN implementation.

Defining the impact of ISDN technology on our organization enabled us to adapt it to the special needs and expectations of our business and employees. These adaptations of the new technology greatly facilitated its use by our customers—the Bell Labs scientists and engineers—and helped us develop stronger relationships with them both during and after the ISDN implementation. Additionally, we used our experiences to help develop implementation processes for other companies, encourage development of new ISDN applications development, and provide feedback to the ISDN technology developers, engineers, and service providers.

Managing the migration to any new technology is generally handled in phases. Only the first phase of our ISDN installation is covered in this chapter. The full deployment took place over three years. From a cost-benefit view, the initial installation must be cost effective. Therefore, the first phase concentrated on offering basic services for basic customer applications. Enhanced capabilities and sophisticated customer applications would be rolled out in later phases.

Customer Service Initiatives

During preliminary ISDN planning, we recognized that our role as telecommunications support specialists had to change. Previously, we had simply responded to employees requesting help with their telephone or PC, but now we needed to involve them in the planning process. ISDN provided many new features, and we needed to know which employees needed which features and capabilities. We also had to anticipate future needs. This type of specific planning was essential for designing the initial ISDN installation.

In any business, the success of a new technology depends on how well the employees are able to use it. The value of ISDN technology in our organization had to be defined in terms of the end user. Employees wanted to know not only how the technology would be used, but also what kind of training would be provided and what specific benefits to expect for their individual jobs.

The initial phase of our ISDN deployment included only basic ISDN feature packages. During planning meetings with employees, however, it became clear that their needs were greater than the basic packages and technical provisioning capabilities of the ISDN service provider (in our case, the local exchange carriers in the various regions). These needs, identified but not met in the initial phase, became the enhanced features and capabilities included in the second phase of our ISDN deployment.

The capacity of a technology service provider or a product supplier to meet your needs becomes an important financial consideration. To get the best prices, a long-term service contract may be required. Obviously, such a commitment needs to be considered in your cost-benefit study.

Finally, because ISDN deployment was moving us from an analog to a digital environment, we needed to come up with new typical user configurations. We also had to develop a system for identifying each employee's needed features and applications. All this had to be completed before the business case analysis. Although we used to do this part of the design during the installation stage, we recognized that these new configurations could change substantially if too much time elapsed between planning and installation.

FINANCIAL IMPLICATIONS

The ISDN financial planning included an ISDN economic analysis, a customer cost-benefit analysis, and capital and expense budgeting. An economic analysis with the ISDN business case examined alternative ISDN scenarios linking the strategic and tactical planning to the service delivery phases of design, installation, and operations.

We chose ISDN because of its potential to provide cost reduction and improved productivity from the new digital features. The replacement of electronic key capabilities, the ease of administration and maintenance, and the upgrade of the premises distribution systems in each location resulted in lower costs in the long term.

ISDN DESIGN AND IMPLEMENTATION

The design and installation stage is considered to be the project management stage. As the new technology was installed, it became part of the total system of telecommunications tools.

ORGANIZATIONAL IMPACT

Because of the significant changes to telecommunications tools from the ISDN implementation, the support people developed new roles and responsibilities. It also required changes in other products and services and in the administrative systems for processing service orders.

From the preliminary design decisions, the purchasing and project implementation schedules must be made. The existing network and hardware inventory tracking systems were upgraded to include ISDN features and equipment. The support people also attended training sessions to learn to operate and manage the new systems, including voice messaging and electronic directory.

CUSTOMER SERVICE INITIATIVES

Employee product education and training was conducted prior to the installation. However, we learned that it's a good idea to do this training within a week of the installation so that the employees don't forget it. With ISDN, the station equipment is different. The features are different. The operation is different. Some employees are anxious to use the newest "bells and whistles." Others are content to use the same old standby equipment. You can often have the service provider develop training programs or tools for your employees to help make the transition as stress free as possible.

In the analog world, end users either have dial tone or they do not. In the world of ISDN, acceptable service goes way beyond dial tone. Are the feature configurations right? Are the features operating correctly? If there's trouble, is it station equipment or the wiring? Or is it the LEC central office? We negotiated formal acceptance agreements with our service provider to ensure that the ISDN features were installed correctly and were operating as expected. This increased attention on how employees will use the technology and the technology service performance resulted in favorable reactions to the new ISDN service from the end users.

FINANCIAL IMPLICATIONS

Because funds had to be budgeted and available, we actually started buying equipment and services during the implementation phase. Digital service was more expensive than straight analog service, but the enhancements and the new tools more than made up for the expense in the form of improved performance and better productivity.

ISDN OPERATIONS, ADMINISTRATION, AND MAINTENANCE

In our experience, the organizational and customer service functions were significantly affected by the conversion to ISDN. Other than the addition of ISDN products, features, and equipment to the inventory and chargeback systems, the impact of ISDN services on ongoing financial systems was slight.

ORGANIZATIONAL IMPACT

Once ISDN was implemented, we needed technical consultants to work with employees and suppliers to develop new and enhanced ISDN applications on an ongoing basis. These consultants also played a key role in planning the second phase of our ISDN deployment project. Site operations personnel needed to have the knowledge to support the desk terminals, the location distribution system, and the ISDN lines.

CUSTOMER SERVICE INITIATIVES

Once deployed, new features and applications were developed to leverage the installed technology. After all, one of the primary benefits of ISDN was the improved productivity. This was the big payoff for installing the technology in the first place.

FINANCIAL IMPLICATIONS

Also, once deployed, costs were real and employee cooperation helped keep ISDN features and applications as cost effective as possible. We developed a new financial process, a "budgeting tracking system," to keep track of the ISDN cash flows and the actual spending for ISDN projects.

SUMMARY OF ISDN MIGRATION

Table 4-2 summarizes the impact of the migration to ISDN technology on our telecommunications management functions during the three main stages of implementation.

Telecommunications Implementation Model

Impact on Management Functions:	Technology Implementation Phase		
	Planning	Design & Installation	Operations
Organization	some	significant	significant
Customer	significant	significant	significant
Financial	some	some	little

Table 4-2

ISDN service was a major component of the overall technical migration strategy for Bell Labs. Its implementation had significant impact during the design and installation stages. We created new jobs to perform the various design and installation functions, and new administrative and operational systems were required for service order provisioning, change management, and so on.

By carefully managing the migration to ISDN technology and using the techniques described above, we successfully integrated our strategic plans with our technical evolution to state-of-the-art telecommunications products and services. New end user interaction processes ensured that the perspective of these users was clearly understood, and improved management processes resulted in better service to the end user. The migration to ISDN technology continued with the implementation of enhanced ISDN applications.

The planning and implementation process outlined in this chapter can be applied to the adoption of any new telecommunications technology. Keep in mind that careful planning is supremely important because telecommunications is such a vital part of any business strategy.

✓ Telecommunications, properly utilized, can give your company a competitive advantage.

✓ Telecommunications, like MIS, is vital to the conduct of business.

✓ Telecommunications allows decentralization of the decision-making process.

✓ The proper technology is key to the success of your management decision-making.

✓ The value and merit of technology is not always self-evident.

✓ The creation of telecommunications capabilities requires trade-offs.

Part

II

Introduction

THIS SECTION SERVES AS A PRIMER on the telecommunications networks used for voice, data, and video applications. The changing telecommunications industry and the technologies behind these networks are examined in detail. My goal is to provide a clear explanation of the technologies and networks available to businesses and corporations of every size, how the technologies and networks work, and how everything fits together in the North American telecommunications infrastructure.

Keep in mind that voice communications and data communications are rapidly converging. A dedicated voice network no longer exists. Everything rides over the same network, and, in fact, data has surpassed voice in volume over the public switched telephone network (PSTN). For this reason, we will cover the telecommunications network in its entirety in this section.

Certain long-distance and backbone segments of the network are segregated, however. For example, the Internet backbone is independent of high-speed voice trunks, although the transmission wires often run side by side in the same multifiber cables and conduit pipes. Also, telephone company switching offices and Internet network access points (NAPs) often share the same facilities.

At first glance, the subject of telecommunications may appear to be quite complex and intimidating. After all, it's a huge industry that uses many sophisticated technologies, from integrated circuits to microwave transmitters to satellites. I have tried to break the subject down into logical pieces to make it easier for you to understand.

The way a subject is presented and organized can help a reader's comprehension immensely. Therefore, I formatted this section in an outline form that makes it easy to see how the various elements relate to one another and fit together. There is a general discussion of the telecommunications industry in Chapter 5, telecom and data networking basics in Chapter 6, and transmission media and signaling in Chapter 7. The remainder of the book is then presented from your perspective as a telecommunications user.

In Chapter 8, we start at your desktop, which is where you physically interact with telecommunications equipment—talking on the telephone or keying data into your computer. This is where we see the end result, or payoff, of telecommunications. Devices such as credit card terminals, pagers, scanners, automated teller machines, printers, and bar code readers connect to networks for the purpose of transmitting information elsewhere. The network itself is useless without devices that can be put to practical use.

Then we progress to how this equipment is hooked up to local networks within the building. In Chapter 9, we discuss local area networks (LANs) for data transmission and private branch exchanges (PBXs) for voice transmission. These are the little networks lying at the very edge of the huge public networks.

The next step is connecting to the outside public networks, which will connect us to locations across the street, across town, or on the other side of the world. In Chapter 10, we discuss the different network access services provided by the telephone company, from a regular dial-up POTS line to T1 service to a dedicated fiber-optic link.

In Chapters 11 and 12, we take a look at the high-speed public networks, including the PSTN, wireless networks, and the Internet. We cover the sophisticated transmission technologies that make these networks operate, and we also discuss asynchronous transfer mode (ATM), frame relay, SONET, and various overlay networks.

Finally, we wrap up the book with a chapter that will hopefully put everything into perspective. In the last chapter (Chapter 13), we trace an actual data path through the Internet. In fact, I suggest that you scan this chapter first, because it will make all the material in this book more meaningful.

Chapter

5

A Changing Telecommunications Industry

· ·

THE TELECOMMUNICATIONS INDUSTRY is in a state of change that few industries have faced. Although deregulation has encouraged new competition, it has also led to confusion. Which company provides what, when, and where? In addition, the convergence of today's technologies has resulted in a melding of the telecommunications, computer/information services, and entertainment industries. This chapter discusses the changes that are occurring, who the players are, and how future changes will impact your business.

A CHANGING INDUSTRY

Telecommunications have always been a critical part of the competitive business world—more so today than ever before. Businesses could not survive without telephones, email, fax machines, and a host of computerized applications. Today's employees are on the road, working from home, and conferencing with global customers at 3 A.M.

Confusing technology, spiraling business costs, and a plethora of new service providers have combined to create unprecedented change and upheaval for the telecommunications industry. Both state and federal legislators, regulators, and the courts have also encouraged change by fostering increased telecommunications competition via industry deregulation.

As innovative equipment vendors continue to develop new technology and systems, service providers (whether telephony, Internet, or wireless) strive to compete with new products, pricing, and support programs. However, the competitive playing field is not always level because many service providers are still subject to regulatory rules and limitations.

COMPETITION

Sixteen years after the 1984 divestiture of AT&T, businesses continue to feel its impact. Further change arrived with the Telecommunications Act of 1996. The intention of federal regulators and legislators was to create a fully competitive telecommunications environment over a short period of time. The Act has indeed led to improved competition, but it has also spawned numerous lawsuits challenging the intent of the Act or seeking to change its requirements.

So far, deregulation has resulted in a wave of major acquisitions and mergers of companies, both large and small. Some will argue convincingly that the result is fewer companies to choose from, thereby diminishing competition. To understand why the government is so interested in creating competition, it will be helpful to understand how the telephone industry was established and nurtured as a natural monopoly in the first place.

THE TELECOMMUNICATIONS INDUSTRY: A NATURAL MONOPOLY

The United States government recognized early on that a nationwide, high-quality communications system was essential for achieving its ambition to be a strong, powerful nation with a thriving economy. To that end, Congress passed the Graham Act of 1921. Its purpose was to eliminate the expense and potential duplication of scarce resources that would result if many companies competed to build a national communications infrastructure.

The Graham Act exempted the telecommunications industry from the Sherman Antitrust Act. In addition, it recognized natural monopolies for AT&T and other existing independent local telephone companies, but, to prevent monopolistic abuses, individual states were empowered to regulate the industry and establish prices and services within their borders. The power to regulate all interstate telecommunications equipment and services was allotted to the Federal Communications Commission (FCC), which Congress created with the passage of the Communications Act of 1934.

From 1934 to 1984, Congress continued to monitor the regulated status of the telecommunications industry. In 1968, however, a crack in AT&T's natural monopoly occurred when the Carterfone Decision allowed equipment manufactured by companies other than Western Electric (AT&T's manufacturing arm) to be connected to the telephone network. Next came the MCI Decision, also in 1968. It permitted non-AT&T companies to offer long-distance service to the public by mandating connection of these new long-distance companies to local service providers' networks. The U.S. Department of Justice antitrust suit, begun in 1974, eventually led to the Consent Decree of 1984 that finally broke up the AT&T monopoly. Under the direction of Judge Harold Greene, this decree forced AT&T to divest itself of the Bell operating companies (BOCs). Subsequently, AT&T no longer provided local telephone service.

DIVESTITURE IMPACTS

After the divestiture of AT&T's natural monopoly, telecommunications services were divided into three new industries: (1) long-distance companies, called interexchange carriers (IXCs); (2) local telecommunications companies, called local exchange carriers (LECs); and (3) a new industry consisting of companies that make customer premises equipment (CPE), such as telephones and fax machines. The IXCs and the CPE providers were deregulated, but the LECs continued to be regulated exactly as they were prior to divestiture.

To obtain telephone services, consumers and business customers now had to deal with three different companies. A problem with your phone service often required calls to all three companies just to find the right company to fix the problem. In addition, customers were expected to buy and install their own equipment (CPE), as the LEC was not allowed to do this anymore. The relationship between long-distance and local services also changed. Because long distance no longer subsidized local services, costs dropped for long-distance services. Without the subsidies, however, the cost for local services increased.

Another major divestiture-related change that impacts us still was the definition of long-distance service. It used to mean out-of-state (interstate) calls. After divestiture, however, each state was divided into small regions called local access transport areas (LATAs). Long-distance calling was now distinguished from local calling by the boundaries of these regions. Because calls made to people outside of each LATA were considered long distance, an IXC had to provide the service. Only intra-LATA calls were considered local service.

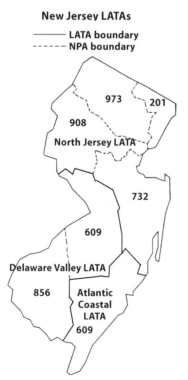

New Jersey LATAs

——— LATA boundary
------ NPA boundary

973
201
908
North Jersey LATA
732
609
Delaware Valley LATA
856   Atlantic
       Coastal
       LATA
609

A state as small as New Jersey is divided into three LATAs: the North Jersey LATA, the Atlantic Coastal LATA, and the Delaware Valley LATA. Whenever you install a new telephone line, you must first pre-subscribe to your inter-LATA service provider. Then, if you are in a state that also has regional toll competition, you must pre-subscribe to the regional toll service provider as well. You could now have three service providers for your telephone service: local, regional toll, and long distance. If you do not choose a long-distance or regional company, a carrier will be randomly assigned to you.

Figure 5-1

Divestiture has created healthy competition in both the IXC and the CPE industries. Many companies now provide long-distance services, and there is no question that competition has driven down the cost of long-distance service. Telephones and other forms of telecommunications equipment are sold in department stores, electronics stores, and grocery stores, through the mail, and over the Internet. There is also a much wider selection of telephone equipment featuring a variety of helpful bells and whistles. Dozens of companies now make CPE in all price ranges for all kinds of specialized uses. It wasn't too long ago that our only choice was either a basic black or beige telephone.

The LECs continue to be regulated today. Many LECs are owned by RBOCs (regional Bell operating companies), which were previously part of AT&T. There were seven original RBOCs—Ameritech, Bell Atlantic, Bell South, NYNEX, Southwestern Bell, Pacific Telesis, and U.S. West. At the time this book was written, mergers had reduced the seven companies to four—Bell Atlantic, Bell South, SBC, and U.S. West. Additional mergers and acquisitions are under way to combine Bell Atlantic with GTE and U.S. West with Global Crossings.

DEREGULATION ISSUES
Proponents of deregulating a portion of the U.S. telecommunications industry hoped to provide better, more economical service and offer new, more flexible products to telecommunications customers. Important deregulation issues are discussed below.

Goals
The primary objective of deregulation is to return industry control to the forces of the open market, where competition for customers determines the products, prices, and services available. Another goal is to offer a choice of service providers for all related telecommunications services. Eventually, one service provider may take care of all your telephony, Internet, and video services, or you may choose different companies for different services.

Depreciation
For tax purposes, a depreciation schedule attempts to account for

the cost of a piece of equipment in relation to its expected life span. The difficulty for incumbent LECs, or ILECs, is that some high-quality equipment continues to be used long after it has been fully depreciated. Conversely, the same equipment may become technically obsolete before it has been fully depreciated. These situations affect both the tariff rates that ILECs charge their customers, as well as decisions to employ new technology.

Universal service

The regulated telecommunications service providers were, and still are, required to provide universal service. The Telecommunications Act of 1996 continues the requirement for universal service because it is feared that deregulating the entire industry would risk leaving many customers underserved. New companies, seeking maximum profits in densely populated urban areas, might choose to ignore rural customers altogether. Prior to the 1984 divestiture, universal service was subsidized by long-distance revenues.

TELECOMMUNICATIONS ACT OF 1996

With the passage of the Telecommunications Act of 1996, Congress took radical steps to restructure the U.S. telecommunications market, expecting that significant benefits to consumers, telecommunications service providers, and equipment manufacturers would result. The intention of the Act was to encourage competition among telecommunications and cable television providers, thereby giving customers more choices, newer services, and lower prices.

Deregulation would also allow a single service provider to offer local and long-distance telephone service, Internet access, and cable TV in a bundled package. Most customers, it was thought, would prefer "one-stop shopping" for all their needs. Key provisions of the Act are discussed below.

Open long distance

The regional Bell operating companies (RBOCs) now offer long distance service outside their local service area boundaries. However, once the RBOCs are considered open and competitive within their local service areas, they will also be allowed to offer long-distance services *within* their boundaries. This means the RBOC will be able to provide inter-LATA services as well as the intra-LATA services they currently provide. In effect, the RBOCs will compete with AT&T and other long-distance carriers, such as MCI WorldCom or Sprint.

Open local service

The LECs must now open up the service areas within the LATA to competitive companies. Long-distance carriers, such as Sprint, MCI WorldCom, and AT&T, are freed from any restrictions on entering local markets, and they will be able to compete with the RBOCs and LECs in offering local telephone service. Conditions that must be met by the RBOCs include permitting the interconnection of competing companies' equipment to their networks, the sale of services to the competition (usually for resale), and local number portability, which allows customers to keep their phone number when changing service providers.

Open cable TV

The new law also allows cable companies to offer telecommunications services. Because coaxial cable has a larger bandwidth capacity than twisted-pair wire, cable companies can exploit their existing networks to deliver Internet access, cable TV, and telephone services to individual homes.

Video programming

The Act gives telecommunications carriers the option to provide video programming. Prior to the Act, carriers could not create the content they relayed, such as 900-number sports scores. Now, they can offer both audio and video content. On March 31, 1999, all services offered by cable television providers were deregulated except basic programming, which includes the educational and public access channels as well as broadcast programs.

Indecent material

The Act requires online providers to restrict minors' access to indecent material. This provision of the law has been ruled unconstitutional, and it is being fought in the courts as I write.

Services for individuals with disabilities

Provisions are included in the Act to promote and increase the availability of telecommunications services that meet the needs of individuals with disabilities. Telecommunications equipment manufacturers and service providers are charged with ensuring that all consumers have access to telecommunications services.

In addition to the provisions we just talked about, the Act addressed a number of other issues. It relaxed rules concerning ownership of radio and television stations, and it provided guidelines for the manufacture of telecommunications equipment. Television manufacturers are now required to equip new TVs with the "V-chip," which allows parents to block violent, sexually explicit, or indecent programming at home.

The Telecommunications Act also introduced a new universal service clause that was intended to ensure Internet access for every school, library, hospital, and medical clinic in the U.S. by the year 2000. To pay for the universal fund, a small charge is added to each customer's monthly service fee. The charges are collected by the carrier and then dispersed to the government.

CONFUSION

It seems that the telecommunications, computer/information services, and entertainment industries all want to be in one another's business. These changes make it hard for each of us to plan, implement, and manage our voice and data telecommunications. Which company should you contact? Which provides the best service? The least expensive service? Global service? Local service? Where will it all lead?

The major players in the telecommunications game are the LECs, the IXCs, government organizations, cable television companies, and wireless providers, but other players include the standards bodies, Internet service providers, and user groups. Let's discuss each of these players in more detail.

LOCAL EXCHANGE CARRIERS (LECS)

The seven original regional Bell operating companies (RBOCs)

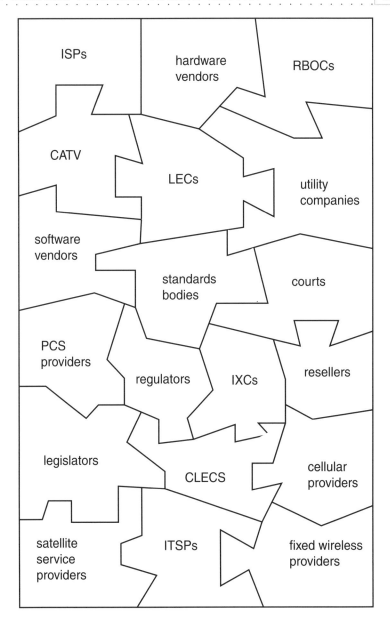

Figure 5-2

that divested from AT&T had been reduced to four by late 1999. Southwestern Bell Company (SBC) acquired Pacific Telesis and merged with Ameritech. Bell Atlantic merged with NYNEX and is also attempting to merge with GTE, the largest independent telephone company in the United States. That leaves Bell South and U.S. West as the remaining RBOCs.

In addition, there are approximately 1,100 independent phone companies, ranging in size from small mom-and-pop operations to GTE, the giant of them all. U.S. and international companies are snapping up these independents on a regular basis, however. Though not as closely regulated as the RBOCs, each LEC still operates as a natural monopoly for local services and is governed by a state regulatory commission. LECs are classified as either incumbent or competitive.

Incumbent LECs (ILECs)

The LECs provide local dial tone through an access line known as the local loop. The local loop is actually the installed connection between your location and the telephone company's central office, which houses its switching equipment. (Types of services and local connections provided by the LECs will be described in later chapters.) The Telecommunications Act of 1996 allowed the RBOCs and LECs to begin providing long-distance services as well, but only outside their established service areas.

Competitive LECs (CLECs)

After the 1984 divestiture, various companies began building metropolitan fiber-optic networks. These networks provide high-speed telecommunications services and are used by large corporations to connect their metropolitan locations to one another and to the interexchange carrier networks. Several of these original competitors to the LECs, called competitive access providers (CAPs), have since been acquired by the interexchange carriers. For example, WorldCom acquired MFS, and AT&T acquired Teleport (TSG).

When the Telecommunications Act of 1996 opened up the local market, a number of companies began offering local services. Because these companies had to be "certified" before connecting their equipment to the LEC networks, they became known as certified LECs, or CLECs. Today, CLECs are called competitive LECs and include several different types of companies, including resellers, facilities-based carriers, and Internet telephony service providers.

The simplest type of competitive LECs are the **resellers**. They provide regional toll or intra-LATA services, but they do not own any of the telecommunications facilities that are used to provide services to the customer. Resellers purchase the ILEC's service at discounted wholesale rates and then sell the services to their customers at retail rates, which are usually just under the LEC tariffs set by the regulators. Customers reach these resellers by either pre-subscribing to the company or by using a 10-10 access code. (Because the fourth number does not need to be a zero, it is technically a 101 access code, but that's not how you see it advertised.)

Facilities-based carriers may own their central office switches plus the local loop, or their switches but not the local loop, or the local loop but not the switches. Their service is a much more expensive proposition. Customers reach the facilities-based carriers through pre-subscription or by dialing a 10-10 access code.

Internet telephony service providers (ITSPs) have begun offering Internet telephone services to consumers and small businesses. Routing calls over the Internet for part of their journey can save you money, particularly on long-distance and international telephone calling. This is because there are no usage charges on the Internet and most people already pay a flat monthly fee for access.

INTEREXCHANGE CARRIERS (IXCs)

IXCs provide public inter-LATA and interstate services, as well as access to the international carriers. They have existed since AT&T's divestiture, and they have extensive long-distance networks in place throughout the United States. The three largest IXCs are AT&T, MCI WorldCom, and Sprint. IXCs provide most of the same services as LECs, but on an inter-LATA basis.

However, as a result of the Telecommunications Act of 1996, some IXCs have started to provide intra-LATA regional toll services. They have done so by acquiring companies with metropolitan networks already in place, by establishing reseller services, or by partnering with other companies that have direct access to the end customers, such as cable TV companies or power companies. AT&T, for example, merged with TCI cable television and is acquiring MediaOne cable services as I write this book. These mergers will allow AT&T to directly connect its long-distance services to over 38 million households via cable-wired connections. Additional services provided by the IXCs—private networking, packet switching, and backbone networking—are described in Chapter 11.

THE GOVERNMENT PLAYERS

The telecommunications industry is subject to regulation by the FCC and state public utility commissions, but Congress and state legislatures also make laws concerning telecommunications issues. Here's how the various government bodies impact the industry.

The Federal Communications Commission (FCC)

Since its inception in 1934, the FCC's appointed board of governors has controlled most interstate telecommunications activities, as well as the radio and television broadcasting industries. The Telecommunications Act of 1996 also tasked the FCC to encourage competition within the local exchange areas. Some believe this should be the responsibility of the state regulatory commissions, not the federal government.

State regulatory commissions

The regulatory commission of each state establishes tariffs, or prices, for that state. It is also responsible for determining which services or capabilities are offered within that state. Each commission's primary goal is to ensure that all citizens have access to telecommunications services. These commissions have a variety of names, such as the Bureau of Public Utilities, Public Service Commission, or Public Utilities Commission.

Federal and state court systems

At times, various telecommunications companies have filed suits asking the courts to interpret or clarify seemingly conflicting, inconsistent, or unfair laws that govern the telecom industry. Depending on the issues, telecommunications companies may side with one another on one issue, but oppose each other on the next. Some of these issues have wound their way through the lower courts up to the Supreme Court. Because full implementation of the Telecommunications Act of 1996 has been delayed by these lawsuits, many feel the benefits of the Act have not yet been realized.

Congress and state legislative bodies

Congress holds the power to make laws affecting the telecommunications industry at the federal level. Examples include the Graham Act of 1921, which created a natural monopoly status for AT&T and the independent telephone companies, and the Telecommunications Act of 1996, which deregulated the local exchange area. States also have the power to make laws affecting the telecommunications industry, providing there is no conflict with federal law.

CABLE TV SERVICE PROVIDERS

Deregulation of the cable industry took effect on March 31, 1999, following the Cable Communications Act of 1992. Due to its existing wired cable infrastructure, community access television (commonly known as cable TV) is now able to compete with the LEC.

AT&T has moved aggressively into the cable TV business by both merging with Tele-Communications, Inc. and negotiating to acquire MediaOne Group (Englewood, Colorado). AT&T's Broadband and Internet Services subsidiary plans to deliver long-distance and local telephone services, cable television, and Internet services over a hybrid fiber/coax (HFC) network that will connect directly to the consumer's home.

WIRELESS SERVICE PROVIDERS

The field of wireless telecommunications has grown from a specialty service for businesses to a consumer product that reaches more than 70 million subscribers in the U.S. alone. In addition to voice services, wireless companies are deploying their networks for data access to the Internet. There are a number of players in this area, and, although wireless will be discussed more fully in Chapter 10, a preliminary overview follows.

Cellular and personal communications service (PCS) providers

Today, it's hard to tell the difference between cellular and PCS service providers. However, there are two main differences: (1) the transmission frequency bands, and (2) whether analog or digital transmission is employed. Some wireless companies offer both, and some offer only one or the other. Marketing plans blur the distinction between the two services even further.

Satellite telephony service providers

Satellite communications have been a part of the telecommunications infrastructure since the first satellites were launched into space. Satellite networks were originally conceived and designed in the mid- to late '80s, giving birth to a new industry that proposed delivery of telephony and data services directly to the consumer via satellite. The idea was to first offer voice services "anywhere, anytime," and later implement data services. Iridium LLC (Washington, DC), the first company in this market, began service trials in September 1998 and revenue service in November 1998. Other direct-to-consumer satellite telephony companies currently in the wings include Globalstar L.P. (San Jose, California) and ICO Global Communications Ltd. (London).

Unfortunately, the future of this technology is doubtful. The deployment of satellite networks costs billions of dollars before the first revenue dollar is ever received, and Iridium is facing severe financial difficulties as I write. This service is also expensive for customers, and the competition from established terrestrial wireless systems is brutal. Satellite telephony may be a technology in search of a market that does not yet exist.

STANDARDS BODIES

One of the greatest advantages of the public telephone network is its capacity to connect to networks all over the globe. This is achieved through the work of the international standards organizations. Standards organizations also influence how and when new telecommunications products and services are offered. A few of the more important organizations are profiled below.

IEEE/ANSI

IEEE/ANSI is the acronym used for the Institute of Electrical and Electronic Engineers and the American National Standards Institute. These organizations recommend procedures to develop and manage voluntary American national standards for electrical or electronic systems, including telecommunications networks.

ITU-TSB

The International Telecommunications Union-Telecommunications Standardization Bureau (another mouthful!) is the international standards group. This organization was formerly known as the International Telegraph and Telephone Consultative Committee (CCITT), and most U.S. carriers and standards bodies are members. Its goal is the worldwide standardization of telecommunications. Members of the ITU-TSB study technical, operating, and tariff issues, and then develop recommendations for the use of new technologies.

Telcordia Technologies (formerly Bellcore)

This organization specializes in research and development that relates to the local telecommunications network. It is the U.S. representative on international standards bodies.

INTERNET SERVICE PROVIDERS (ISPS)

Internet service providers offer customers access to the Internet or other computer services, usually via a telephone line and a modem. These are commercial companies, and they charge a fee for their services. The Internet will be discussed fully in Chapter 12.

USER AND INDUSTRY TECHNOLOGY GROUPS

The user technology groups represent you and your colleagues. These organizations identify user needs and influence the development of interoperability agreements. They also help to prioritize whatever additional development may be necessary to meet these needs. Usually, equipment vendors and service providers are active participants in these groups. Some industry technology groups, however, are restricted to equipment vendors and service providers only.

The North American ISDN Users Forum (NIUF)

Originally sponsored under the auspices of the National Institute of Standards and Technology (NIST), NIUF was the grandfather of the user groups. Over time, it was split into two organizations—the ISDN Users group (IUW) and the ISDN Implementers Working group (IIW). In addition to developing national ISDN interoperability agreements, these groups have identified over 125 ISDN business applications.

Internet Engineering Task Force (IETF)

The IETF is a subsidiary of the Internet Architecture Board. It handles the day-to-day operational aspects of managing the Internet and develops inter-industry agreements to deal with technical Internet issues.

Asynchronous Transfer Mode (ATM) Forum

Founded in 1991, the ATM Forum is responsible for developing the interoperability agreements necessary to standardize technology interconnections between network service providers and equipment. Representing their individual technologies, members of this group work with other industry groups to devise ways of handing off traffic between different types of networks. For example, the ATM Forum and IETF have jointly developed protocols, or agreements, that deal with switching and transporting Internet Protocol (IP) traffic on public ATM networks.

Others

CPE and public network equipment manufacturers, consultants, agents, and value-added resellers also impact the development of standards. Industry leaders, such as Lucent, Nortel, Motorola, or Cisco, will often agree on standards so that their equipment is mutually compatible. Because of their leadership in the industry, the de facto standards of these companies then become universally adopted.

Chapter

6

Telecommunications and Data Networking Basics

· ·

THE EASIEST WAY TO LEARN about telecommunications networks is to break the subject down into its logical components. We can start at the most basic level by looking at the actual signals used to transfer information and by understanding how they are created and encoded. Next we can learn about the methods used to move and transmit these signals over the physical media. After figuring out how to move a signal down a wire, we can then learn how to route it through various network nodes to reach its intended destination. When the signal has reached its destination, our last task is to learn about the methods used to decipher, or decode, the signal so the information is intelligible to us.

Telecommunications and data networking people use just such a stepped, or layered, approach to understand and teach their subject. They also used this layered approach to establish guidelines for building and designing networks capable of interoperating with one another. Their efforts resulted in the development of the Open Systems Interconnection (OSI) Model, which is an international standard for the interconnection of all data equipment and networks.

OPEN SYSTEMS INTERCONNECTION (OSI) MODEL

Until recently, one of the major problems with data communications was that different data applications required different networks. There was little compatibility among the various architectures, systems, and equipment. Different vendors often had incompatible equipment even for the same data applications. This situation forced end customers to select one vendor to supply all the equipment for each system.

In response to these problems, the International Organization for Standardization (ISO) developed the Open Systems Interconnection-Reference Model (OSI-RM). It serves as a standard for data network design, and it also delineates product standards for the computer industry and other technical fields. This model is very useful for explaining how all the components of the communications process work together and connect with one another.

The OSI model consists of seven layers, each describing a specific aspect of the communications process. The seven layers are then divided into two groups. The first three layers are referred to as the telecommunications group, and the remaining four layers are referred to as the upper layers. The ultimate goal of the model is for the telecommunications network to be able to transmit any application independent of the upper layers.

Each layer communicates with both the layer above it and below it. As data is transmitted from one end user (or computer) to another end user, the data actually moves down through each layer and is transformed into whatever code is necessary to be understood by the adjacent layer. At the other end of the transmission, the transformed data moves in reverse through the layers. In this way, the data is in the proper format to be understood by the receiving end user.

In general, the lower layers deal with hardware and connections, while the higher layers are software based. The lower layers are relatively uncomplicated and have very fast transmission speeds. They don't really care what kind of data they're transporting—they just do it fast and indiscriminately. The higher layers incorporate more software and are largely found inside the computer device at each end of the data transmission. Most of this book is about the lowest three layers, the telecommunications group. These layers define how signals and data get transported through networks.

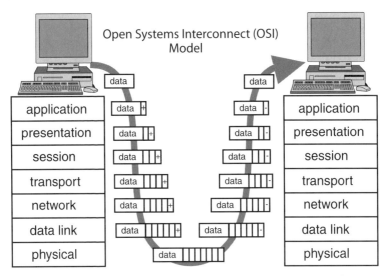

When data is transmitted over a network, it must pass through each layer of the OSI model. As the data passes through each layer, information is added in order to help format, route, and transmit the data properly. When the data reaches its destination, it passes through the layers in the reverse direction, and the information is in turn removed from the data at each layer.

Figure 6-1

Layer 1—Physical Layer

This layer deals with the actual transmission of the bit stream over the physical transmission medium. It describes how the transmission cable or wire connects to the equipment and dictates the mechanical, electrical, functional, and procedural characteristics necessary to access the physical medium. The Physical Layer is concerned with the interface between the terminal equipment and the communications network, as well as the premises distribution system within the work location. It also specifies how electrical signals are transmitted over the medium (wire) and how the various modulation and multiplexing schemes are performed.

Layer 2—Data Link Layer

The Data Link Layer insures the reliable, error-free transmission of data across the physical link. It specifies how to package the information into units for transmission, whether packets, frames, or cells. This layer defines the synchronization, error control, and flow control necessary for transmission over the Physical Layer.

Layer 3—Network Layer

This layer is the interface between the telecommunications group and the upper layers. The Network Layer is responsible for routing, switching, establishing, maintaining, and terminating the end-to-end (device-to-device) connections. This is essentially an addressing layer, where computers are identified on the network and data is routed along a path to its intended destination.

Layer 4—Transport Layer

The reliable and transparent transfer of data between the end users' equipment is maintained by the Transport Layer. It provides end-to-end error recovery and flow control to ensure that all the data arrives at the far end correctly.

Layer 5—Session Layer

The Session Layer, determines how connections are established, maintained, and terminated. In addition, it provides the control structure for how the data is exchanged.

Layer 6—Presentation Layer

For the communications process to begin, the end user's information must be translated by the Presentation Layer into an appropriate format for the application software.

Layer 7—Applications Layer

This layer governs how the end user interfaces with the OSI environment for data transmission. User applications, such as file transfer, email, and other distributed information services, are supported when each end user communicating on the network is using the same applications software.

As I mentioned earlier, OSI Layers 4 through 7 are pretty much disregarded for the purposes of this book. The functions in those layers are performed primarily by software loaded in the computers involved at either end of the data session. This book will cover what happens in the bottom three layers.

COMMUNICATIONS PROTOCOLS

Protocols are sets of rules that control the interaction between people, people and machines, and machines and machines. The English language can be thought of as such a protocol. When official standardization bodies adopt and publish protocols, they are called standards.

All devices in a data network communicate via protocols that define how the machines "talk" to one another. Communications protocols have names such as Ethernet, TCP/IP, or ATM. These protocols define what happens at various layers of the OSI Model, and they may be implemented in either the software or the hardware.

In the past, the proliferation of incompatible protocols was a major problem in the communications industry. Many manufacturers developed proprietary protocols to use exclusively with their own product lines. Think of a conference of international businessmen, each insisting on speaking his native language, and you will get an idea of the problems that faced users trying to accommodate these multiple protocols in a complex environment.

This unwieldy situation was addressed by the development of the OSI layered approach. Because the functions of each layer can be developed independently, equipment and protocols from many different vendors can now operate with equipment and protocols designed for other layers of the OSI Model.

The OSI Model and other layered descriptions of communications protocols are often called "protocol stacks." These stacks offer us a coherent structure for understanding the whole communications process. Though confusing at first, there *is* a method to the madness. Different protocols are used between the various layers, and many different protocols are needed for any given communication. By knowing that your device or technology is operating at a particular layer, you can relate it properly to devices operating at the layers above or below it.

DEVICE-TO-DEVICE HANDSHAKING PROTOCOLS

Also known as data link protocols, device-to-device handshaking protocols are employed to establish data communications circuits, manage the flow of traffic between and among telecommunications devices, and terminate the connections. The most common handshaking protocols and their functions are:

> **Communications start-up**—Establishes communications between devices
>
> **Character identification and framing**—Defines differences between text and control characters
>
> **Message identification**—Separates or combines characters into messages
>
> **Line control**—Regulates data transmission (a receiving device declares that the data is good and requests the next block of data)
>
> **Error control**—Gives instructions on how to handle cases of error, communications links breakdown, and communications reestablishment
>
> **Message termination**—Defines and identifies both normal and abnormal terminations of the telecommunications connection

BASIC COMPONENTS OF A DATA COMMUNICATIONS SYSTEM

Regardless of how complex a data communications system may initially seem, it is really quite simple when broken down into its basic components. Three components are required in all data communications systems: a transmitting device, a receiving device, and some type of medium to carry data between the two. Furthermore, every part of a network can be categorized as one of these three components.

The transmitting device can take many forms. It may be an end user computer or a specialized communications device, such as a modem or a multiplexer. The same is true for the receiving device. It may be an end user computer, a receiving modem, or a receiving multiplexer. The medium also takes many forms, such as a copper wire that transmits the user data by means of an electrical signal or an over-the-air radio wave that is altered in various ways to represent data. The medium may even be an optical fiber that changes the user data into light patterns for transmission.

TYPES OF COMMUNICATIONS EQUIPMENT

In today's networks, the data communications process involves several classes of equipment: data terminal equipment, data communications equipment, and data switching exchange equipment. The diagram below provides an overview of the communications process.

Data terminal equipment

The communications process starts with the application that the end user is working with. The user's data application originates in the desktop equipment, known as the data terminal equipment (DTE). Although data terminal equipment describes all end user machines, it usually means a computer or a terminal. End user application processes and data files are also found in the data terminal equipment.

Basic Components of a Data Communications System

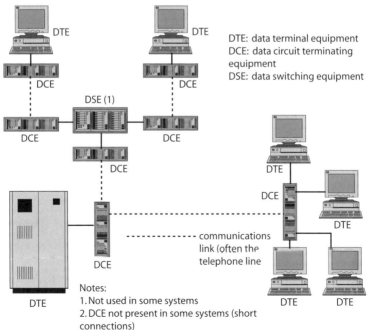

Figure 6-2

Data communications equipment

DCE, the second class of customer data equipment, is also called data circuit-termination equipment. The function of the data communications equipment is to interconnect DTEs in order to share resources, exchange data, or provide backup support for one another. The functions of DCE include the conversion and coding of each individual communications signal, as well as establishing, maintaining, and releasing the connection between the DTE and the transmission line. Modems are an example of DCE.

Data switching exchanges (DSE)

A data switching exchange (DSE) actually connects the transmission links described below. A switch located within the business site allows the DTEs to use individual channels to communicate with other user devices in the same location. The DSE are used for circuit switching, packet switching, or message switching, and they also include necessary routing functions from end to end.

TRANSMISSION LINKS

The transmission paths between the DTEs are referred to as lines, links, circuits, or channels, and they have different functions based on the number of devices involved. Together, these paths are also known as the transmission media, and they consist of copper wires using electrical transmission signals, microwave paths using radio signals, and fiber-optic cables using light or optical transmissions.

The different names can get confusing, but it's important to understand the distinction between them.

Channels are individual communications paths between users. They represent the lowest common denominator in the hierarchy of links. When transmitting data communications, a sender and a receiver are connected by a channel. Channels may go through any physical media for transmission, not simply wires. They are thought of as one-way communications. Many channels can exist on one circuit or physical wire. A telephone call or a two-way data session using the PSTN uses one channel in each direction.

Circuits are the physical means used to connect two points for communications. Sometimes they are called "pipes." A circuit can be a two-way link (two one-way channels), or it can be divided into multiple channels.

Trunks are similar to circuits. They are capable of carrying multiple channels over one physical connection, such as the circuits that interconnect switches and central offices.

Paths are the specific routes that signals follow between any two nodes on a network. A path can follow a channel, a circuit, or a trunk.

Transmission media are the physical links, such as copper wire, coaxial cable, or fiber-optic cable. One unit of the physical medium (one strand of fiber, a coax cable, or a pair of twisted copper wires) is generally considered the same as a circuit. With the right technology at either end, each unit is capable of transporting multiple channels.

Link configurations

The links that form the communications networks may be configured in one of two ways: point-to-point or multipoint.

Point-to-point refers to two machines connected via a single communications link. Here, the communications link protocol controls the sending and receiving of data between the machines. If the machines are of equal or relative standing, then this link is also referred to as a peer-to-peer connection.

Different forms of **multipoint** connections include star networks, ring networks, and switched networks. The multipoint configuration connects three or more machines via a number of communications links. This setup can only be used if the link has excess capacity that would allow multiple devices to use the medium simultaneously. An advantage to placing multiple devices on one transmission medium is an overall reduction in the cost of the network.

Link speeds

Compared to the computer world, the data communications world travels at a snail's pace. This is because most data communications utilize a telephone line (still the most convenient and readily available connection). Unfortunately, data transmission rates over telephone lines are painfully slow, but newer technologies have been designed to increase the speed of data communications. Data communications speeds are measured in bits per second (bps), and the table below illustrates the link speeds of various applications.

When we talk about data transmission speed, we're really talking about the throughput. The actual electrical (or light) signals transmitted across the wires all travel at the same speed. Variation occurs in the amount of data that can be carried by the signal.

Use this book as an example. The characters and formatting add up to a total of about 1.03 megabytes, and the graphics represent

Link Speeds (bps)	Typical Applications
0-600	telegraph telemetry older terminals
600-28,000	human-operated terminals personal computers batch and file transfer operations
32,000-64,000	digital voice
64,000-128,000	integrated digital voice & data desktop video
128,000-1,544,000	very high speed for multiple users computer to computer videoconferencing backbone links for networks frame relay data transmission
1,544,000-45,000,000	backbone links for networks high-quality video multiplexed digital voice & data SMDS transmission
45,000,000 and greater	broadband integrated voice, data, and video transmission ATM integrated transmission

Table 6-1

another 26.3 megabytes or so (graphics always require more bytes than text to be represented with any degree of acuity). Thus, the entire book is represented by about 27.33 megabytes, which equals 218,640,000 bits (27.33 x 1,000,000 x 8). Here's how long it would take to transmit this book over the following links (assuming ideal conditions and ignoring overhead bytes or line impairments):

56 kbps modem	65 minutes
128 kbps ISDN	28 minutes
1.5 Mbps T1	2.4 minutes
45 Mbps T3	5 seconds

Interesting, isn't it? Be careful you don't get bits and bytes mixed up. Data speeds are always measured as bits per second, while data is usually represented in kilobytes or megabytes. Before you do any speed calculations, make sure you convert the data to bits by multiplying the bytes by the number eight.

BASIC DATA NETWORKING CONCEPTS

Before we go any further in this book, I want to introduce a few basic data networking concepts. We have already talked about the important concept of communications protocols, but we also need to consider such ideas as session connections, synchronization, and access methodology, among others. Don't worry. This discussion won't take up much space, and you will learn a lot about how your network operates.

Let's start with how our original signal is created and encoded for transmission over the network.

COMMUNICATIONS CODES

Digital codes, based on binary numbers, are the "language" that directs the actions of computing machines. The familiar decimal number system uses the numbers 0 through 9, but computers use only two signal states, 0 and 1. The example below illustrates how the value 110001010 in the binary system is calculated to equal 394 in the decimal system.

Base 10	Binary	Decimal
2^8	1	= 256
2^7	1	= 128
2^6	0	= 0
2^5	0	= 0
2^4	0	= 0
2^3	1	= 8
2^2	0	= 0
2^1	1	= 2
2^0	0	= 0
	394	394

Table 6-2

Each binary digit is called a bit, and a group of eight bits is a byte, or octet. Several signaling techniques are used to represent binary numbers and codes. One technique transmits data by switching electrical current on (1) or off (0), and then measuring the current and its associated electromagnetic field. Another technique uses the positive and negative voltage of the current to represent 1s and 0s, respectively. Binary signals can also be transmitted through fiber-optic cables by using light pulses to represent 1s and 0s.

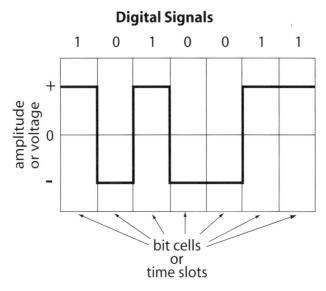

Figure 6-3

One example of the many different codes used is the 7-bit ASCII code (American Standard Code for Information Interchange), which is managed by the American National Standards Institute (ANSI). We have included a table of this code on the facing page.

SESSION CONNECTIONS
Now that we have an encoded signal, let's send it somewhere.

Bit Positions			7 >	0	0	0	0	1	1	1	1
			6 >	0	0	1	1	0	0	1	1
			5 >	0	1	0	1	0	1	0	1
4	3	2	1								
0	0	0	0	NUL	DLE	SP	0	@	P	\	p
0	0	0	1	SOH	DC1	!	1	A	Q	a	q
0	0	1	0	STX	DC2	"	2	B	R	b	r
0	0	1	1	ETX	DC3	#	3	C	S	c	s
0	1	0	0	EOT	DC4	$	4	D	T	d	t
0	1	0	1	ENQ	NAK	%	5	E	U	e	u
0	1	1	0	ACK	SYN	&	6	F	V	f	v
0	1	1	1	BEL	ETB	'	7	G	W	g	w
1	0	0	0	BS	CAN	(	8	H	X	h	x
1	0	0	1	HT	EM	)	9	I	Y	i	y
1	0	1	0	LF	SUB	*	:	J	Z	j	z
1	0	1	1	VT	ESQ	+	;	K	[	k	{
1	1	0	0	FF	FS	`	<	L	\	l	:
1	1	0	1	CR	GS	-	=	M	]	m	}
1	1	1	0	SO	RS	.	>	N	^	n	~
1	1	1	1	SI	US	/	?	O	-	o	DEL

Table 6-3   ASCII Code

Data communications sessions can occur on a network in two ways: (1) a connection-oriented session, and (2) a connectionless session. A network may be a mixture of both connection-oriented and connectionless techniques.

Connection-oriented session

Before transmission between two devices can actually take place, a circuit must be set up end to end. This is very similar to placing a phone call. When you telephone someone, the PSTN uses the phone number you dialed to establish a circuit and then provides ringing to alert the called party. If the call is answered, the circuit is established and you can start talking. Data devices must go through a similar procedure, known as a "handshake." (Hence, the handshake protocols that we discussed in the first part of this chapter.) Once the connection is established, data is exchanged.

Connectionless network

A connectionless network does not require a formal call or circuit setup prior to the transmission of the signal. The transmitting data is divided into packets, which may take different paths through the network and arrive at the destination end at different times. Although two devices are communicating, there is no fixed path or circuit between them. Because all the devices in a connectionless network share the same channels, transmission speeds may be faster than the connection-oriented network. Examples of connectionless networks are x.25 packet networks and SMDS metropolitan area networks.

SYNCHRONIZING THE COMMUNICATIONS

For data communications to occur, the computers and terminals must first notify each other that they are about to transmit data. They also need to provide a method of tracking the status of the ongoing transmission. The sending DTE is known as the transmitter, and the destination DTE is called the receiver. This part of the communications process, the setup and tracking, is referred to as synchronization.

Connections over a short distance often use a separate line to provide the synchronization, which is also known as clocking. Clocking signals perform two functions: they synchronize the receiver before the data actually arrives, and they keep the receiver synchronized with the incoming data bits. When connections are transmitted over a long distance, it is both impractical and expensive to have a separate clocking channel. Therefore, the clocking signals are coded into the actual transmission signal.

Synchronous vs. asynchronous transmission

Asynchronous communications systems transmit each character separately from all other characters, or one at a time. There is no connection or synchronization between the characters. Asynchronous transmission is widely used because the cost of the interface between the DTEs and the DCEs is inexpensive. Most personal computers use asynchronous interfaces. Most packet-switched networks also use an asynchronous transmission method, so that each data packet is transmitted independently of the others.

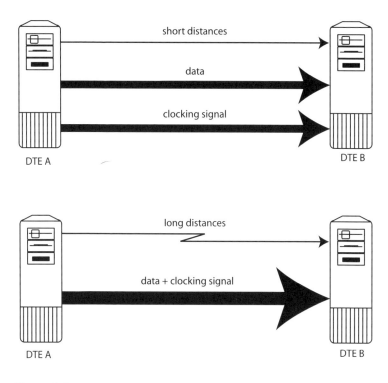

Figure 6-4

On the other hand, synchronous communications require both the sender and the receiver of the transmitted data to synchronize, or use exactly the same timing, for communicating entire blocks of data during one session. Transmissions that require speedy delivery use synchronous transmission, such as the digital backbone of the public switched telephone network (PSTN).

Synchronization formatting

Two data formats are used to help achieve synchronization, whether

asynchronous or synchronous in nature. In asynchronous formatting, each data character is provided with both a start and stop bit.
These bits act as the synchronization, or timing, signals. Because
the receiver clock is not synchronized with the sender clock, the
start bit serves to synchronize the receiver with each arriving character.

Two other functions of the start and stop bits are: (1) to alert the
receiver that data is arriving, and (2) to give the receiver sufficient
time to perform certain timing functions before the next character arrives.

In synchronous transmissions, separate clocking channels or self-
clocking codes are used, thus eliminating the start bit. The receiver is alerted to incoming user data by sync (synchronization)
bytes, flags, or preambles that indicate the beginning and ending
of the data stream. This alerting function is known as framing.
The actual content is protocol specific and connection dependent.
All synchronous protocols contain a header with information on
the destination and length of the message, a payload (data section), and a trailer that includes methods for error detection.

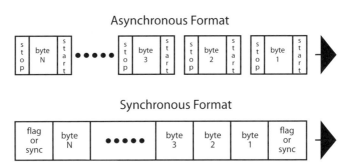

Figure 6-5

ERROR DETECTION METHODS

Noise or electrical interference can sometimes cause a spike in the
electrical signal of a transmission. If this spike is misinterpreted as
a 1 or a 0 in the wrong place, the result is an error in the transmission. To ensure reliability, error detection methods are used to

Common Error Detection Methods

Method	Features	Characteristics
echo checking	simplest	Echoes back each character via full duplex. The user verifies the correct transmission by looking at it (visual verification).
parity checking	simplest for asynchronous data	Adds a parity bit to each character to validate that the correct character was received. For "even parity," the modem adds (sums) the number of 1s in the character being sent and adds a 1 or a 0 in the parity bit position to make the number of 1s even. "Odd parity" is the same except the number of 1s should be odd. The modem at the other end performs the same calculation and compares the results with the parity bit.
longitudinal redundancy checking	better reliability, used for blocks of data	The modem adds a a byte of data, called the block check character (BCC), to the block of data. The first bit of the BCC is the parity check bit of all the first bits of all bytes of data in the block. The second bit of the BCC is the parity check bit of all the second bits of all bytes of data in the block. This continues through all positions. This provides a much better chance of detecting any errors.
checksum	simplest, used for blocks of data	The modem sums all the data in the block of data and places a number in the checksum BCC byte. When the receiving modem performs the same calculation and compares the checksum. If its different, it sends a negative acknowledgement requiring the transmitting modem to resend the block of data.
cyclic redundancy checking	most complex, most reliable, used for synchronous communicaitons	The block of data is divided by a polynomial producing a value and a remainder based on the coefficient, k, which is the degree of the polynomial. The computed remainder is the CRC character transmitted in the BCC position. The receiving modem makes the same calculation and compares the remainders. If they are different, a negative acknowledgement is sent requesting the retransmission of the original block of data.

Table 6-4

check, notify, and correct data that may have been corrupted by noise or transmission impairments.

Access Methodologies

Many employees may share the same LAN, so a control method is needed to determine when each employee can use or access the network. A good analogy might be our highway system. If you consider how cars entering an intersection are controlled by traffic signals, you will have an idea of how network access controls work. Two common access methods are carrier sense multiple access with collision detection (CSMA/CD) and token passing.

Carrier sense multiple access with collision detection (CSMA/CD)

This method allows anyone access to the network at any time. A few collisions are a small price to pay for its simplicity. Envision a single-lane residential street with a driveway on each side directly opposite each other. Then picture a car backing out of each of these driveways at the same time. As the drivers pull out into the one-lane street, they see that they will collide, so they both pull back into their driveways. Each driver then waits a different, predetermined period of time before pulling out again. If the first driver waits two seconds and the second driver waits five seconds, each should be able to pull out without colliding. This is the essence of the CSMA/CD method.

What does "carrier sense multiple access" actually mean? The carrier signal is the electrical transmission coming over the transmitting medium, and each PC on the LAN is listening to the carrier signal to see if anyone is using it—this is the carrier sense. If no one is using the carrier signal, then the PC can transmit without additional permission—this is the multiple access. Transmissions will collide if more than one PC transmits at the same time, so transmission detection lets the devices know that the data was not delivered and needs resending. Each PC then waits a specific time to retransmit. Ethernet LANs use CSMA/CD, but if the LAN is very busy, this type of access degrades the overall network performance. We'll discuss both LANs and Ethernet in Chapter 9.

Token passing

This access method requires permission from the network in the form of a "token." Just as a green light allows your car to enter a busy intersection, the token allows your PC to access the network. As long as you have the token, your PC can transmit until finished.

The transmitting PC changes the token (after receiving it) from "free" to "busy" and transmission begins. Then, after receiving notification that the transmission was delivered, the PC changes the token back to free and passes it on to the next device. Because there are no collisions, token passing is very effective at higher speeds.

LOGICAL TOPOLOGY

How messages are passed from device to device until reaching their ultimate destination is described by logical topology. Two methods for message passing are sequential and broadcast. In the **sequential** method, also known as ring message passing, the message is transferred from one PC or device to the next until it reaches its ultimate destination on the LAN.

Broadcast message passing is a one-to-many transmission, meaning that one communications device transmits to multiple devices simultaneously. This method is used in commercial TV and radio broadcasting, where one station is transmitting to many receivers.

Because it is relatively easy to send the signal to all stations on a limited number of media, the broadcast method is widely used in networks where the machines are in close proximity. In addition, broadcast is quite popular for satellite transmissions, wherein the satellite station transmits traffic to potentially thousands of receivers.

CONCENTRATOR TECHNIQUES

A concentrator is a line-sharing device that combines data from several sources into a single communications line. Multiplexers and concentrators are used for many of the same operations, but concentrators are also able to process data and make changes. A concentrator typically combines the transmissions of many low-speed channels into one or more high-speed channels. Two basic concentrator techniques for a multimedia environment are consolidation and grooming.

Both data packets and empty packets arrive in sequence through a number of different input channels. The **consolidation** technique removes the empty packets and redundant packets, thus compressing the data into a single output stream. The **grooming** technique sorts mixed signals arriving from separate input channels into groups of similar signals. The ensuing output streams then carry only one type of data signal.

I hope you are beginning to feel comfortable with the language and concepts of data networking introduced in this chapter. In the next chapter, we will dive into a more thorough examination of transmission media and signaling.

Chapter

7

Transmission Media and Signals

· ·

THIS CHAPTER DESCRIBES THE VARIOUS SIGNALS—electrical, radio frequency, or light—that are used to transport data, as well as the physical media that carry the signals. We will also discuss the methods used to superimpose intelligence (in the form of digital bits) onto these signals. The signals move the bits over the physical medium, but the bits carry the message.

TRANSMISSION SIGNAL CHARACTERISTICS

Speaking is our most basic means of communication. As we speak, the vibration of our vocal chords produces changes in the surrounding air pressure. In turn, these changes in air pressure generate the sound waves our ears detect, and we recognize combinations of sounds as words and language.

The telephone is designed to convert these same sound waves into basic electrical (analog) signals. Telephone wires then transmit the signals to a receiving telephone, where they are converted back to sound. The telephone frequency used for voice transmission is called the voice spectrum, or voice band. It ranges in frequency from 300–3000 Hz, and most human speech falls within this range.

Prior to the 1970s, the entire infrastructure of the public switched telephone network used analog signaling. Analog switching, transmission equipment, and connecting facilities worked well enough for simple voice communications services (though long-distance calls were never very clear or reliable). However, in the last 25 years, the demand for data transmission services and more complex voice services has grown at an unprecedented rate. It was necessary to adopt a technology capable of handling large volumes of traffic.

Digital was the solution. Digital signaling transmits data and voice more efficiently and reliably than analog ever could. For this reason, today's network infrastructure has migrated to digital. The local connection, however, is still analog, so we need to understand both analog and digital transmission techniques.

ANALOG SIGNALS

As we have just explained, the basic electrical signals used in telephones themselves and in the local access network are analog signals. This signaling system converts the acoustic energy (sound) to electrical energy, and then creates an electrical waveform that is analogous to the original sound waveform. The analog signal takes

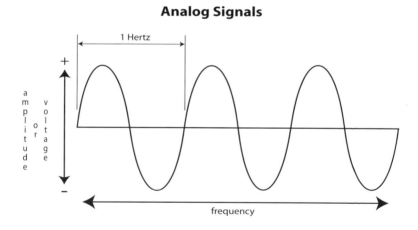

Analog Signals

- continuous signal
- gradually changes
- periodically reverses its voltage
- one complete cycle equals one Hertz

Figure 7-1

the form of a sine wave, which consists of two constantly changing variables: the amplitude and the frequency.

Amplitude refers to the height of the wave, and frequency (measured in Hertz) counts the number of cycles a wave travels over a fixed period of time. For example, 300 Hertz equals 300 cycles per second. Amplitude varies with the loudness of a voice, while the tone, or pitch, of a voice varies the frequency. Analog signaling voltage alternately reverses its polarity in the pattern of a sine wave—zero to positive to zero to negative and back to zero again.

DIGITAL SIGNALS

The digital signal is a "discrete" signal, meaning it is assigned a specific value for a given period of time. The value is determined by the communications equipment device being used, such as a modem, computer, switch, or other transmission equipment. A digital circuit uses the value "0" to indicate the absence of voltage and the value "1" to indicate the presence of voltage.

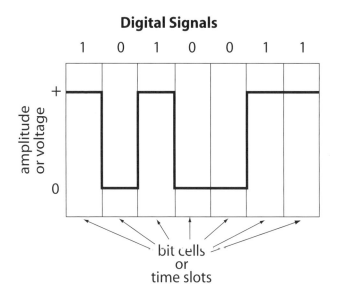

Figure 7-2

Computers are digital machines using only 0s and 1s, so it is easy to see that digital signaling is ideal for transmitting data traffic over networks that link computers together. Digital signaling is also an efficient way to transmit voice. In the public telephone network, analog voice signals from the local lines are first converted to digital signals. Then the signals are switched and transmitted over the digital backbone trunks that link the central offices together.

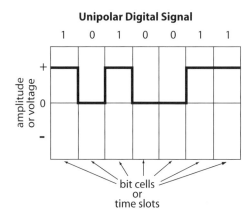

Unipolar Digital Signal

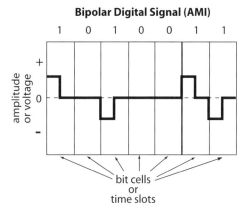

Bipolar Digital Signal (AMI)

Figure 7-3

The public telephone network uses two standard types of digital signaling: unipolar and bipolar. In unipolar signaling, a positive voltage (+3 volts) represents "1" and the absence of voltage represents "0." The positive voltage is known as a pulse, or mark. In bipolar signaling, the voltage representing "1" alternates between positive and negative. Alternate mark inversion (AMI) is another name for bipolar signaling.

Noise distortion is a common problem when transmitting analog signals over long distances. The problem occurs because the amplifiers used to boost the original analog signal also amplify any accompanying noise. On the other hand, digital signals are regenerated, or repeated, rather than amplified. Because regeneration affects only the presence or absence of voltage, there is no associated noise accompanying the signal. The resulting transmission is cleaner, quieter, and more accurate than an analog transmission.

Finally, digital signals can be multiplexed, meaning several channels from different sources may be grouped onto one transmission facility. The advantages of multiplexing include faster speeds, reduced maintenance, better efficiency, and lower overall costs. You can read about multiplexing techniques later in this chapter.

TRANSMISSION IMPAIRMENTS

A variety of impairments may degrade the performance of a signal as it is transmitted over a circuit or channel, especially when transmitting analog signals over copper wires. To reduce these impairments, telephone companies "condition" the basic analog line by adding equipment that improves the quality of the transmission.

Impairments are categorized as either predictable or unpredictable. Predictable impairments are always present, but can be overcome. For example, attenuation can be corrected by circuit design or special equipment, and certain forms of distortion may also be eliminated with the correct equipment.

Unpredictable impairments, however, are random, transient, and difficult to overcome. No specific engineering or installation procedures exist that will totally eliminate these types of impairments. The most common impairments are discussed below.

Attenuation

As an electrical signal travels along its transmission path, its strength, or amplitude, diminishes. We can get a good idea of how this occurs by envisioning what happens when a rock is thrown into a pool of water. Waves generated from the rock's entry point become smaller and smaller as they move outward, and eventually fade altogether. Resistance in the transmission wire causes the same thing to happen to an electrical signal. This loss of signal strength is called attenuation.

Amplifiers installed every 15,000 to 18,000 feet along the transmission path boost the signal strength. One or more amplifiers may be needed, depending on the distance between your telephone and the end central office.

Noise

An unwanted or random electrical signal that interferes with the communications signal may sound like static over the telephone connection. This noise commonly results from splicing two wires together. Accordingly, telephone engineers try to minimize the number of splices on any given circuit.

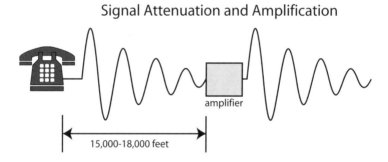

Figure 7-4

Because amplifiers don't discriminate, noise and extraneous electrical interference are amplified along with the original analog signal. Amplification repeated several times over a long distance may cause the talk path to become so noisy that the conversation cannot be understood. In this case, it is best to hang up and make the call again. If the static or noise persists, then you should call your local telephone service provider to check the physical transmission path.

Using noisy analog lines for data transmission significantly degrades the accuracy and speed of the transmission. However, the POTS line is intended for voice transmission, not data. To ensure clear and accurate data transmission, a digital line should be installed. Equipment added to the circuit to improve the analog performance (such as an amplifier) is removed for a digital line. This process is known as "deconditioning" the line, and the improved data transmission performance is well worth the extra cost.

Echoes
Using different gauges, or thickness, of wire in a transmission path may cause reflection of the signal that, in turn, creates an echo. When this occurs during a telephone call, we hear the echo of our own voice.

Cross talk
When electromagnetic radiation effectively connects the signals on two parallel channels and mixes them together, you are able to hear someone else's conversation. This is known as cross talk. It often results when long lengths of inexpensive telephone connecting wires are used, such as the extension wires found at Staples or Radio Shack. In these wires, the conductors are parallel to one another. Twisted-pair copper wire helps to eliminate this problem.

Distortion
Distortion is defined as any change in the shape, or waveform, of the transmission signal (whether analog or digital) that leads to misinterpretation or errors in the original transmission. Two common types of distortion are "jitter" and "bias." Jitter refers to the intermittent shortening or lengthening of the signal, while bias indicates signal intervals that are too long or too short.

CONTROL SIGNALING
Control signals help to manage the telephone network by providing information such as caller ID or a busy signal on the line you are trying to reach. Control signals are transmitted on the telephone network as either "in-band" or "common channel."

In-band, or in-channel, signaling uses the same transmission channel for both control signals and the actual voice or data transmission. In the past, most signaling was in-band.

Common channel signaling, or out-of-band signaling, uses one dedicated channel for all the signaling functions of a group of telephone channels. In addition, voice and data are transmitted over separate channels. The Signaling System 7 (SS7) network, discussed later, is the latest evolution of out-of-band signaling.

MODULATION

Modulation is used in many common applications, such as AM/ FM radio, TV, and telephone modems. It refers to any method that modifies one signal with another signal, thus enabling us to send intelligible signals over a line.

Analog telephone lines include a carrier wave (similar to a sine wave) that transmits a continuous signal over the local loop, but, other than telling us that the channel is functioning, the carrier wave conveys no information unless it is changed by another signal. A carrier wave's amplitude, frequency, phase, or any combination of these can be modified to transport digital bits.

A modulator/demodulator, commonly known as a modem, is a device used to modulate the carrier wave with a second signal at the transmitting end and then demodulate the wave at the receiving end. However, modulation is not limited to modems. Radio and TV stations also use various forms of modulation to transmit their signals.

Modulation techniques may be used together. For example, quadrature amplitude modulation (QAM) combines phase and amplitude modulation to achieve faster data transmission speeds. What is common to all modulation schemes is that information, whether analog or digital, is superimposed on the analog carrier signal.

The terminology here can get a little confusing, but don't be intimidated. Though some terms may be used interchangeably, it is

Analog Signal Modulation

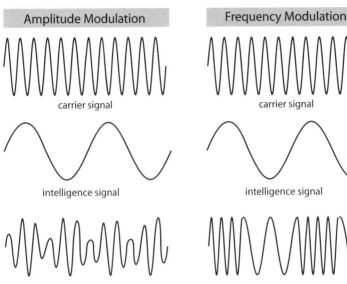

An example of analog modulation is a voice conversation over a POTS line. The analog voice signal is modulated onto the analog telephone circuit carrier signal. The modulation process takes place inside the electronics of the telephone.

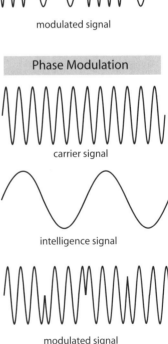

Figure 7-5

Digital Signal Modulation

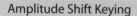

Amplitude Shift Keying

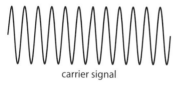

carrier signal

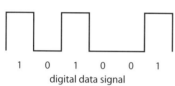

1   0   1   0   0   1
digital data signal

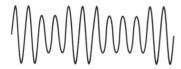

modulated signal

Frequency Shift Keying

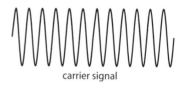

carrier signal

1   0   1   0   0   1
digital data signal

modulated signal

Phase Shift Keying

carrier signal

An example of digital modulation is a modem transmitting over a POTS line. The modem modulates the attached computer's digital bits onto the analog telephone circuit carrier signal. A modem at the other end performs the reverse function by removing the digital bits from the analog carrier signal.

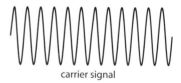

1   0   1   0   0   1
digital data signal

Figure 7-6

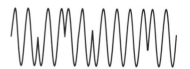

modulated signal

not necessarily wrong. For example, frequency modulation or frequency shift keying can properly describe either analog or digital modulation of an analog carrier; and amplitude shift keying is also a type of amplitude modulation that refers specifically to a digital signal superimposed on an analog carrier.

Throughout this book, however, we will differentiate between analog modulation and digital modulation as described below.

ANALOG MODULATION

Your home telephone uses this modulation method to convert the sound waves of your voice into analogous electrical signals. These signals are then transmitted over the phone line.

For voice applications, analog modulation uses three techniques to put an analog input signal on an analog carrier. They are:

Amplitude modulation (AM)—Depending on the input signal, the height of the carrier wave is increased or decreased as necessary.
Frequency modulation (FM)—The cycle of the carrier wave is modified.
Phase modulation (PM)—The timing of the basic waveform is modified.

DIGITAL MODULATION

This modulation method uses modems to convert digital computer signals into a form that can be sent over an analog phone line. Digital modulation also uses three basic techniques for modulating a digital input signal onto an analog carrier. They are:

Amplitude shift keying (ASK)—The height of the carrier wave is modified when the input signal is "1," but there is no carrier when the input signal is "0."
Frequency shift keying (FSK)—Binary FSK is the most common form of frequency shift keying. The frequency of the carrier wave is modified by using two frequencies to represent two discrete states, such as the "0" or "1" of a digital transmission.

Phase shift keying (PSK)—The timing of the basic waveform is modified. The most common form of phase shift keying, 2-PSK, represents each discrete state by one of two phases located 180° apart.

Multiple phase shift keying is also quite common. Quadrature PSK (4-PSK) uses one of four phases located 90° apart, and 8-PSK uses one of eight phases, 45° apart. Because phase shift keying allows more information to be packed onto the carrier wave, some form of it is used by all of today's modems.

DIGITAL SUBSCRIBER LINE (DSL) MODULATION

Many, many people connect to the Internet on dial-up modems via the local access loop, and, once connected, the trend is to spend more time than ever before surfing the 'Net. Consequently, the PSTN overloads and users are unable to connect at peak hours. Also, even if connected, downloading data from the Internet to one's PC can be maddeningly slow.

Digital subscriber line (DSL) technologies offer much higher data transmission speeds than analog POTS lines. So, rather than re-placing or reengineering the local loop to increase transmission speeds, a digital subscriber line is used. These lines modulate digital signals onto an analog carrier, just like a POTS line, but sophisticated modulation schemes allow the DSL to carry significantly greater quantities of data.

Although DSL services are offered by the local telephone companies, they require special modems to connect to the POTS line. Various DSL services are discussed at length in Chapter 10.

One of the more popular DSL offerings is asymmetric DSL (ADSL) service. In this chapter, we will focus on the modulation techniques used by ADSL: carrierless amplitude phase (CAP) modulation and discrete multitone (DMT) modulation. These two techniques refer to the line coding (how the bits are sent) and the frame structure on the line (how the bits are organized). Differences between these techniques affect performance, cost effectiveness, and signal processing delay.

Carrierless amplitude/phase (CAP) modulation

The CAP modulation technique divides a channel into three subchannels, each using different frequencies. The lowest channel, 0–4 kHz baseband, is the band used today for standard voice communications over the POTS line.

The upper bandwidth is divided into two separate channels by the process of frequency-division multiplexing (described below). The frequencies used for upstream transmission range from 20–200 kHz, and the frequencies used for downstream transmission range from 240 kHz to 1.1 MHz.

CAP is based on quadrature amplitude modulation, a technique that has been in use for many years. Due to its simplicity and the minimal latency experienced with this technique, CAP modulation is more widely used than discrete multitone modulation.

Discrete multitone (DMT) modulation

Beginning at 0 Hz, the discrete multitone modulation technique divides the entire bandwidth range of 1.1 MHz into 256 equally spaced subchannels. Subchannels 1 through 6 are used for analog voice transmission. Usually, there are 32 upstream channels and 250 downstream channels. Because a modified frequency-division multiplexing scheme is used where the upstream and downstream bands overlap, some form of echo cancellation is required.

DMT is considered better than CAP at rate adaptation, which is the ability to change speeds in variable line conditions. When varying loop conditions exist, such as bridge taps and mixed wire gauges that occur in typical neighborhoods, DMT is also the better choice.

ANALOG/DIGITAL CONVERSION

In the last section we discussed modulating either digital or analog signals onto an analog carrier because that's how voice or data is moved along the analog local loop. Now we are going beyond the local loop onto the backbone of the PSTN.

The entire backbone of the PSTN—switching, interoffice, and long-haul transmission facilities—is purely digital, so we need to learn about the special equipment and techniques that are required to convert analog signals (sine waves) to digital signals (pulses).

PULSE CODE MODULATION (PCM)

The most common method of converting analog voice signals to digital signals is pulse code modulation. PCM employs a method of sampling called pulse amplitude modulation that is entirely transparent to end users. It consists of a four-step process that ultimately digitizes an analog voice signal into a channel output of 64 kbps.

Digital signal level 0 is the basic digital communications channel, and each individual voice conversation requires its own dedicated DS-0 channel. It is important to understand that DS-0 is the building block of all digital voice transmissions. Many different transmission speeds are used in the public telephone network, but each one is a multiple of 64 kbps, the basic DS-0 channel.

To obtain an adequate representation of the original analog signal, analog voltages must be sampled at twice the rate of the highest frequency being reproduced. The highest voice frequency is approximately 4000 Hz. Therefore, the analog sine wave needs to be measured at least 8000 times per second to be reproduced properly at the other end of the transmission. A conversation sampled at only 4000 Hz may be understandable, but you may not recognize the voice, or even whether it's male or female.

Let's take a look at the four steps of the PCM sampling process: sampling, measuring, translating, and transmitting.

> **Step 1**—The original signal is sampled 8000 times per second. Each sample represents a specific point (amplitude) on the analog sine wave at the particular time the sample is taken.
> **Step 2**—Sample values are first measured, then rounded and converted to pulses by using a process known as pulse amplitude modulation (PAM). There are 256 possible sample points.

Step 3—Next, the pulse amplitude points are translated into digital language by assigning an eight-bit binary code to each of the 256 possible points. For example, point number 87 is represented by 01010111, while point number 19 is represented by 00010011. The converted analog signal now consists of 8000 samples multiplied by eight bits (for each sample point), resulting in a transmission speed of 64,000 bits per second (64 kbps).

Pulse Code Modulation (PCM)

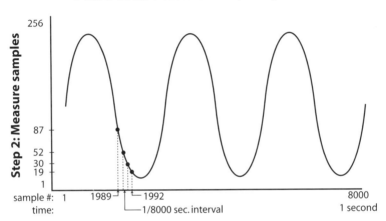

Step 2: Measure samples

sample #: 1   1989 — 1992   8000
time: 1/8000 sec. interval   1 second

Step 1: Sample signal 8000 times per second

Step 3: Translate measurements into binary numbers

Sample point	Measurement	Binary number
1989	87	01010111
1990	52	00110100
1991	30	00011110
1992	19	00010011

Step 4: Pulse bit stream over circuit

Sample #:	1989	1990	1991	1992
Bit stream:	0 1 0 1 0 1 1 1	0 0 1 1 0 1 0 0	0 0 0 1 1 1 1 0	0 0 0 1 0 0 1 1

AMI pulses:

Figure 7-7

Step 4—Finally, transmission takes place when the 64,000 0s and 1s are electrically "pulsed" over the channel using the appropriate coding scheme (alternate mark inversion [AMI] for the telephone network). At the receiving end of the circuit, the PCM eight-bit codes are converted back to 8000 voltage points and smoothed into an analog sine wave signal by a low-pass filter.

An important point to remember is that the central office takes all incoming analog signals—analog voice modulated onto the analog carrier or digital bits modulated onto the analog carrier by a modem—and performs the PCM process on these already modulated signals. The result is modulation on top of modulation.

Every incoming transmission from the local loop is a type of modulated analog signal, whether from a modem or a voice conversation. They all get treated the same way by the PCM process. The high-speed digital transmission facilities of the PSTN don't care what kind of bits are carried. It simply turns everything into 64 kbps channels and lets smarter devices at the other end decipher what the bits represent. Remember the OSI Model layers? PCM is operating at Layer 1, the lowest layer of the model. It is fast, efficient, and indiscriminate.

MULTIPLEXING TECHNIQUES

Digital telephone networks are able to transmit more than one information channel over the same physical medium by using multiplexing techniques. For example, placing special multiplexing equipment at either end of the transmission path enables a T1 connection to transmit 24 separate voice channels over a single twisted pair of copper wires. Fiber-optic transmission offers an enormous range of light wavelengths for use in multiplexing schemes over one strand of fiber.

Multiplexed circuits are described as point-to-point or networked. Point-to-point circuits employ multiplexing to increase the overall data rate of the channel. This is accomplished by combining a number of slower data channels into a single high-speed digital channel. Instead of transmitting 24 separate voice channels at 64 kbps each, a T1 circuit can serve as one huge data channel featuring a collective bandwidth of 1.54 Mbps (64 kbps times 24 plus 8000 framing bits).

In networked systems, many users are actively connected to the same network at the same time. Multiplexing allows a large number of individual calls to be aggregated at the central office, then sent over one physical medium (such as twisted-pair or fiber-optic cable) to another central office. The result is a substantial savings in network resources.

FREQUENCY-DIVISION MULTIPLEXING (FDM)

Frequency-division multiplexing (FDM) divides the available bandwidth of a circuit into multiple channels, each of which carries an individual voice or data transmission. In addition, each transmission is assigned a frequency range within the "pipe," or transmission medium, that defines how much bandwidth that channel can support.

FDM is fundamentally an analog technology that uses multiple analog carrier signals to convey analog or digital information. Figure 7-8 depicts a circuit with a total bandwidth of 24 kHz (60–84 kHz) that has been divided into six channels of 4 kHz each. The center frequency of each channel (at 62, 66, 70, 74, 78, and 82 kHz) serves as the carrier frequency upon which the intelligence signal is modulated. The center carrier frequency is isolated on each side by a 2 kHz band (resulting in 4 kHz per channel) so that the signals do not interfere with one another. Either analog or digital signals may be modulated onto the six carrier frequencies in our example, but the sum of the bandwidth of each individual channel can never exceed the maximum overall bandwidth of the circuit.

Commercial radio provides us with a good example of frequency-division multiplexing. Each radio station is assigned a specific frequency, and you use the radio dial to tune into the carrier frequency for the station you want to hear. Naturally, the best reception is obtained when you are closest to that carrier frequency. The carrier frequency tone, unmodulated by an intelligence signal, is what we hear when the radio station tests its equipment from time to time. Limited available bandwidth requires radio stations to restrict the extent of their transmission range (by limiting the wattage, or power, of their transmitters) so that the same frequencies can be reused in other serving areas.

Analog FDM was previously used for point-to-point microwave radio transmission and on coaxial cable. Presently, FDM is used for cable TV, broadband LANs, satellite transmissions, and lightwave transmission. The number of channels obtainable by employing FDM is limited by the medium used. For example, coaxial cable TV can be divided into a maximum of about 200 channels. Keep this number in mind when we compare FDM with time-division multiplexing (TDM), which is discussed next.

Frequency-Division Multiplexing (FDM)

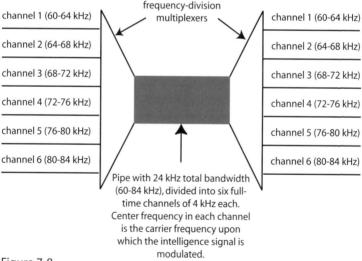

Figure 7-8

TIME-DIVISION MULTIPLEXING (TDM)

Time-division multiplexing (also called synchronous TDM) is a unique form of multiplexing because it is strictly digital. It uses digital pulses only. Analog signals must first be converted into digital signals through pulse code modulation (PCM) before they can be time-division multiplexed. TDM permanently partitions the bandwidth of a data communications line into equal time slots, each of which is dedicated to an individual user or channel. Separate data input streams are then collected and interleaved onto the single shared transmission pipe.

For example, if four PCs needed 2400 bps access to a remote location, one 9,600 bps line with a time-division multiplexer could be installed. Each computer would take its turn accessing the line for a few microseconds in a set sequence that is repeated over and over very quickly. In this way, each device would have full use of the 9,600 bps capacity for one quarter of the time.

TDM multiplexers are simple to implement and are well suited for real-time, delay-sensitive applications. However, if a channel is idle, its time slot is wasted. Therefore, basic TDM is potentially inefficient in low-traffic applications.

It is important to understand the distinction between FDM and TDM. FDM divides a circuit into multiple channels that exist side by side. A multilane highway is a good analogy. On the other hand, TDM consists of only one lane, but far more traffic travels on this single lane than the multilane highway because the speed of the cars can be increased and the intervals between them decreased. Thus, TDM is capable of carrying many more channels than FDM.

The digital backbone of the PSTN uses time-division multiplexing, or the variation described below, to move bits throughout the network. The smallest backbone pipe in the PSTN is the T1, which has a total capacity of 1.54 Mbps (24 voice channels), and the largest is the OC-192, with a capacity of nearly 10 billion bits per second (129,024 voice channels). The only difference between the two is the rate at which the bits are pulsed on the line. The capacity, or bandwidth, of the pipe increases as the bit rate is speeded up. It is nothing short of amazing that the PSTN backbone equipment can both generate and keep track of bit pulses transmitting at a rate of 10 Gbps.

Statistical Time-division Multiplexing (STDM)

Statistical time-division multiplexing (STDM) is also referred to as asynchronous TDM. As we mentioned above, basic TDM may waste bandwidth because it divides a transmission line into equal time slots for each user, whether needed at a given moment or not. STDM eliminates this waste by continuously adjusting the allocation of bandwidth according to the needs of the transmitting devices.

STDM operates on the principle that not all input channels are transmitting data at the same time. Nonetheless, the possibility

Time-Division Multiplexing (TDM)

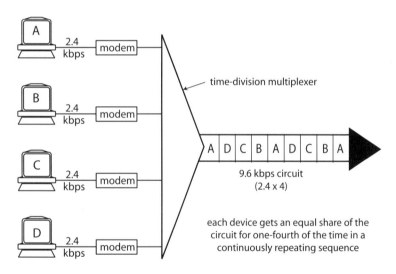

Figure 7-9

exists that all channels could transmit simultaneously and "overbook" the transmission line. In other words, the sum of the data speed requirements of the transmitting devices may exceed the capacity of the facility. Therefore, STDM devices must be able to temporarily store, or buffer, some of the data.

A stat mux is an STDM device that incorporates both a buffer and a processor. It is essentially a "smart" time-division multiplexer.

STDM devices may also offer additional network management functions, such as speed and protocol conversion, error detection and correction, polling, and the addition of synchronizing codes. STDM is generally used by packet switching data networks, while circuit-switched telephone networks use synchronous TDM.

WAVE-DIVISION MULTIPLEXING
Wave-division multiplexing (WDM) is a form of frequency-division multiplexing that is used in optical transmissions. Because the light spectrum consists of many different colors, all at different frequencies, an enormous number of independent channels can be established on a single fiber. A distinct hierarchy of communication channels that do not overlap is created, greatly increasing the data rate capability of each individual optical fiber. We will discuss WDM further in Chapter 11.

TIME-DIVISION MULTIPLE ACCESS (TDMA)
In analog cellular systems, the number of simultaneous users in any cell is limited. Wireless service providers are therefore converting their networks to digital systems to accommodate a greater number of users. Digital radio technologies have improved dramatically over the last several years. In addition to better voice quality, less noise, and less interference, these technologies now provide wireless data and messaging services.

Wireless service providers primarily use three digital radio multiplexing techniques: time-division multiple access (TDMA), code-division multiple access (CDMA), and Global System for Mobile Communications (GSM).

Time-division multiple access is based on the proven techniques of time-division multiplexing. Multiple signals on a single radio frequency are time interleaved together to provide simultaneous transmission. A major advantage of TDMA is its simplicity.

CODE-DIVISION MULTIPLE ACCESS (CDMA)
This wireless multiplexing technology is employed by some digital cellular and PCS (personal communications service) providers in their communications networks. CDMA is also referred to as a

"spread spectrum" technology. Transmissions are first converted into data packets that contain identification information; then they are literally "spread" over a wide range of frequencies. Spreading transmissions in this way allows a specified range of frequencies to carry up to ten distinct transmissions simultaneously. A comparable analog transmission channel is only able to carry one transmission.

After being transformed to a digital format, the data relayed via CDMA spreads out to occupy the entire available bandwidth. When more than one call needs to use the same route, a unique sequence code is assigned to the bits of speech of each call. This unique digital code can only be received by the specific wireless phone it is intended for. Once received by the intended party, the code is translated back into speech.

CDMA transmissions are more secure than analog cellular transmissions, which can be overheard by others, and because more simultaneous channels are available, CDMA has greater capacity than TDMA.

GLOBAL SYSTEM FOR MOBILE COMMUNICATIONS (GSM)
Global System for Mobile Communications (GSM) was originally the European standard for international cellular technology. It is a combination of both networking and radio technologies. Many personal communications service (PCS) providers in North America use a form of GSM, namely the PCS 1900 network (GSM digital cellular system at 1900 MHz).

GSM employs a type of time-division multiple access. However, it is not compatible with North American TDMA because the GSM radio band is much wider than the TDMA bands. Each GSM radio channel is 200 kHz wide as opposed to the 25–30 kHz bandwidth of TDMA channels. Carriers in North America are working to provide a transparent interface between the different digital cellular systems.

WIRED TRANSMISSION MEDIA
Communications signals are transmitted over a variety of physical

media, such as copper wire or fiber-optic cable. In the telephone industry, the term "medium" refers to the physical path used to transport customer-generated signals.

Factors that will determine which medium to use include the following: the number of users and the demand for service; the required bandwidth; the cost of the medium; the physical and electrical environment surrounding the cabling; and the expected life of the system. Wired communications media are generally limited to twisted-pair copper wire, coaxial cable, and fiber-optic cable.

TWISTED-PAIR COPPER WIRE

This basic wire is formed by two copper wires twisted together at a rate of two to twelve twists per foot. Each of the twisted wires is covered with plastic insulation. The twisting improves transmission performance by reducing interference effects (cross talk) in adjacent pairs. Twisted-pair cable is inexpensive, readily available, and easily installed. Special equipment is often added to improve the performance of the voice-grade line and to minimize transmission impairments, such as attenuation, distortion, and echo. This is called "conditioning" the line.

Twisted-pair wire may be either unshielded twisted pair (UTP) or shielded twisted pair (STP). Originally, UTP was used for voice communications and was available in two, three, four, or twenty-five pairs of twisted copper wire. UTP is considered a balanced system, meaning both wires carry similar types of electrical signals and have similar characteristics.

The properties of UTP have been standardized by the Electronics Industries Association/Telecommunications Industries Association (EIA/TIA). Five categories were created that specify performance guidelines for wiring, jacks, plugs, and cross-connect panels. The standard defines the minimum level of performance required for each category, and a higher level of performance is dictated for each ascending category.

For data communications, STP used to be the choice because it outperformed UTP in so many ways. STP was able to reduce cross talk, transmit over greater distances than UTP, and protect from grounds, faults, electromagnetic interference (EMI), and radio frequency interference (RFI).

Today, UTP cable has such improved performance that STP is used only for specialized applications in environments where electrical or magnetic interference may occur, such as high-voltage lines or large electric motors. UTP is used in the outside local loop, and, currently, most LANs use Category 5 UTP.

Type	Wire Size (AWG)	Description and Use
Category 1 UTP	22 or 24	Voice grade cable, certified for voice conversation use.
Category 2 UTP	22 or 24	Data grade cable, certified to handle data transmissions up to 1 Mbps.
Category 3 UTP	24	Data grade cable, commonly used for all voice and mid-speed data transmissions, certified to handle data transmission up to 16 Mbps. Generally used for 4 Mbps token ring and 10 Mbps Ethernet LANs.
Category 4 UTP	22 or 24	Data grade cable, certified to handle data transmission up to 20 Mbps.
Category 5 UTP	22 or 24	Data grade cable, certified to handle data transmission up to 100 Mbps. This is the most commonly installed UTP today, used for Ethernet LANs with wire runs not exceeding 100 meters.

Table 7-1

To save on installation costs, some companies use a different category of wire for different applications. In my experience, however, these initial savings are quickly eaten up by the cost of managing different wire types (voice wire vs. data wire) as employees move around and require changes in their telecommunications connections. Keeping track of an assortment of wires costs a lot more in the long run. It's much easier to use one type for all your needs, as long as the most stringent requirements of your system are met.

Unless I knew a higher speed would be necessary, I would wire an entire building with a minimum of four 4-pair Category 3 wires to every workstation. If the computer manager insisted on Category 5 for all data connections, then I would install a minimum of four 4-pair Category 5 wires to each workstation.

COAXIAL COPPER CABLE (COAX)

Coax consists of a single inner core conductor of solid copper wire surrounded by three outer layers of material. The innermost layer is a type of insulation, such as plastic, followed by a solid aluminum or braided copper shield. A final jacket of PVC or Teflon protects the conductors and prevents interference from outside signals. Coax is considered an unbalanced medium—the main signal is transmitted through the inner core conductor, while the other conductor, the aluminum or braided copper shield, acts as a ground.

Coax cables were once used in long-distance telephone networks and local area data networks (LANs), but they are now primarily used for cable TV installations. Coax utilizes frequency bandwidths of either 50-350 MHz or 50-750 MHz to transmit analog TV signals. The number of TV channels received is limited to 50 or 100, respectively, but this number can be increased in a variety of ways. Digitizing the signals and multiplexing three digital channels onto each analog channel is one option. Another option is to use a physical medium offering greater bandwidth.

Coaxial cable is described as either broadband or baseband, referring to the nature of the signal transmission. (Broadband and baseband will be covered later in this chapter.) Advantages to using coaxial cable include:

High bandwidth—A large number of channels can be sent over one cable.

Negligible cross talk—The shielded nature of coax design virtually eliminates cross talk.

Minimum delay distortion—The signal velocity ensures that user frequencies arrive at the far end close together in time.

High propagation speeds—The likelihood of echo problems is reduced during transmission.

Disadvantages of coaxial cable include:

Media cost—Coax cable is considerably more expensive than twisted-pair cabling.
Repeaters—Coax repeaters for long-haul systems are not as efficient as repeaters for other media.
Attenuation—Signal loss is quite significant in high-capacity systems.

Coaxial Cable (Coax)

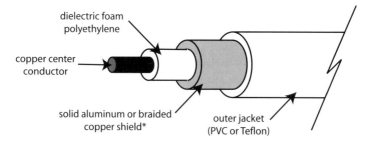

(*broadband coax would use only a solid shield)

Figure 7-10

FIBER-OPTIC CABLE

Two types of media can transport light waves for telecommunications signals: space (over the air) and fiber-optic cable. The transmission of infrared light signals through space will be saved for a later discussion, but, right now, let's take a closer look at fiber-optic transmission.

A fiber-optic circuit consists of a light source (either a laser or light-emitting diode) at the transmitting end and a light detector at the receiving end. Digital signals are modulated over light beams transmitted through the fibers, and equipment at each end converts the electrical signal to a light signal and vice versa. A notable advantage of fiber-optic cabling is its ability to remain unaffected by surrounding electromagnetic or electrical interference.

Fiber-optic cables are composed of one-way glass, fused silica, or plastic threads capable of carrying light signals. Each cable features two layers of glass or plastic—a small, central transparent core, known as the fiber thread, surrounded by a second layer, or cladding. The cladding has a different refractive index than the center core, and its purpose is to keep the light energy within the core. An outer covering of tough polyethylene plastic protects the fiber from environmental hazards. If the cable is to be pulled through conduit or strung from poles, a strength cable, such as steel, is bundled together with the fiber.

Fiber-optic cables have become the preferred media for transmitting huge quantities of information from one location to another. Two types of fiber-optic cable exist: single mode and multimode. Multimode fibers are used to cover distances of 10 to 100 kilometers in local area networks. They provide modest data transmission rates, ranging from 10 to 100 Mbps (megabits per second).

Single mode fiber-optic cable is used to cover medium to long distances. It provides greater bandwidth than multimode, and it achieves transmission speeds in the gigabit-per-second range. (Terabit speeds—a trillion bits per second—have been documented in the laboratory!) However, the greatest reason to use fiber-optic cable for communications, whether single mode or multimode, is its capacity to convey optical energy over a long distance without significant loss, or attenuation.

Because single mode fiber transmits digital signals at faster speeds and for longer distances than multimode fiber, it is used for the telephone trunk transmission network, which is the backbone of the telephone network. Multiple fiber threads, each isolated from the others, are banded into a single cable to provide many individual transmission channels. Some backbone cables carry 600 to 800 strands of fiber. Theoretically, one strand of fiber can transmit a trillion bits per second, which is the equivalent of more than 15 million simultaneous telephone conversations. If you multiply

15 million conversations by 600 to 800 strands, you will get an idea of the data capacity of the fiber-optic cable backbones being installed by numerous telephone companies today.

Fiber-optic cable is also being used in some LANs. It is used for high-speed data transmission beyond the capabilities of Category 5 UTP, and it is often found in the vertical riser systems of large office buildings. Because fiber-optic signals are not affected by

Single Mode Fiber Cable

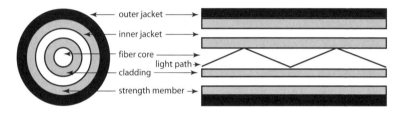

Multimode Fiber Cable

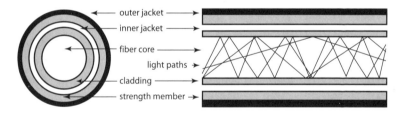

Figure 7-11

surrounding electromagnetic or electrical interference, they are very reliable and secure.

Although the cost of fiber-optic cable is declining rapidly, it is still too expensive to use for individual stations in the horizontal cable system. Therefore, UTP is used for most applications. Also, fiber is physically more fragile than UTP. We'll talk more about premises cabling arrangements in Chapter 9.

HYBRID CABLES

To increase the capacity of local distribution cable, both telephone companies and local cable TV companies have been installing more and more fiber-optic cable. Fiber-optic cable extends switching capabilities further out into the neighborhoods and allows these providers to offer high-speed services to their subscribers. Two types of hybrid cable are described below.

Hybrid fiber copper (HFCop)

This cable is most often used in the local loop to extend the electronics of the central office to the neighborhood. Today, the feeder cables, or backbone, of the local distribution plant are fiber-optic cables. Signals from the central office terminal (COT) are carried over these cables to the remote optical terminals (ROT) located in the neighborhood. The signals are then converted from optical to electrical and transmitted via twisted-pair copper wires to the subscriber's home or business location.

Hybrid fiber coax (HFC)

Cable TV companies are the primary users of hybrid fiber coax. HFC increases the bandwidth of the physical medium, thereby increasing the number of channels available to end customers. Because HFC uses the coaxial cable already installed in the neighborhood distribution system, companies need to replace only the feeder cable with fiber-optic cable. In this way, high-quality signaling is achieved without the expense of fiber-optic cables and amplifiers end to end.

HFC also provides a bidirectional signal that an end user may employ for interactive commands. If cable TV analog modems are attached to the HFC cable, the line becomes a two-way communications channel shared by all users. The bandwidth would depend on both the available capacity of the two-way channel and the number of users accessing the channel at the same time.

WIRELESS TRANSMISSION MEDIA

In 1888, Heinrich Rudolf Hertz was the first to prove that energy could be transmitted over the air. Today, continuously improving technology has made wireless the fastest growing telecommunications service, claiming more than 100 million users in the year 2000.

Radio was the earliest wireless application for consumers. The broad electromagnetic spectrum (illustrated below) includes not only radio frequency waves, but visible light, ultraviolet, and infrared waves as well.

The frequency range for commercial AM radio is 550–1.6 MHz, while FM radio uses the frequency range of 88–108 MHz (between TV channels 6 and 7). The commercial broadcast television frequencies (air medium) are 50–212 MHz for VHF and 400–950 MHz for UHF. Other frequencies within the spectrum have been reserved for telecommunications applications. For example, the bands at 800 and 1900 MHz are reserved for cellular and personal communications services (PCS).

Wireless systems are now being used in LANs. One inherent advantage of a wireless premises system stands out: cabling does not have to be installed, cross-connected, or terminated. After wired systems are installed, a major expense of any telecommunications system is moving and rearranging connections. To overcome this, many employees will use their cellular or personal communications systems (PCS) telephones rather than the wired terminals.

Wireless LANs use either infrared or radio-based systems, discussed below. Though still fairly expensive to install, wireless LANs incur very few ongoing expenses. They are fast becoming a viable alternative to wired systems, which require extensive planning and maintenance.

RADIO SYSTEMS

Radio waves are transmitted, or broadcast, in many directions through the earth's atmosphere. Radio transmitters and receivers, such as those used for AM and FM radio and television programs, also possess telecommunications capabilities. The lowest frequencies are not recommended for high-speed, high-capacity data communications systems, but they are adequate for simple applications, such as stock market quotations and personal pagers. Taxi, police, and fire communications systems needing to contact remote vehicles also use these low frequencies.

In general, a radio system transmits one signal to all the receivers within its range in a local area. How far the signal may be transmitted depends on the power of the transmitter (ranging from 50 to 50,000 watts), the height of the antenna, the actual terrain (natural or man-made obstructions), and weather conditions.

Broad Electromagnetic Spectrum

Frequency (Hertz)	Band	Communications Application
3 Hz - 30 kHz	very low frequency (VLF)	
30kHz - 300 kHz	low frequency (LF)	
300 kHz - 3 MHz	medium frequency (MF)	**Terrestrial Systems:** - AM radio (550-1,650 kHz)
3 MHz - 30 MHz	high frequency (HF)	
30 MHz - 300 MHz	very high frequency (VHF)	-portable telephone (34 MHz) -VHF TV (54-216 MHz) -FM radio (88-108 MHz)
300 MHz - 3 GHz	ultra-high frequency (UHF)	-UHF TV (220-500 MHz) -radio astronomy (608-614 MHz) -cellular telephone (800 MHz) -portable telephone (900 MHz) -PCS (1.85-2.2 GHz) **Satellite Systems:** -L band (1-2 GHz)
3 GHz - 30 GHz	super-high frequency (SHF)	-S band (2-4 GHz) -C band (4-8 GHz) -X band (8-12 GHz) -Ku band (12-18 GHz) -K band (18-27 GHz)
30 GHz - 300 GHz	extremely high frequency (EHF)	-Ka band (27-40 GHz)
10^3 - 10^7 GHz	infrared, visible light, ultraviolet light	TV remote controller security detection sensors

Table 7-2

MICROWAVE RADIO SYSTEMS

Microwave systems use line-of-sight radio waves to carry frequency- or time-division multiplexed voice and data signals. Originally, microwave radio systems were installed for nationwide television transmission. Then, as demand for long-distance telephone service increased, microwave transmission was used as an economical way to distribute voice circuits.

In 1931, the International Telephone & Telegraph Company installed the first commercial microwave system for transmission across the English Channel. The first U.S. system was installed in 1948 and operated between New York and Boston. Today, much of this long-distance transmission takes place through fiber-optic cables, but in remote areas where the cost of physical wireline facilities is prohibitive, telephone companies still use microwave extensively.

Like coaxial cable, microwave transmission supports very high data rates over long distances. A microwave facility requires fewer amplifiers or repeaters than coax cable, but it does require a line of sight. This means there must be a direct, unobstructed path between the transmitter and the receiver. Microwave systems may also be used for short-haul systems between buildings, for closed circuit TV (CCTV), or as a data link between LANs. The ability of microwave transmission to span natural barriers and obstructions, such as canyons, bodies of water, and heavily wooded areas, is a clear advantage.

Although microwave covers a wide range of the frequency spectrum, it is sometimes difficult to obtain frequency assignments in large cities due to the limited availability of channels in the radio spectrum. Typically, frequencies range from 2–40 GHz, although most network systems operate in the range of 2–18 GHz. The lower-frequency systems are used for voice and data at transmission rates up to 12 Mbps; the higher-frequency systems (18 GHz) provide data transmission rates up to 274 Mbps.

Attenuation (signal loss) is a major problem for microwave systems because distance, wavelength, and the weather all affect the signal. Interference from other overlapping transmissions is also a common problem.

Local multipoint (microwave) distribution systems (LMDS)

Microwave transmission in the 10 GHz band is being used as an alternative to the wired local loop for digital data and video transmission in small regions or cells (up to a six-mile radius). Called "fixed wireless" (because the subscribers are stationary), LMDS offers a high-bandwidth alternative to the local loop. Some competitive LECs are using LMDS to gain customers rather than building out a wired network.

SATELLITE SYSTEMS

The first international communications satellite, INTELSAT I, was launched in the late 1960s. The international satellite telephone industry has grown rapidly ever since. In the U.S., satellites are used for television program distribution and for corporate voice and data networks. Although the initial outlay for satellite systems is high, subscriber cost is low because so many customers are served by one satellite. Expenses for customer premises equipment will vary widely. The frequencies allocated for satellite communications are in the super-high-frequency (SHF) and extremely high-frequency (EHF) bands.

Satellite transmission has several significant advantages when compared to terrestrial systems. It has extremely high bandwidth that is matched only by fiber-optic media, and noise is not a serious impairment because there is less interference from adjacent signals, terrestrial microwave, and weather conditions. The quality of the transmission makes it an excellent choice for broadcast or one-way transmission, communications with mobile stations, and data communications. Also, satellite transmission has fewer distance limitations than terrestrial microwave because it overcomes the natural obstruction imposed by the curvature of the earth.

Satellite networks do have disadvantages, however. Most notable is the up-front expense, which runs into billions of dollars, but there are performance disadvantages as well. The time it takes to transmit up and back from the satellite is known as propagation delay, and it is responsible for echo problems in voice transmission. In addition, the total round-trip delay of a satellite transmission may result in unacceptable response times for real-time voice and video applications. Locating a satellite closer to the earth is not a very practical solution for minimizing delay. More serious problems involving gravitational pull result, and, in fact, low-earth orbit (LEO) satellites do not stay aloft for more than three to five years.

INFRARED SYSTEMS

Infrared is the invisible portion of the broad spectrum's optical section. Short signals receive good resolution at this wavelength, but only for minimal distances. Therefore, infrared's primary use is for TV remote controllers, security detection units, and similar devices.

Infrared signals are line-of-sight beams, transmitting at high speeds. For example, laptop-to-laptop infrared services run at 16 Mbps. Unlike unidirectional radio waves, infrared signals are omnidirectional, and, because they are light waves, they are immune to electrical interference and eavesdropping.

BANDWIDTH

We have used the term "bandwidth" frequently in this chapter, but what does it really mean? In the most general sense, bandwidth refers to the total data volume capacity of a transmission medium—the higher the bandwidth, the more data that can be transported over a link in a given period of time. A variety of different technologies and signaling schemes are used to increase the bandwidth of a transmission medium.

Most people in this industry talk about data or transmission speed as though it is the same thing as bandwidth. It is easy to think that higher bandwidth must equal faster speed. This isn't technically correct, however, because the electrical (or optical) signals traveling down the wire all go at about the same speed. Higher bandwidth refers to how much data can be loaded (by modulation and multiplexing) onto the signal.

Greater carrying capacity means that a given block of data will arrive at its destination faster. This explains the use of the term "speed," but volume would be a more accurate measure of the rate of data flow. Therefore, when speaking of bandwidth, a larger transmission pipe provides a higher volume of data flow.

NARROWBAND VS. WIDEBAND

Narrowband and wideband are relative terms that allude to the data capacity of a link. Generally, narrowband refers to one voice channel, consisting of either 4 kHz on an analog line or 64 kbps on a digital line.

Wideband is considered anything beyond narrowband and refers to more than one voice channel. In telecommunications, wideband and broadband, described below, are often used interchangeably.

BROADBAND SIGNALS

Broadband signals are analog in nature. The total bandwidth of a broadband transmission link equals the difference between the upper and lower frequencies, expressed in Hertz. Within that range, the frequency band can be divided into numerous separate channels. For example, a frequency range from 4–48 Hz will equal 44 Hz (48 minus 4) total bandwidth. Within this bandwidth, there might be 11 separate 4 Hz channels (44 divided by 11).

In the middle of each channel is an analog carrier frequency, which is modulated by the signal carrying the data or intelligence part of the transmission. The intelligence signal can be anything—voice, data, video, or broadcast TV. The main input signals are then modulated onto an analog carrier wave for transport through the system.

Broadband systems provide a very large bandwidth over very long distances. If overall frequency bandwidth is widened at the same time individual frequency channels are narrowed, the net result is an increase in the number of independent data channels that can be transmitted. Cable TV is one example of a broadband system that offers the potential of hundreds of channels, each carrying complex video and audio signals (either analog or digital).

BASEBAND

A signal in its original form, unchanged by any other signal (such as an analog carrier), is referred to as baseband. All digital signals start out as baseband signals, utilizing 1s and 0s to represent the presence or absence of voltage on the line.

Baseband systems are much easier to engineer, install, and maintain than broadband systems. Although baseband cable has limited bandwidth and range for telephone applications, it is excellent for local area networks, such as Ethernet networks. The total bandwidth of a baseband system is expressed as its maximum data volume in bits per second (for example, a 10 Mbps Ethernet LAN).

Chapter

8

Desktop Equipment

· ·

NOW THAT YOU HAVE A HANDLE on the fundamentals, we can begin discussing data networks in more detail. We'll start with the desktop equipment familiar to you, such as PCs, telephones, and modems. Then, in the following chapters, we'll step up to LANs and keep moving up to ever larger networks. I hope this logical progression from your desktop to worldwide public networks makes sense to you. My intention is to present the material from your perspective. All interaction with data networks starts at your desktop, so you naturally view everything from that standpoint.

BUSINESS COMPUTING

For many employees, the desktop is the primary work area. This is where customers are contacted, sales data is generated, and marketing plans are produced. Whether a typical office desk or a retail sales counter, it's the place where telecommunications conversations, transactions, and file transfers are started and finished. It is also where the telecommunications features and applications that reside on employees' business telephones, PCs, and other equipment are located. In other words, it's where their telecom tools are located, and it's where communications begin and end.

The communications process originates from the various applications located within the DTE (usually a computer or terminal). These applications may be in the form of a word processing program, a spreadsheet program, or an email program on your PC.

As mentioned in Chapter 6, the data communications process involves several classifications of equipment. In this chapter, we will concentrate on the desktop equipment employed directly by the end user in a business environment. This equipment includes data terminal equipment (DTE), user interface equipment, and data communications equipment (DCE).

DESKTOP DATA TERMINAL EQUIPMENT

Both the cost and size of business computers continue to shrink even as computing capabilities grow ever more powerful. Business computers can be categorized according to their computing power, and they range from supercomputers to desktop PCs. Portable, or mobile, computers are common in the business world, and specialized handheld devices are widely used for limited applications such as scheduling, contact management, or email messaging. Business computers can be connected to one another through networks, or they can be stand-alone machines, such as a workstation or a laptop.

Supercomputers

These computers are generally the largest in size, and they have the greatest computing power. Corporations, universities, and military facilities engaging in scientific and/or military research use supercomputers. When it is necessary to process huge amounts of data, such as forecasting weather patterns, processing space exploration data, or creating graphic-intensive digital movies, supercomputers do the work.

Mainframes

Second in size to supercomputers, mainframes are usually found in enclosed computer centers. Many corporations use mainframes for centralized data processing and to manage large databases. Early business computer systems were entirely mainframe until distributed computing—networked PCs—decreased their role.

Mainframes are often called host computers because end users access the system through so-called "dumb" terminals connected directly to the mainframe. In contrast, the client in a client/server network is usually a personal computer (PC) that can also function indepen- dently. Because centralized data processing mainframes require programmers and computer operators to keep them running, most small businesses cannot afford the expense of a mainframe com- puter center.

Minicomputers

Though smaller than mainframes, minicomputers perform many of the same functions as the larger mainframe. They are consid- ered mid-range computers and are used to perform specific tasks, such as engineering applications or scientific research. The first minicomputers I worked with handled electronic mail and simple word processing systems. Minicomputers offer the flexibility needed by smaller corporate departments or companies with mul- tiple physical locations.

Technical workstations

Some people define a workstation as any device connected to a network, but I consider workstations to be the specialized, power- ful desktop computing devices employed by many scientists and engineers. Featuring high-resolution color displays, these comput- ers are used for high-speed calculations and whenever greater com- puting levels are required. The Sun Workstation, manufactured by Sun Microsystems, is an example of a technical workstation. An interesting fact, however, is that today's newest PCs are more powerful than the technical workstations of only a few years ago.

Microcomputers

The smallest general-purpose computers are called microcomputers or personal computers (PCs). The IBM microcomputer has been the dominant business computing device, and most PCs are con- sidered IBM-compatible devices. The primary advantage of PCs is that employees have direct computing power at their desks, in- dependent of the huge computer mainframes.

PCs costing as little as $299 may fit the needs of many small busi- nesses. These low-cost PCs have joined the ranks of basic con- sumer products, such as TVs and VCRs. They are acceptable for such basic applications as word processing, but they are not able to support multimedia applications (integrated voice, data, and video) or high-volume Web surfing.

PCs can be categorized as desktops, portables, laptops (or notebooks), and palmtops.

Laptop, or notebook, computers are fully powered portable PCs that enable employees to work from any location. Connections to corporate networks or the Internet are made via wired or wireless modems.

Palmtop, or handheld, computers are often specialized devices for data collection, personal contacts, calendars, and email messaging. The data can be transferred to corporate systems as required.

Pen-based **notepads** are used to take notes, edit text, or modify drawings.

Personal digital assistants (PDAs) have the ability to input or retrieve data from corporate systems by using wireless interfaces. Other applications currently being developed will allow us to use PDAs as mobile phones and for portable email.

Network computers

These are the most basic computers found on many networks. Although they must have the capability to work with the appropriate network operating systems, they do not have to interface with other networks. Network computers (NCs), or thin clients, are similar to PCs, but they have less hardware and software installed. In addition to being less complicated, they also cost less and require less support than stand-alone PCs. However, any savings realized by substituting network computers for PCs is usually offset by the costs of the network administration and management.

USER INTERFACES

Character-based and graphical-based hardware and software enable the user to interact with the computer. End users may type in character-based instructions on keyboards, or they may use a mouse or touch pad to select icons (little pictures) or menu options provided by a graphical user interface (GUI). These interfaces are also necessary for communications between the user and the network. The Windows operating system uses an easy-to-navigate GUI that most of us are familiar with. It's a big improvement over the old text-based DOS (disk operating system) days!

Input Devices

Keyboards and pointing devices are the most common methods of inputting data to computers. Keyboarding is not efficient for large amounts of data, however, and often leads to entry errors.

Employees who do not type find pointing devices make it easy to interact with the computer. The mouse is used most often to move the cursor on the computer screen, but trackballs, touch pads, touch screens, or special pens are also commonly used. Other data entry options that do not require typing include bar code or image scanners, smart cards, and voice response devices.

Bar code scanners

Bar codes are widely used to deliver price and product information in manufacturing and sales situations. Bar code scanners create a digitized picture of a bar code, such as the Universal Product Code (UPC), perhaps the most familiar bar code to many people.

Image scanners

Photographs, drawings, and other images can be converted into a digital format by an image scanner, and then saved in the computer.

Smart cards

Although they look like credit cards, smart cards carry enormous amounts of data on chips, magnetic strips, or laser-optic fields. Also, smart cards have much better security features than credit cards. They are used for point-of-sale transactions, automatic teller machine entries, pay phone calling, and security access to protected PCs.

Voice response system

In voice response systems, the user speaks commands, such as words or numbers, and voice recognition software then deciphers the spoken word and translates it into text or specific commands. Voice recognition systems and Touch-Tone telephones are often used for data entry and database access.

OUTPUT DEVICES

The two primary types of computer output devices are monitors and printers. Monitors display video images, and printers produce paper documents.

Monitors

The computer video screen displays information in a visual format as text, graphics, or both. Most monitors display in full color, and the resolution is actually superior to that of a television. Standard desktop monitors have become larger than earlier models. Today's monitors measure 17 inches, or even 21 inches, diagonally. At the same time, displays have become smaller for laptops and PDAs. Current devices employing Windows software can display different programs on the screen simultaneously.

Printers

People needing a hard copy of data or information obtain it from a printer. Printers are categorized as either impact or nonimpact. Impact printers, such as the dot matrix printer, are similar to typewriters, where the letter key strikes the paper and imprints ink. Nonimpact printers, such as ink-jet or laser printers, spray the image on the paper or burn it onto the paper. The output of these printers can be in either color or black and white. Plotters are ink-jet printers used to produce graphical output, such as engineering and architectural drawings, on large rolls or sheets of paper.

Photo printers

The new digital cameras have many applications for businesses and individuals. It is no longer necessary to send film out to be processed, and the photos can be manipulated with special software to add special effects, graphics, or text. It is easy to capture and store the images, then download them into a computer. Also, new photo-quality printers now make it possible to print the digital image at a reasonable cost. Older systems required a PC to do the processing, but the newer photo printers have their own computer processing power and memory-card readers. Ink-jet printers use a glossy paper to resemble traditional photographs, while other printers use a heat process to produce the images on special photo paper.

ADD-IN CARDS FOR MICROCOMPUTERS

Different types of add-in cards may be placed in the PC's expansion slots to improve the performance of the PC or to connect various input or output devices. Commonly used cards include:

Accelerator card—Upgrades older machines or boosts the processing speed

Adapter card—Connects peripheral devices, such as a mouse, tape backup system, or zip drive

Emulator card—Allows the PC to operate as if it is a terminal connected to a large host computer

Fax card—Now your PC doubles as a facsimile device (fax)!

Network interface card (NIC)—Connects your PC to other PCs, file servers, or LANs

Sound card—Provides audio recording and playback capability for multimedia systems

Video card—Allows you to display video images in multimedia systems or desktop videoconferencing applications

DESKTOP DATA COMMUNICATIONS EQUIPMENT

Now that we have covered the desktop computer equipment (DTE) you use to do your work, we can address the other classification of desktop data equipment, data communications equipment (DCE).

As I mentioned in Chapter 6, the function of the DCE is to interconnect DTEs so they can "talk" to each other—share resources, exchange data, or provide backup support. The DCE establishes, maintains, and terminates the communications connection between the DTEs, which could be two PCs, a mainframe host and a remote terminal, or any other combination. DCE also provides the conversion and coding of each individual communications signal.

Modems and terminal adapters are two types of DCE familiar to many of us. A modem is used if the communications line uses analog signaling, while a terminal adapter, or line driver, is used if the line uses digital signaling. A new type of DCE beginning to be used in business and residential applications is the cable TV modem, which uses the cable TV wire to access the Internet. Because most businesses do not provide cable TV access to their employees' desktops, cable TV companies are developing Internet business applications as a way of expanding their market beyond the traditional residential market.

TELEPHONE LINE MODEMS

Modems are usually associated with data transmission over twisted-pair copper analog lines, the standard telephone lines. In fact, this is the most common way for homes and small businesses to connect to the Internet. The modem is an inexpensive device that usually operates at connection speeds of 28,000 bps to 56,000 bps (bits per second). It is also used to connect desktop computers or technical workstations, via a standard communications line, to a host computer or to desktop computers in other locations.

The modem converts the PC's digital language into signals suitable for transmitting over an analog telephone line by modulating, or changing, the analog signal characteristics (amplitude, frequency, or phase) to represent digital bits. The modulated analog signal is then demodulated to its original digital form on the other end of the transmission. (The term "modem" is actually a shortened version of modulator/demodulator.) Different modems use different types of modulation techniques. When transmitting data communications over an analog POTS (plain old telephone service) line, the analog signals carrying the modulated digital bits are eventually converted to digital telephone signals. These signals are then switched and transmitted over the main trunks of the public switched telephone network (PSTN).

Not all modems can talk to one another. Modems must be paired with a compatible modem at each end of the circuit. They may be dial-up for regular telephone lines or dedicated for special leased or private lines. Because dial-up modems operate on the POTS telephone line, they must have some of the same capabilities as telephones, including the ability to generate Touch-Tone signals or rotary dial pulses, detect ringing, and convert from the four-wire transmission of the computer to the two-wire transmission of the local telephone loop.

A wide array of optional features and protocols for modems exists, but to communicate with one another, modems must use compatible protocols.

Modulation protocols

The basic rules of communications governing speed, parity, and bit synchronization are also important for modems and dial-up connections. Modulation protocols are the basic rules used by different types of modems.

Rate of transmission

Modems are capable of transmission speeds ranging from 100 bps to 56,000 bps, but the actual modulated transmission rate on a POTS line is limited by a variety of factors encountered on that line. Remember, the POTS line has been engineered to enhance the performance of voice traffic, not data. Thus, the use of a voice-grade POTS line is not optimum for data transmission because the actual bit transmission will hover around 18,000 bps to 22,000 bps. Much depends on both the distance traveled from the telephone central office and the equipment that has been added to improve voice services. A 56K modem actually uses data compression techniques to improve the throughput of the data transmission.

Data compression

There are many different types of data compression, but the same type must be used on both ends of the transmission. Let's say we want to send an email: "Good morning, James, how are you today?" Data compression might change the message to: "Hi, James." This is the compressed version that is actually transmitted across the communications channel. At the other end, the modem checks its clock, sees that it is 11 A.M., and knows to decompress the message to: "Good morning, James, how are you today?" The throughput is seven words, while the actual transmission was only two words.

Data compression is intended to speed up transmission by decreasing the number of bits transmitted. Not all information files can be compressed, so transmission speeds may slow considerably depending on the type of data being transmitted. It is important to understand that throughput and transmission bandwidth are both concerned with the transmission of the data, but they are not always measuring the same thing. To ensure the accurate delivery of decompressed data, modems that perform data compression must also be able to do error checking.

Error control

It is vital that the transmission equipment does not cause or create errors in the data bits, so error detecting and error correcting protocols are included in most data equipment. Error potential and error prevention in data transmissions directly affect all aspects of data flow (retransmission time, reliability, maintenance, and failure rate) as well as its overall cost.

Modems use echo checking—sending the data twice to make sure it matches—or the more sophisticated cyclic redundancy checking, which uses mathematical functions to check the before and after transmissions. (Refer to Chapter 6, Table 6-4, for detailed information on error control methods.)

Turnaround time

Half-duplex modems use the same communications channel for both sending and receiving, but transmission occurs in only one direction at a time. Turnaround time, usually expressed in milliseconds, is the length of time the modem requires to reset from sending mode to receiving mode. Full-duplex modems send and receive signals at the same time.

MODEMS AND DATA NETWORKS

In the simplest networks, a dedicated phone line and modem is provided for each user. This system requires an Internet service provider to set up individual accounts for each user. As more employees are added, however, costs can become expensive.

If a data network already exists, it is much less expensive to install the modems on the network server computer rather than the employees' desktops. Separate modem-sharing software is required for network users to access the modems as shared devices.

Installing only one modem limits Internet access to one network user at a time. If more than one employee needs access to the Internet at the same time, a separate communications server with several modems will accommodate multiple network users. Modem-sharing software will still be necessary for the server to share its modems with the network.

ISDN TERMINAL ADAPTERS

ISDN (integrated services digital network) is a digital telephone service. It transmits data at rates of up to 128 kbps, versus the 33.6 kbps or 56 kbps of a modem on a conventional analog phone line. Like modems, ISDN lines can also be shared by network users. The difference is that a special device combines multiple users over the same digital transmission connection. In addition, a single ISDN line really consists of two channels, allowing you to have a voice conversation even when your computer is connected to the Internet. We'll talk more about ISDN in Chapter 10.

The ISDN terminal adapter can be a stand-alone desktop box connecting the line to the PC; it can be an interface card inserted into the PC; or it can be found in the telephone closets, where the local premises wiring from several employees is connected to the ISDN lines. Wherever it may be located, an ISDN terminal adapter's primary function is to change the computer digital language into a telephone digital transmission.

CABLE TV MODEMS

Cable TV coaxial wiring is one of the newest methods for connecting to the Internet. Because cable TV is an analog transmission, a cable modem is required to perform the same modulation functions as the telephone modem. Cable modems will also be discussed further in Chapter 10.

We are finally ready to move off the desktop. In the next chapter, we will review everything else that is required to make up the local premises network for voice, data, and video services.

Chapter 9

Your Work Location: LANs and Telephone Systems

· ·

IN CHAPTER 8, WE DISCUSSED the different types of equipment used by employees at their desks. In this chapter, we will review everything else that is required to make up the local premises network for voice, data, and video services.

The premises distribution system (PDS) is the skeleton of an organization's communications system. The function of a PDS is to connect employees and their desktop equipment to the voice and data switches, the computing equipment, and the outside world. A well-designed premises distribution system allows the transmission of voice, data, and video signals for all business applications. Clearly, it is a critical element for business communications.

The optimal network for any business would be a single premises network capable of handling all telecommunications needs. Although current technology is not quite there yet, it is definitely heading in that direction.

PDS DESIGN AND COMPONENTS

Telephone company services end and your business system begins at a location known as the building entrance point, or "demarc." The PDS then carries the telecommunications signal from the demarc to each telephone or communications device within your business location. It also carries the telecommunications signal to all the telecommunications devices within each individual workstation.

Table 9-1 lists design considerations that must be evaluated when laying out a PDS for any particular location. We will discuss some of these factors more fully in subsequent sections of this chapter.

Depending on the size of your location, PDS components include the building entrance hardware and the main distribution frame, the equipment room, the vertical riser system and related telephone closets, and the horizontal wiring system that connects voice and data devices. The actual vertical and horizontal wiring system is composed of twisted-pair cable, coaxial cable, or fiber optics, and, for wireless systems, air waves.

Building entrance

The entrance facility consists of the telephone company's outside plant cables, the connecting hardware (including the main distribution frame), any protection devices, and the power equipment necessary to connect the services to the PDS. The actual handoff point of the service, the demarc, defines the boundary between the telephone company's responsibility and your responsibility as a business owner. Large commercial buildings often have two or more facility entrances to provide backup services.

Equipment room

The equipment room, or switch room, contains centralized computers, switches, power sources, uninterrupted (backup) power sources (UPS), and grounding and protection hardware. Many transmission services today have distance limitations. Therefore, the equipment room should be located on the middle floor of a building to minimize the distance traveled by the telecommunications signal to the farthest stations on any floor. In addition, a controlled environment is required because of the sensitivity of this equipment. Other special considerations for the equipment room include security systems, such as alarms and protective doors, and whether or not there will be offices in the same room.

PDS Design Considerations

Design Consideration	Issues	Examples
Terminal or device communications	What devices are to be connected? How will communications occur? What is the physical connector?	Analog or digital phones, dumb terminals, personal computers, printers, storage devices
Transmission media and bandwidth	What type of physical connection is necessary between the equipment? What are the transmission speeds?	UTP copper, STP copper, coaxial cable, fiber-optic cable, wireless options
Network topology and size	The physical arrangement of all the interconnected terminals and devices.	Star, bus, ring, mesh, tree
Network protocols	The specific transmission services or protocols used to carry the signals.	ISDN, Ethernet, token ring, FDDI, ATM, TCP/IP
Centralized communications	What types of concentrators or centralized functions are needed? How many current and future users?	Stand-alone hubs, expandable hubs, LAN switches, voice switches
Internetworking	How will traffic move from local network to local network?	Bridges, routers, brouters
Wide area networking	How will traffic move from local networks to the outside world? What access services will need terminating equipment in the building?	ISDN, frame relay, dedicated (leased) access lines and trunks, ATM
Reliability	Who troubleshoots? Who repairs? What are the contingency plans for failures and disasters?	Uninterrupted power supplies (UPS), replacement equipment, off-site back-up contracts, service level agreements
Management - including security, cost, installation, service, and repair	Who manages the system? How are users (ports) moved, added, and changed? What operating systems are compatible with management systems? Will you use remote management? Can the systems be upgraded? What security is used?	Management software, security hardware & software, remote management software

Table 9-1

Vertical riser system

The vertical riser system consists of cables and connectors that transmit the telecommunications signal up and down between the floors of a building. When designing the vertical riser system, you must consider the number of floors in your building, the number of separate riser runs, or paths, required, and the number of closets needed to serve each riser. Your design must also take into consideration the expected capacity for each run and what type of transmission medium should be used, such as twisted-pair copper, optical fiber, or future fiber.

Because it's safe to assume that fiber will be necessary one day, you will save money by planning for its use when the copper cabling is first installed. This is done by installing either interduct or plastic tubes with special threads that will be used for pulling future fiber through the tubes.

Telephone closets

Telephone closets, also called satellite or telecommunications closets, provide the necessary cross-connects (connections) from the vertical cable to the horizontal cable. The cross-connects are made up of patch panels and jumper wires. If an employee moves to a new cubical, changes are easily made by simply moving the individual's service to a different desk connection. The design of the telephone closet will be determined by the number of stations being served, the need for any type of centralized data equipment, and the need for initial and backup power.

The size of the closet should be large enough for a worker to physically access the conduit and duct systems for the floor, plus allow room for making cross-connects or other changes to station connections. The closet also needs to be large enough to handle a potential increase in the number of stations it serves.

Horizontal cabling

The horizontal cabling should be a direct connection, traveling from each desktop to the appropriate cross-connect in the telephone closet. It consists of the connector at the desktop, the connector in the closet, and the cable itself, which may be twisted-pair copper wire, coax, fiber-optic cable, or even wireless. The cable is run through cavities in the floor construction, under raised computer flooring, or through overhead ceiling ducts with ceiling drop poles. When installing the horizontal cabling, distance is an important factor to keep in mind due to limitations that may be imposed by the LAN technology in use.

VOICE AND DATA SWITCHING

Without switches, telecommunications take place only between those devices that are directly wired together. Imagine having to string a separate, dedicated phone line to everyone you needed to talk to! Obviously, such a situation would be totally impractical.

Switching allows us to connect to anyone who has access to the same switch. Switches may also be connected to other switches, thereby providing access to people and machines connected to a different switch than yours. In addition, these network switches route incoming calls to the intended party. Switches may be voice oriented, such as private branch exchanges (PBXs) or key systems; data oriented, such as LAN switches; or integrated voice and data systems.

Business owners are responsible for supplying their business locations with adequate facilities and attendants to ensure that incoming calls are handled promptly and efficiently. Several types of switching systems are available. The simplest is a key system, which is typically used for voice services. Another common switching system is the private branch exchange (PBX). These systems vary widely in complexity, from a basic voice system to an integrated voice and data switch featuring hundreds of options.

Businesses may also choose to forego switches entirely on their premises. Instead, they can outsource their communications to the local exchange carrier (LEC) by using Centrex integrated voice and data services. (More about Centrex in a later chapter.)

KEY SYSTEMS

Key systems were the earliest forms of business-specific telephones, but they are not actually switches. Six-button telephones, referred to as multibutton or multiline telephones, had a button for your own individual line as well as buttons for your coworkers' lines. This was a great feature for businesses—no more running to answer other folks' phones if they were away from their desks!

Today, key systems are known as electronic key telephone systems (EKTS). The key system unit (KSU), which is the brain or control part of the system, is connected to the public switched telephone network (PSTN) through basic analog business lines. However, multibutton telephones require an individual pair of wires for each button (or line) running from the desk to the KSU in the telephone closet.

Originally, this equipment was leased from the telephone company, but business owners are now required to operate and maintain their own equipment. Although a number of companies make key equipment, the systems generally use proprietary technology, which means only the manufacturer's telephones can be connected to the KSU. Some key systems offer many PBX-type features and are often used by small or medium-sized companies that do not handle a large volume of calls.

PRIVATE BRANCH EXCHANGES (PBXS)

PBXs are privately owned switching systems for business applications that are planned, installed, and operated by the business. An operator/receptionist and a manual switchboard were the earliest forms of business switches. These first PBXs were analog switches, but today's PBXs are digital and are able to provide digital connectivity all the way to the digital telephone or data terminal. Ideally, a single premises switch will one day handle all your voice, data, and multimedia needs.

PBXs provide switching connections to the end user telephones or stations (the end user's desktop device). Additionally, they provide business capabilities, such as individual station features and system features. Basic functions include:

✓ Station-to-station calling with four- or five-digit dialing

✓ Connection of end stations to the LEC central office access trunks (for connection to the PSTN and private virtual networks)
✓ Centralized handling of incoming calls from LEC central office trunks
✓ Integration of voice and data features and applications (such as PBX-to-host interfaces, data interfaces to data devices, and ISDN voice and LAN services)

The software, or operating system, of the PBX develops many of its features. Station features are developed directly for the end users and include call forwarding, call transfer, conferencing, and speed dialing. In addition to intercom calling and attendant services, PBX systems may include the features discussed below.

Least cost routing (LCR), also called automatic route selection, allows the PBX to automatically select the least expensive outgoing trunk. The route is chosen based on the number being called, the time of day, and the service provider being used.

Call message detail recording (CMDR) keeps track of all calls made by a business and subsequently transfers the data to a call accounting computer system. Rather than splitting toll costs evenly among departments or employees, a monthly bill is generated for the actual usage of each employee or department. Hopefully, this monthly bill and call data will help individuals and departments manage their costs better.

Direct-inward dial (DID) network access allows an outside caller to directly dial an employee's telephone number. This access eliminates the intermediate steps of calling a general business number and being switched by a receptionist or automatic attendant to the extension of the employee. **Direct-outward dial (DOD)** lines function in the opposite direction. Dialing "9" or "8" before the number you want to reach gets you directly to your party. Otherwise, you need to ask the receptionist to give you an "outside" line before dialing your call.

Toll-free calling allows your customers or vendors to call you "collect" without obtaining permission for each call. Most of us are familiar with the toll-free 800, 888, or 877 numbers. These numbers may also be combined with "vanity" numbers that use names instead of digits. For example, 1-800-FLOWERS makes it easy for customers to remember your number.

The opposite of toll-free calling is **WATS** calling, or **wide area telephone service**. It lets you define the specific areas, such as counties or states, that your business calls most often. Then, instead of paying toll charges on a per call basis, you pay a fixed monthly rate to have unlimited calling within those areas.

Wide area networks or virtual private networks (VPNs) are often installed by large and mid-sized companies consisting of multiple business locations. **Access to virtual private networks (VPNs)** in the form of a dedicated or switched line is offered by both LECs and IXCs, plus a number of competitive telephone companies. Refer to Chapter 10 for more information on these services.

Advantages of digital PBXs
Companies that install PBXs on their business premises become, in effect, mini-telephone companies. Many of the same switching functions performed by the local exchange carrier's (LEC) central office (CO) become the responsibility of the business.

However, when businesses install PBXs rather than lease Centrex service from the LEC, they acquire considerable benefits. State-of-the art digital communications voice features, advanced switching technology, information management applications, and data interconnection with host computers and terminals are some of the reasons a business will install a PBX. Other advantages are discussed below.

Local control
Your business can manage and monitor its system's performance by using the administrative and control functions of the PBX. You will need several people trained to do this, or it is a wasted capability. Feature packages may be customized or changed as needs

change, and day-to-day management issues can be responded to promptly. In addition to saving money, your business will control its own private network.

I once worked with a small company that was having trouble with its network about six months after installing its PBX. When I asked to see the management reports to troubleshoot the system, the company owner didn't know what I meant. The PBX sales rep had left him with the impression that the PBX did everything internally. As it turned out, this company had not made any back-ups, kept any record of changes, or updated any routing tables. We had to start from scratch to get the system running again.

Local area switching

A PBX gives your business the ability to interconnect various us-ers, plus switch voice and data calls from desk to desk. In this way, the cost of interconnecting onsite users via individual lines to and from the LEC central office is eliminated. LEC charges would include trunk charges, usage charges, and local access charges, so, if most of the calling is in-house, the savings can be great. On the other hand, if most of the calling is to outside locations, a PBX may offer no cost advantage.

Common premises distribution system

PBXs permit separate voice and data traffic to be transmitted over the same twisted pairs of copper wire, thus allowing the use of integrated voice and data equipment. Wiring to the workstations is minimized, and valuable space is freed up by eliminating sepa-rate equipment for voice and data.

Predictable monthly costs

Once the PBX is installed, monthly costs for the system can be budgeted exactly. These costs include depreciation for the capital equipment, monthly charges for access lines and trunks from the local exchange company, and staff salaries for operating and main-taining the system.

Enhanced services and host-to-computer services

PBXs have more features and capabilities than most companies will ever use. Nonetheless, your company can select those features and capabilities that will provide it with a competitive advantage.

Disadvantages of PBXs

Small and mid-sized companies sometimes lack the staff and expertise to maintain a PBX. These companies should seriously consider outsourcing their needs to a third party maintenance organization or using Centrex services from the LEC. Possible disadvantages of PBXs should be weighed carefully against the advantages.

Capital expenditure

Depending on the size of the system, a major capital outlay may be needed for the PBX and its related equipment. Managers often think of this as a one-time cost, but there will also be ongoing costs for maintenance and system upgrades, such as new hardware and software.

Obsolete technology

Telecommunications technology changes rapidly. The system you choose should be designed to handle your business needs for at least five years. Start with the latest, state-of-the-art technology even if it's not immediately needed. Naturally, you don't want to pay for what you don't use, but this tactic gives you the option of growing into your system's capabilities. In addition, be sure that your technology can be upgraded to capabilities you might want in the future.

Equipment room and power requirements

You will need space in your building for the PBX and its auxiliary equipment. Most companies also require power backups or uninterrupted power supplies for their PBX and computer equipment. Depending on the size of your system, this expense can be considerable.

Staff and training requirements

If your employees require 24-hour, seven-days-a-week communications access, you will need a trained staff to maintain your PBX. Large companies often have these people on staff anyway, but small and medium-sized companies may not be able to afford the additional help.

Integrated voice and data PBX technology

Traditional switching integrates voice and data by giving each terminal its own unique address. In digital telecommunications, however, both voice and data are transmitted as digital bits over a high-speed time-division multiplexed (TDM) carrier. The next generation of PBXs not only combines voice and data, but also integrates LANs with voice communications. In addition, some data equipment vendors are developing LANs that handle data and voice without the need for switches.

Auxiliary voice processing services

Auxiliary, or add-on, systems provide PBXs with additional capabilities. Voice processing services include automated attendant, automatic call distribution, voice messaging, and interactive voice response (IVR).

Automated attendant

When your call is answered by a recording that directs you to enter an extension number or spell the name of the person you are calling, you have reached the automated attendant. This service is also used to distribute calls to different departments within a business (1 for sales, 2 for human resources, 3 for customer support, and so on). The key to successful use of this feature is to make sure a live representative always answers the transfer to "operator" or is otherwise easily available. Keep in mind the needs of the caller, your customer, who is frequently annoyed when not able to speak with a real person.

Automatic call distributor (ACD)

Some PBXs have ACDs built in, while others require separate equipment for interconnection. The function of an ACD is to switch a large number of incoming calls to different agents or answering positions. Because only one telephone number is needed, businesses that employ call centers for reservations, catalog sales, or customer support can maximize their efficiency with the ACD. If all agents are busy, the ACD notifies the callers (via a recording) and places them in a queue. The calls are then answered in the order received as agents become available.

Voice messaging systems

Voice mail systems allow employees to leave specific greetings for their callers. Like electronic mail, the resulting voice messages can be saved, forwarded to others, or deleted. If a caller does not want to leave a message and your system allows a transfer to "0," make sure a live person always answers the transfer. Otherwise, callers transfer from greeting to greeting to greeting without ever talking to anyone. This is bad for business!

Interactive voice response (IVR)

Voice response systems offer callers a menu of choices that allow them to conduct transactions, such as making reservations, checking bank account balances, or reviewing event schedules. Callers generally like IVR systems as long as a live person is available for questions.

PBXs for the small office/home office (SOHO) market

Professionals working out of their home office or starting small businesses have greatly increased their demand for small PBXs. It is one of the fastest growing equipment markets today. These small PBXs have the same capabilities and features as the larger PBXs, but cost considerably less. Small businesses can choose features such as automated attendants, integration of cell phones and pagers, voice mail, ISDN support, and computer telephony applications driven by caller ID.

COMPUTER TELEPHONY INTEGRATION (CTI)

Computer telephony integration joins two of the most common communications devices—the computer and the telephone—to create a whole new field of business applications. One common application uses caller ID to automatically access a customer's account record. The record, which resides on a database server, is displayed on the agent's screen even before the agent has answered the incoming call. All the relevant client information is immediately available, thus allowing the agent to better respond to the client's needs.

Another new CTI feature is unified messaging. This service accesses and responds to all voice mail, email, faxes, and pager messages from a common mailbox. Most of us are familiar with how email messages are stored and forwarded. Unified messaging handles voice messages, faxes, and pager messages in the same way. As we discussed earlier, other applications, such as interactive voice response and automated attendants, also employ CTI.

LOCAL AREA NETWORKS (LANs)

Whether located in the same building, the same city, or at a distance, the employees of any business need to be connected effectively. The purpose of a LAN is very simple—to transport data between employees and their terminals (usually PCs). The components of a data communications network may be complex, but everything is designed to meet this common goal.

A variety of LANs may be installed on a single floor, within a section of a building, or throughout an entire building. Each of these networks may use different types of data network equipment. If data managers adopt certain proprietary equipment, they should be aware that it may not work with other vendors' proprietary equipment and thus lock them into certain types of networks.

LAN BACKGROUND

In the past, new data applications were developed to be function specific. For example, only finance people used financial applications, and only engineers used engineering applications. Each application required a separate data network to connect its users to the host computer. Local area networks (LANs) evolved as a way to connect multiple users to the host computer where a specialized application resided. Because each application was different—accounting, engineering, production—protocols were developed for each LAN without regard for connectivity between LANs of different types. Why would the bean counters in accounting need to communicate with the techies in engineering?

Today, we recognize the value of enterprise-wide communications and interconnectivity. Different types of LANs must be interconnected, or new networks must be developed, so that everyone can connect to everyone else.

LAN COMPONENTS

To be connected to a LAN, every computer or shared peripheral device must have the appropriate hardware and software, plus a transmission medium that physically connects each device. The result is called a shared-media LAN. Hardware and software on each device may be obtained from various manufacturers, but all must be compatible and "speak" the same data language. Data networks perform services for the data communications user in the same manner that the telephone network does for a telephone user.

Network hardware

A network interface card (NIC) must be installed on each device or node on the LAN. The NIC acts as a go-between by taking messages from the computer, converting them to the proper LAN language, and then sending them to other computers or devices on the LAN. In addition, the LAN will need some type of network hub or wiring center to physically connect the devices. The hub provides the connecting point for all the devices.

Other types of data network hardware include the host mainframe and the front-end processor. Databases are stored in the mainframe, while the front-end processor's purpose is to off-load communications tasks from the host computer. In this way, the host computer is free to devote its processor to user applications and database operations. IBM pioneered this type of network.

Networking software

PCs share resources, such as printers, data, and applications, via their networking software. Stand-alone PCs need an operating system to interface between the applications (such as word processing) and the CPU (the PC's brain). The specific software that permits PCs to log onto the LAN and communicate with other devices is called client-network software.

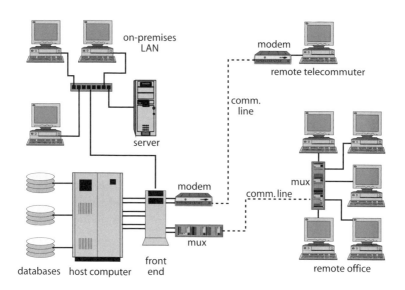

Figure 9-1

Client PCs communicate not only with each other, but also with servers, such as application servers or print servers. These servers are actually PCs that perform central functions for the LAN, and they require specific server software. Two popular networking software programs are Windows NT (2000) and Novell NetWare.

Transmission media

Factors influencing which media to use include the transmission speed needed, the type of NIC used, security requirements, and the physical environment. The transmission media must be installed carefully and be fully compatible with the LAN hardware. Refer to Chapter 7 for a discussion of the various types of transmission media currently available.

Internetworking

As organizations increased their use of data communications systems and LANs, it became necessary to connect the LANs together for the purpose of sharing servers and host computers. The additional component needed to interconnect these LANs is called an internetworking unit (IWU).

The IWU relays traffic between the networks, and it may also provide protocol conversion functions if the networks' protocols differ. Internetworking equipment includes bridges, routers, brouters, and gateways. All these devices are described later in this chapter.

LAN SELECTION CRITERIA

Before installing LAN protocols and components, a LAN manager must assess his company's specific needs. Determining the needs of the end users is critical to the success of the installation. Important considerations are outlined in the following sections.

COST

LAN managers do not have unlimited budgets. (If they did, they would immediately install the biggest and fastest LAN possible!) Therefore, cost is the most basic constraint when determining the best LAN for your business. Costs for site preparation, design, and documentation need to be added to the actual hardware and software costs. Then, there are the installation costs, which include cabling, hardware, software applications, and testing. Finally, training costs for administrators, operators, and end users must be added as well.

Often, cost benefit studies do not consider the annual or recurring costs necessary to operate the LAN effectively. These costs include hardware and software maintenance (approximately 7 to 10 percent of the hardware costs), LAN management personnel costs, consumable supplies, and training for new users and administrators.

Size

When considering the cost and design of a LAN, size is certainly a factor. Because each end user is physically connected to the LAN, the number and type of workstations or personal computers is critical. Do you use Apple Macintoshes or IBM-compatible equipment or both in your business? LANs also have distance limitations. The geographical coverage of a LAN is based on the type of cabling installed and the transmission speed required.

LAN speeds are determined by the data transmission rates of the media being used. However, this speed is not constant, nor does each workstation have its own transmission capability. All workstations share the total LAN transmission capability. Therefore, the actual data speed between any two machines depends on the total number of devices connected to the LAN and how many of them are transmitting at the same time. Common LAN speeds range from 1 Mbps to 100 Mbps.

Usage

Probably the most crucial design considerations are: How is the LAN is going to be used? What application software packages will be run on the LAN? Are the existing user applications LAN-compatible, or will they need to be modified? What interfaces or application program interfaces (APIs) are necessary for the applications to communicate over the network?

The LAN's performance is directly affected by the number of users accessing it at the same time. In fact, LAN responsiveness is the primary complaint of most LAN users. In addition to workstations and users, LANs also serve printers and other devices, such as optical storage disks, that contribute to the overall workload. What are these devices and how many are there per LAN? How are they connected to the LAN?

LAN SOFTWARE AND HARDWARE

Once the cost, design, and usage requirements and constraints are defined, the LAN software and hardware can be chosen. Can you use your existing software and hardware, or must they be replaced? Many different proprietary LANs were installed over the years, and some, such as Ethernet, became de facto standards.

A number of vendors make compatible hardware and software for standards-based LANs, so a distinct advantage to using this type of network is being able to choose your vendor. In addition, LAN experts better understand the characteristics and capabilities of LANs designed around predictable standards.

CONNECTIVITY TO OTHER NETWORKS

Although each LAN is a stand-alone network, users on the LAN need to communicate with users on other LANs, whether in the same building or in other company locations. Many users also need to communicate with customers and vendors via public networks. This is the point where businesses need to determine how they will connect with other networks.

Security becomes a critical element when LAN interconnectivity is allowed. Who has access to data stored on the LAN? Who manages each file? How is the LAN protected from unauthorized access? These are all questions that must be considered.

MANAGEMENT

The ongoing management of a LAN is as important as the initial installation. The LAN's expandability must be considered up front. What will be the maximum number of users? How will the new workstations be attached to the cabling? How will this affect speed and performance?

Even a very small LAN requires a manager to add or remove users and applications, create data backups, and provide equipment and user support. The LAN manager can be assisted in these tasks by special LAN management software, and the vendors that provided the LAN hardware and software are also good sources for support.

SHARED LAN ARCHITECTURES AND LAN PROTOCOLS

Logical topology and physical topology describe two basic ways LANs may differ. Logical topology is the method used to transmit data over the network, while physical topology refers to the physical arrangement of all the devices.

In a shared LAN topology, such as Ethernet or token ring, users take turns transmitting data. Newer switched LAN architectures provide point-to-point connections, allowing multiple users to communicate at the same time.

The Institute of Electrical and Electronics Engineers (IEEE) publishes several recommended standards for LANs that are widely accepted. These standards are important because they encourage the use of common approaches for LAN protocols and interfaces. We see the direct benefits of standardization when, for example, chip manufacturers are willing to develop inexpensive hardware in anticipation of a large market. The IEEE LAN standards are defined in:

IEEE 802.1	High-level interface (and MAC bridges)
IEEE 802.2	Logical link control (LLC)
IEEE 802.3	Carrier sense multiple access/collision detection (CSMA/CD)
IEEE 802.4	Token bus
IEEE 802.5	Token ring
IEEE 802.6	Metropolitan Area Networks
IEEE 802.7	Broadband LANs
IEEE 802.8	Fiber-optic LANs
IEEE 802.9	Integrated data and voice networks
IEEE 802.10	Security
IEEE 802.11	Wireless networks

In the following sections, we will discuss the three most common LAN protocols: Ethernet, token ring, and FDDI. It is important to keep in mind how these LAN protocols relate to other data networking protocols. They are designed for relatively short distances, and their only purpose is to move bits through a local network. These protocols end at the edge of the local network, and other protocols take over if the data is being transmitted via the PSTN or over a WAN.

Think of these protocols as local delivery trucks. They pick up parcels of data from one PC and deliver it to another PC in the same neighborhood. The driver knows all the neighborhood PC addresses, but he wouldn't have a clue how to deliver a parcel across the country. For out-of-neighborhood parcels, he would simply deliver it to a shipping hub and let them take care of it from there.

To take the analogy a step further, let's assume the delivery truck can accept parcels of different sizes with different contents. The contents could be a higher-level protocol, such as TCP/IP. If the parcel is addressed to an outside location, it gets delivered to the shipping hub where the handlers open the parcel and find several envelopes with numerous different addresses in other cities. These envelopes are TCP/IP packets, each with its own address.

The handlers now place these packets in another type of box, perhaps a frame-relay frame, and sent them on their way. This is the essence of protocol conversion. The envelope containing the original data, the TCP/IP packet, hasn't been changed at all. It is simply riding in a different transport vehicle.

This basic concept pervades data communications at all levels. The task of the lowest layers on the OSI Model, Layers 1 and 2, is to move whatever parcels are presented to them as efficiently as possible. LAN protocols are at these levels.

ETHERNET

The most common LAN protocol is Ethernet. In the 1980s, Robert Metcalfe developed this proprietary network protocol for

Xerox's internal data networks. Due to its popularity, the IEEE subsequently standardized the Ethernet protocols, and most data hardware and software manufacturers now make Ethernet-compatible products. Ethernet uses CSMA/CD access methodology to control the transmission of data on the network. Compared to other types of data protocols, Ethernet is inexpensive.

Depending on the specific type of Ethernet system used, data can be transferred at different speeds. Most Ethernet LANs transfer data at a rate of 10 Mbps, but newer Ethernet networks, such as fast Ethernet, transfer data at a rate of 100 Mbps. Even faster gigabit Ethernet networks are being developed to transmit images and video clips. As outlined below, data transmission speeds will dictate the type of cabling, NICs, and connectors required by an Ethernet system.

Smaller departments of large companies use **10Base2 Ethernet**. It uses coax to transfer data over distances up to 607 feet at a rate of 10 Mbps.

Thicknet, a thicker coax, is used by **10Base5 Ethernet**. It transmits data up to 1,640 feet at a rate of 10 Mbps, and it is used in newer installations. Transceivers installed in this cable communicate with the network interface card (NIC) residing in the PC.

10BaseT Ethernet is the form of Ethernet most often used today. It consists of unshielded twisted-pair (UTP) copper wire and transmits data up to 328 feet at 10 Mbps.

100BaseT Ethernet is similar to 10BaseT. It transmits data at a rate of 100 Mbps.

Token Ring
The IEEE 802.5 token ring specification defines the token-passing ring network. Each multistation access unit (MAU) connected to the ring can accommodate up to eight individual workstation connections. The ring covers a maximum distance of 770 meters with a maximum of 260 nodes, and it operates at 4, 16, or 100 Mbps.

A major advantage of the token ring LAN is the predictability of its performance, which is due to the nature of the token-passing access methodology described in Chapter 6. There is no chance of a data collision. Both the maximum time and the average time needed for each station to transmit its message can be calculated. Ethernet LANs usually have a lower speed-per-station cost than a token ring, but the token ring provides better performance for those LANs serving many stations and transmitting heavy traffic.

FIBER DISTRIBUTED DATA INTERFACE (FDDI)

High-speed LANs may be used as backbone networks to inter-connect other LANs. The American National Standards Institute (ANSI) established FDDI as the backbone standard for networks using fiber-optic cable. The specification calls for the token ring LAN to operate at 100 Mbps over distances up to 200 kilometers, with a maximum of 1000 nodes connected to the ring.

Because the distance is so great, FDDI is not a true LAN trans-mitting only one message at a time. The FDDI protocol permits multiple messages to be transmitted simultaneously by the use of a dual counter-rotating ring structure for high-speed token pass-ing. FDDI's use has been primarily limited to backbone applica-tions as its cost is considerably more than copper-based LANs. FDDI is often used for multi-building campus data backbones.

SWITCHED LAN NETWORKS

Switched networks are designed to connect large numbers of in-dividual users to other individual users, all at the same time. An individual transmission is sent to a switch, and the switch then determines how to route the data.

LAN switching uses concentrators and hubs to shorten the length of the LAN, thereby increasing its performance without changing its basic characteristics. Only one station can transmit at a time on a shared LAN, but a switching hub or LAN switch allows mul-tiple users to transmit at LAN speeds simultaneously. Thus, every device on a 100 Mbps LAN can communicate with every other device at the full 100 Mbps.

LAN switches are available for Ethernet, token ring, and FDDI. In addition, high-end LAN switches support asynchronous transfer mode (ATM). When the bandwidth needs of a shared-media LAN exceed the available bandwidth, installing a LAN switch may be the simplest way to increase data throughput speeds. The appropriate LAN switch replaces the shared-media hub.

A variety of LAN switches exists, including cut-through switches, store-and-forward switches, and ATM switches. How the data packets or frames are switched will determine which type of LAN switch is used.

CUT-THROUGH SWITCHES

The first task of a cut-through switch is to determine the final destination of the incoming data. Next, it establishes a point-to-point connection with the correct switch port for that destination, and the incoming data is then forwarded. Cut-through switching is very fast. The receiving destination, however, must do the error checking and request retransmission if any data frames are incorrect. If there are lots of errors, the overall transmission through the switch is increased.

STORE-AND-FORWARD SWITCHES

These switches store the entire frame of data in a memory buffer, and then perform error checking to ensure that the stored data is the same as the original transmission. If not, it requests the necessary retransmission. If the data is correct, the switch finds the correct port, establishes the point-to-point connection, and forwards the data to the destination. This type of switching is slower than cut-through switching, but it is completely accurate.

ATM SWITCHING FOR LANs

Asynchronous transfer mode (ATM) is a connection-oriented, packet-switched transmission protocol that works in both local and wide area data networks. Because it is fast and it is switched, it can send a continuous stream of data over one transmission path to deliver real-time, packetized voice and video as well as data.

ATM uses a fixed-length, 53-byte packet, which is known as a cell. The fixed length greatly simplifies troubleshooting, administration, setup, and design of an ATM switch. ATM transmits in the local area at rates up to 100 Mbps using UTP Category 5 twisted-pair copper wire, or at a rate of 155 Mbps over multimode fiber-optic cable. We will talk more about ATM in Chapter 11.

Shared Media LAN Architecture

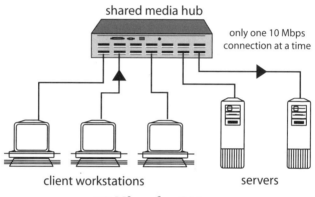

10 Mbps for ALL

Switch-based LAN Architecture

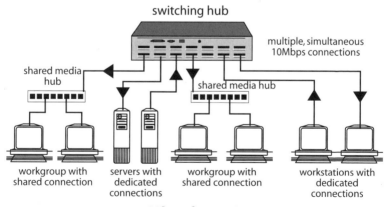

10 Mbps for EACH

Figure 9-2

DATA NETWORKING EQUIPMENT AND DEVICES

Data networks exist for the purpose of interconnecting data terminal equipment (such as computers)—this is their only reason for being. Data terminal equipment (DTE) and data communications equipment (DCE) were covered in the last chapter, and we have already talked about the physical media used to link devices, such as twisted-pair copper wire. We now turn our attention to the equipment that links DTE and DCE together in a network.

Network Interface Card (NIC)

As I mentioned earlier, LANs must have network interface cards (NIC) installed in each device. The NIC acts as the go-between, connecting personal computers and peripheral devices to the network. It takes messages from the computer, converts them to the proper LAN language, and sends them to other computers or devices on the LAN. The LAN protocol employed will dictate the type of NIC to use. An Ethernet card, for example, is a NIC card that takes TCP/IP packets from the PC and places them into the Ethernet frame delivery vehicle.

Front-end Processor

Pioneered by IBM, the front-end processor is a special-purpose computer on the network that functions as an assistant to the host computer. Many computer networks contain a front-end processor. Its primary job is to off-load communications tasks from the host computer. The host computer is then free to devote its CPU cycles to user applications and database operations. The front-end processor also performs other tasks, such as protocol conversion, line control, error control, and message handling.

Modems and Line Drivers

Modems for telephone lines were discussed in the previous chapter, but modems are also used in data networks to increase the distance covered by the transmission line. If workstations and other computers are located more than a few hundred feet from the host computer (or the front end), modems are used to terminate the communications line between the host computer and remote

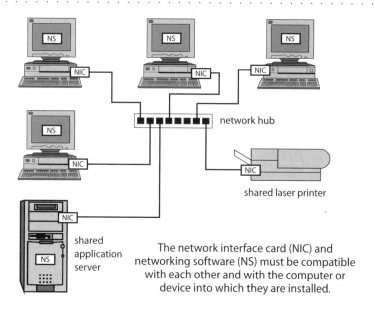

The network interface card (NIC) and networking software (NS) must be compatible with each other and with the computer or device into which they are installed.

Figure 9-3

workstations. The digital signals are then modulated onto an analog carrier to achieve transmission distances of several miles.

In some installations, modems are not used. Instead, a line driver, a modem-like device, provides the signaling interface. If the communications line transmits via analog signaling, a modem is used, but line drivers are used for digital signaling.

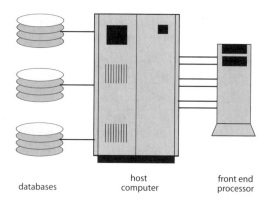

Figure 9-4

MULTIPLEXERS

A multiplexer (MUX) is a device that groups multiple inputs into an aggregate signal, which is then transmitted through a single channel. Refer to Chapter 7 for a detailed discussion of multiplexing.

HUBS

Network devices are physically connected to one another by cables, and a hub is basically a box containing a bunch of cable connectors. If your network uses twisted-pair cable, it probably has a network hub. The cable to the hub connects each computer on the network, and the hub, in turn, connects all the computers to one another. If your network uses coax cable, a hub isn't used because the cable goes directly from computer to computer. Network hubs are also used to concentrate data.

A hub with cables radiating out to various PCs may look like a star network configuration. However, a star network topology is not necessarily created. The hub itself can be internally wired for virtually any network topology, such as a bus, ring, star, or mesh network. Hubs simply offer a convenient way to interconnect network devices and may be characterized in a variety of ways.

Repeater hub

This hub device is used on Ethernet LANs. It emulates a shared bus topology by interconnecting all the ports and sequentially copying, or repeating, the signal to each connected device.

Multistation access unit (MAU)

Also called a wiring concentrator, this type of hub creates a ring topology for token ring networks.

Workgroup and enterprise hubs

These are basically concentrator devices that smaller, stand-alone hubs connect to. Their purpose is to make the network wiring scheme easier to design, install, and manage.

Stackable hubs are single protocol units designed to link various hubs, thereby effectively creating one interconnected LAN.

Modular hubs are built on a chassis with multiple slots for plug-in modules. They use a high-speed data bus to link various unit modules, which may be a mixture of repeater hubs, MAUs, routers, or other network devices.

Switchable hubs feature ports that permit additional stackable hubs to be connected for expanded capacity. Special software is used to reassign the ports or switch the ports off and on.

Device	Links	Function	Pros	Cons
Concentrator	multiple sources	single transmission	processes data	needs reassembly
ATM Concentrator	Ethernets, T1s, T3s	uses virtual circuits, discards cells	efficient bandwidth use	most expensive
Modular Hubs	multiple protocols	connects physical cables	mixes protocols (FDDI, Ethernet, etc.)	installed in the physical closets
Stackable Hubs	single protocols	adds units by stacking	fits more units together	cannot connect different network protocols
Switchable Hubs	multiple protocols	software reassigns ports	saves physical connections	more expensive
ATM (future)	LAN to ATM technology	more efficient ATM	allows quality-of-service priorities	most expensive

Table 9-2

REPEATERS

The function of a repeater is to receive a digital signal and regenerate it. Repeaters are used to solve the problem of reduced signal strength over distance, known as attenuation. Its analog cousin is an amplifier. All long-distance digital systems use repeaters to maintain adequate signal strength across the network. Because a repeater forms a new signal, any distortion in the old signal is removed. This is one reason that long-distance communications are so reliable today.

INTERNETWORKING EQUIPMENT

If everyone you needed to communicate with or exchange data with was located near you, each data device would be directly connected together. However, this is not the case in today's business world.

Data networks must have some form of internetwork connection. The devices that perform this function are internetworking units (IWUs). Internetworking is not always easy to do because a variety of protocols and applications are used and installed on different LANs. Therefore, some form of internetworking unit needs to be attached to each LAN. Different types of IWUs, including bridges, routers, and gateways, may have slightly different functions, but their primary purpose is to relay traffic between networks. These devices may also act as repeaters.

Bridges

Separate LANs or various segments of a network that share the same high-level protocols can be connected by a bridge. Users on two small LANs that have been bridged together will be able to communicate as if they were on one large LAN. A bridge reads the destination of each data packet and then forwards it to the appropriate user on the network or across the bridge to the other network.

Conversely, bridges may be used to divide a large, congested LAN into two smaller LANs. Overall transmission performance is improved because collisions and other problems arising in one LAN segment are isolated within that segment, thereby preventing the rest of the LAN from being degraded.

Routers

Routers are similar to bridges, only much smarter. In addition to linking networks together and directing information to its correct destination, routers are able to select the best transmission path or route in any large network that offers multiple paths for users. An intelligent router can also detect whether parts of the network are not working correctly and reroute data packets accordingly. Traffic congestion is prevented by the use of software control.

To connect different types of networks together, routers are able to translate the data into the proper protocols so users on other LANs can understand it. Routers are often used to connect LANs over a wide area as well.

A router will contain an index of all the potential routes an individual packet could travel to reach its destination. When a data packet is received, the router transfers it to the next network on the chosen route, where another router transfers it to the next network, and so on until reaching its final destination. A router can be likened to a knowledgeable traffic cop who, aware of all the roads leading to a given destination, sends a driver along the shortest route with the lightest traffic for that particular time of day.

Brouters

Combining the best features of both bridges and routers, a brouter works with different LANs using high-level protocols to find the most expedient transmission route for data. A brouter performs as a router when it transfers data that arrives in protocols it supports, and it perfoms as a bridge when it cannot translate data. However, brouters are expensive and difficult to install.

Gateways

Gateways are complex, specialized computers that operate at all seven layers of the OSI Model. They connect networks with differing architectures by using software that converts one protocol to another. In addition, gateways may contain a variety of communications devices, such as rate converters or signal translators, to facilitate communication between the two networks. For example, a gateway is used to transfer data between a PC network and a Mac network. When email messages are sent from a LAN to the public Internet and on to a specialized email system, such as America Online, they often pass through various gateways.

CHANNEL SERVICE UNIT (CSU) AND
DIGITAL SERVICE UNIT (DSU)

CSUs and DSUs are usually combined into one device and are used with T1 (and other T-carrier) digital circuits. These are the devices that terminate the T1 circuit at each end. They are located on the customer's premises and act as the demarcation point at the customer's location.

The CSU isolates the customer's DTE and network from the telephone company's network. In this way, disruptive signals or stray voltages can be blocked. One of the main functions of the CSU is to ensure the integrity of the T-carrier facilities in the telephone network. It achieves this by performing tests for the phone company, storing usage statistics, and protecting both telephone company and user equipment from lightning strikes or other electrical problems.

The DSU, also called a data service unit, converts the digital signals into bipolar signals for transmission over the T1 circuit. (All digital signals transmitted over the PSTN are in the bipolar, or alternate mark inversion, format.) The DSU performs this function for T-carrier transmission systems.

CSU/DSUs may also serve as repeaters by reconstituting digital signals that are passed on to either the telephone network or the customer's private data network. Figure 9-5 shows how a CSU/DSU is connected in a typical customer's premises.

CSU/DSU Connections

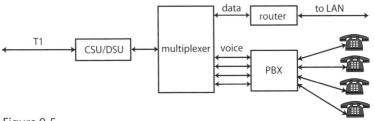

Figure 9-5

NETWORK SECURITY

Network security is no longer a luxury. Today's competitive global economy demands a security system that protects your business data from those who have no "business" accessing it. Many users consider passwords and log-in procedures as inconvenient, but network security should be a top concern for all users and providers. Depending on its function, all customer premises equipment should be located in secured or restricted areas. What about the data itself? As the role of electronic commerce in business grows, so too does the need to protect all online transactions.

USER IDENTIFICATION AND AUTHENTICATION

The first level of security is to determine the identity of the user. Next, some type of authentication is required to verify the user's identity. User identification systems can range from simple first-name passwords to sophisticated systems that employ voice prints or fingerprints for identification. Naturally, the sensitivity of the data being accessed dictates what type of identification system should be used.

FIREWALLS

The delivery of information between an organization's internal network and any outside network, such as the Internet, can be controlled by firewalls. They create a buffer zone that protects the information assets of the company from tampering, destruction, and theft. A firewall will prevent unauthorized individuals from accessing particular parts of a private network or the entire network.

The hardware and software components of a firewall serve as a gateway, allowing data to travel out to the public network, but restricting incoming data. If data does not come from an approved source, it is discarded. Some firewalls are sophisticated enough to filter the data, transferring certain data while blocking other data.

ENCRYPTION

There are circumstances when a physical security system does not provide enough protection. Encryption is the process of scrambling data to be transmitted at the sending end and unscrambling the data at the receiving end. It is used to conceal sensitive information, such as credit card numbers, from unauthorized users.

The Data Encryption Standard (DES) is a sophisticated type of encryption that uses an algorithm to change data into an encoded form for transmission. In addition to transmitting the encrypted data, the key to decipher the data must also be transmitted. These complex encryption keys are measured in bits, and, until recently, a 40-bit encryption key was considered sufficient for sensitive information. Now, however, 64-bit and 128-bit keys are required to thwart increasingly savvy code breakers.

DATA NETWORKING SOFTWARE

For any network to function, lots of software has to be set up just right. The setup programs that come with the various network operating systems (NOS) will configure the network software automatically, but it is usually necessary to do a bit of tweaking as well.

A variety of network software exists, and your choice will depend on end user needs and the type of hardware your business has installed. Client network software allows PCs to run, log onto the LAN, and communicate with other devices on the LAN. In client-server networks, both the clients and the servers need to use the same network operating systems.

Network Operating Systems

A network computer or server runs the network operating system (NOS), which, in turn, controls all the activity on the network. In some cases, the NOS runs on many different servers, each performing a different function. Examples of network operating systems include Windows 95 (98), Windows NT (2000), NetWare, and UNIX.

Windows 95 (98)

Because Windows 95 (98) is installed on most personal computers, this standard PC operating system can be an inexpensive way to build a network operating system. It is used for peer-to-peer networks where each computer exchanges resources and information with other computers on the network. Because of the popularity of Windows 95, many types of network hardware, such as network interface cards, are designed to work with Windows 95. Many end user applications have also been developed.

Windows NT (2000)

Windows NT (2000) is an upgrade of earlier Windows versions. It can be used on peer-to-peer networks, but it is more commonly used on client-server networks for both the network servers and the end clients. It employs a graphical user interface (GUI) for many administrative tasks, making it an easy system to use. Numerous companies provide certified technical support for all aspects of planning, operating, and maintaining a Windows NT (2000) network.

NetWare

Novell developed NetWare for use on client-server networks. Different versions permit different numbers of simultaneous computer connections, and, because it is modular in design, programs may be added as needed. NetWare is well supported by a large bank of certified technicians, and a variety of network applications and hardware has been developed specifically for this system.

UNIX

Developed by AT&T Bell Laboratories in the late 1960s, UNIX is the oldest network operating system. It is a powerful system, but it is also difficult to install and maintain. Special multitasking software allows clients to work on different functions at the same time. Today, UNIX is commonly used for servers on the Internet.

The table below compares and contrasts the network operating systems we have discussed.

APPLICATION SOFTWARE

Application software does not need the full processing capability of the server, so it may be stored on either a central computer or on individual computers. Typical business applications include file services, print services, messaging services, and database services.

File services

These services organize and store your files on secure, centralized file servers. In addition to allowing all users to share files and work together, file services save space on individual PCs. Security systems are used to control user access, and all information is backed up on the server to protect your files from any system failures.

Comparison of Network Operating Systems				
	Windows 95	**Windows NT**	**NetWare**	**UNIX**
Peer-to-peer	X			X
Client-server		X	X	X
Password encryption	X	X	X	X
Audit trails		X	X	X
TCP/IP	X	X	X	
GUI network administration		X		X

Table 9-3

Print services

The purpose of print services is to allow users, whether local or remote, to share the same printer or access specialized printers on the network. The result is an overall decrease in printing costs. If the printers are overloaded, print jobs can be stored or queued. Other types of print services are used for faxing.

Messaging services

Email is the most common type of messaging service used by LANs. Some applications can also exchange word processing documents, spreadsheets, sound files, and video files. Enterprise messaging services combine email, fax, and voice-mail messaging into one integrated system.

Database services

Large amounts of information are stored and managed by databases. Database servers are powerful computers that usually require a lot of maintenance. They are used to manipulate information in the database and handle requests for specific information. Database services provide secure access to restricted data, and they also allow clients to save processing power on their individual computers.

MANAGEMENT SOFTWARE

Administrators can organize, configure, and manage a network more efficiently by using management software. Typically, network administration software is used to activate or shut down devices, control local user access to the network, and permit remote users to connect to the network.

When considering steps to improve network performance, network traffic control and possible network expansion are two areas of concern. By defining where traffic congestion occurs (as well as detecting malfunctioning equipment), management software aids the decision-making process.

WIRELESS LANs

Wireless LANs are especially appropriate for providing data interconnectivity to small branch offices, individual departments, project teams, or temporary work groups. They are also valuable for areas not easily served by wired LANs. For example, historic buildings might require wiring that would be unsuited to the building's character or simply too expensive and disruptive. Some locations are actually too hazardous to support wired installations. Wireless LANs are certainly the best choice for emergency situations or one-time events that require a temporary network.

The freedom to move without restriction and still have access to critical information increases the flexibility and productivity of your workers. If your business employs people who must move around within the building, but still require access to transactions, queries, and messaging, as well as follow-up, collaboration, and troubleshooting data, it may be cost effective to install a wireless LAN. Also, businesses that move or reorganize frequently will encounter considerable costs for network rewiring and reconfiguration. For these businesses, wireless LANs can actually be cheaper in the long run.

Roaming, privacy, and security are issues that will need to be addressed when considering the installation of a wireless LAN, but the benefits will likely outweigh any shortcomings.

It is interesting to note that the first LANs were, in fact, wireless. As wired Ethernet evolved, it replaced wireless to become the preferred LAN. Wireless LANs and wired LANs usually use the same end equipment, but they do not use the same transmission medium. To interconnect with the computer, server, or mainframe, a wireless LAN requires specific wireless connection equipment. Today, wireless LANs use infrared signaling, spread-spectrum radio services, and cellular services to communicate among devices.

Chapter

10

Telecommunications Connection Services

NOW THAT OUR OFFICES are all wired up with a LAN and a phone system, how do we connect to the outside world? Through the telephone company, or something similar, such as a competitive LEC or an ISP. The distinction between the various service providers is currently blurring and will eventually vanish altogether.

Telecommunications service providers offer many options for connecting to the public telecommunications network. These services range from plain old telephone service (POTS) to dedicated, fiber-optic access at speeds of 45 megabits per second (Mbps). Your business requirements will determine which services you will choose.

This chapter describes these basic packaged services—what they do, how they differ, and why you might consider using them. Advanced networking packages are also discussed. Companies use these services to interconnect customers, suppliers, and multiple business locations. The various network packages include metropolitan area networks (MANs), wide area networks (WANs), and, the newest business network package, virtual private networks (VPNs).

INTRODUCTION TO TELECOMMUNICATIONS SERVICES

Each state has a regulatory body that controls local telephone services. The regulatory bodies determine which services, features, or capabilities the local service providers may offer, as well as the rates, or tariffs, for specific services. Tariffs, published by the state, describe the particular services, the necessary equipment, and the prices the local telephone company is allowed to collect. The telephone company may offer a service in one state, but not in another state; or a service may be offered for a certain price in one state, but at a different price in another state.

Your basic telephone service, or dial tone service, is provided by a telephone company called the local exchange carrier (LEC). The LEC also provides your connection to the public switched telephone network (PSTN). This access includes services and features available from the network such as local calling, regional toll services, long-distance services, and international telephone network services. The basic telephone services provided by a typical LEC are outlined below.

Dial tone
This is the tone you hear when you pick up your telephone. The dial tone is the network's way of telling you that it's okay to make your phone call. Dialing the telephone number tells the network who you want to call and where this person's telephone is located.

Single or multiparty line
Telephone users are connected to the network by a line from the LEC's central office. Usually, one subscriber is connected to each line, but in rural areas where access lines are scarce, more than one party may have to share the same line. This situation is exactly the same as having multiple telephone extensions on one line in your house. Only one person at a time can use the line, but instead of your teenage daughter tying up the line, it might be your neighbor's daughter!

Residential or business services
Local telecommunications services are designated as either residential or business. The distinction is based on what features are provided and how the services are tariffed. Although business services are rarely different from residential services, many public utility commissions allow telephone companies to charge more

for the business service. However, telephone companies will often tailor service packages for small, medium, or large businesses.

BASIC CALL PROCESSING

A simple telephone or dial-up data call on the PSTN consists of five major steps: call recognition, digit collection and interpretation, switching and routing, network completion, and billing.

CALL RECOGNITION

The central office switch continuously checks the status of every subscriber=s line for two possible conditions: (1) "on-hook," where the telephone is idle, or (2) "off-hook," where the telephone handset is picked up to make a call. Every telephone line is equipped with a sensor that monitors the status of its electrical current. When the current is flowing from the telephone to the switch, the telephone is off-hook, and when the current is absent, the telephone is on-hook. The switch compares the status of the current to the previous scanned condition. If it is the same, the switch continues to scan other lines, but if there is a change, the switch takes the appropriate action.

Lifting your telephone handset changes the condition of your line from on-hook to off-hook, and the central office switch interprets this current flow as a request for service. Next, the switch checks its database to determine whether you are permitted to make outgoing calls and whether you are using Touch-Tone (an AT&T trademark) or dial-pulse signaling. (The generic name for Touch-Tone signaling is dual tone multifrequency [DTMF].) As soon as the switch knows who you are, it puts dial tone on your line, which is your signal to begin dialing.

DIGIT COLLECTION AND INTERPRETATION

The digits of any telephone number you dial are collected by receivers and stored in the call register assigned to your line. Changes in your telephone line from off-hook to on-hook (known as "pulses" in dial-pulse signaling) are counted and stored for each number you dial. The number "6," for example, would generate six pulses as the dial returns to its original position.

In Touch-Tone signaling, a different tone is assigned to each vertical row and each horizontal row on your telephone's push-button keypad. When you push a number or symbol, the tone you hear is a combination of the vertical and horizontal tones for that position. Thus, a unique tone is created for each number and symbol. Touch-Tone signaling is a good example of in-band signaling, which we discussed in an earlier chapter. In this instance, telephone network control and other call-related information is carried back and forth over the same transmission path used for voice conversation.

Dual Tone Multifrequency

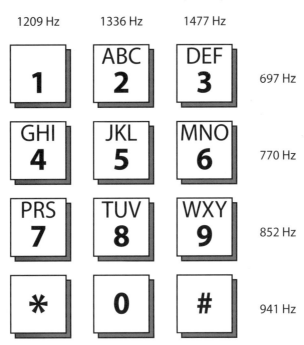

Figure 10-1

When placing a phone call, the number of digits you dial can vary from one to more than fifteen. The switch will make the appropriate connection for you based on the number of digits you dialed. For example, dialing "0" will connect you to an operator, while dialing three digits will connect you to a special service line, such as emergency (911) or repair (611).

If you dial more than seven digits, the switch looks for a "1" or a "0" to decide whether the long-distance call is direct dialed or operator assisted; dialing "011" at the beginning of your call alerts the switch that you want to make an international call; and dialing an access code (10-10-XXX) before a ten-digit telephone number (a 17-digit call) tells the switch to route this call to the appropriate service provider. After you finish dialing, the switch determines:

- ❐ Whether you are permitted to make the call;
- ❐ What routing the switch should use (through or out of the switch);
- ❐ If applicable, what interexchange carrier should be used;
- ❐ What information (time zone, services requested, etc.) to store in the call register for billing;
- ❐ And what information must be forwarded to other switches to complete the call.

SWITCHING AND ROUTING

Switching is the process of identifying, reserving, establishing, and terminating all the connections necessary to complete a call through a switch. Specific paths are required for supplying a dial tone, connecting to customers on the same switch, or connecting to customers outside of your local switch. To establish these paths, the switch accesses its memory for information related to the call that has been stored in various tables and translation areas. Based on this information, the switch then "decides" which circuit to use, the location of the circuit, and which path to establish that will ultimately reach the dialed party's line.

Determining the most efficient route for a call is known as routing. The type of call you place, your service provider preferences, and the location of the party you are calling all influence how your call is routed. Call completion may occur:

- ✓ Within the switch (for a local toll-free call)
- ✓ By a direct connection to another switch within the LATA (for a local area toll-free call)
- ✓ By a direct connection to a tandem or hub switch, and then to another switch within the LATA (for a regional toll call)
- ✓ By a direct connection to a tandem switch, and then to an interexchange carrier point of presence, or POP (for a long-distance call)

Let's look at an example of a direct-dialed long-distance call: 1-715-555-1234. The initial "1" indicates that the call does not require operator assistance and that it is not an international call. The next three digits—7,1,5—represent the NPA (numbering plan area), more commonly known as the area code. The following seven digits—5,5,5,1,2,3,4—indicate the local number within the area code being dialed. It includes the exchange number (555) of the local switch and the subscriber number (1234) of the party being called from that local switch.

Additionally, routing is determined by six-digit translation tables. These are used in switches that have more than one area code in their LATAs. (For example, northern New Jersey has four NPAs: 201, 908, 973, 596.) Routing information would be based on the combined six digits of the NPA and the exchange (908-647, 908-651, etc.). In some cases, there are locations where the local telephone company can complete calls across the LATA boundary without using an IXC. These areas, referred to as metropolitan calling areas, were established before AT&T's divestiture. Examples are the New York/New Jersey region and the Washington, DC area.

NETWORK COMPLETION

The process of network completion involves finding, reserving, establishing, and, ultimately, tearing down the talk path you use to communicate with another party. Once the basic route is determined, your switch compiles this information and forwards it to the network signaling system.

Your local switch then sends the information required to complete the call to the Signaling System 7 (SS7) network via a dedicated circuit. This circuit passes only signaling and call-related information between the central office switch and the SS7 network. This type of signaling is called "out-of-band" because it does not use any active network talk paths. SS7 makes efficient use of the message network and will be covered fully in the next chapter.

SUPERVISION AND BILLING

Telephone companies offer customers a number of services that are activated by the "flashing" of the telephone switch hook. Only by constantly checking on the line status can the switch recognize the request and provide the appropriate service connection to the line. There is a credit card calling feature, for example, that allows pay phone users to make multiple calls and charge them to their credit card without having to reenter the card number for each call. Supervision plays a key role in this service. When the parties hang up after completion of a call, the switch notifies the network (via SS7) to tear down the talk path connection.

Billing is a very important function (to the telephone company, at least), because it is how the telephone company collects its revenue. The call register collects the following information in order to generate a bill for the call:

- Duration of call
- Time of day
- Calling number
- Called number
- Number of message units per time unit
- Interexchange carrier used
- Calling card information

This information is forwarded to a revenue accounting center via a dedicated data line or by magnetic tape. All the call data is consolidated each month resulting in the telephone bill sent out to you. In many cases, the local telephone company serves as the billing agent for the long-distance telephone company as well.

The local telephone company collects a fee for this service and forwards the collected funds to the appropriate IXC.

THE LOCAL LOOP—CONNECTING TO THE PSTN

Each subscriber to basic telephone service is connected to the serving switch in the central office by a twisted pair of copper wires known by various names—outside plant, the local loop, or the access loop. Cross-connecting your telephone line to the serving switch in this way provides you with various telephone services, such as call waiting or voice mail, as well as connectivity to any location in the world.

Take a moment to consider how our highway networks are designed. The large interstate highways that connect our cities branch off into major arterial streets within the urban area. Then, these major arteries branch off into key streets in our neighborhoods that ultimately lead to the individual streets we live on. The local distribution system of a telephone network is designed in much the same way.

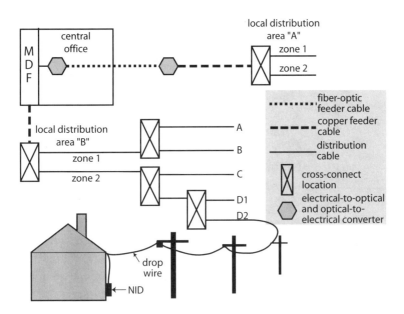

Figure 10-2

The components of the local distribution system are the feeder cables (major arteries), the distribution cables (key streets), and the actual wires, or drop wires, that connect homes and work locations to the network. All cabling originates from the local distribution plant, which is the single largest investment in the telephone network infrastructure. The cabling may be run overhead on telephone poles, or it may be buried underground.

FEEDER CABLES

These large-capacity cables originate at the main distribution frame (MDF) in the central office. From there, they follow individual routes to the local distribution areas. The MDF is actually a series of cabinets, each containing hundreds of wire connectors. These connectors are used to attach your telephone line to the central office switch, and there is one wire connector for every individual subscriber line served by the office.

Feeder cables may contain 1800 pairs or more of twisted copper wire, or they may be composed of fiber-optic threads. The feeder system is predesigned to provide maximum capacity for each specific geographical area.

DISTRIBUTION CABLES

These smaller cables, containing 25–200 pairs of twisted copper wire, are connected to the end of a feeder cable. From there, they travel out into neighborhoods or down individual streets. The distribution system is designed so that lines may be added, changed, or rearranged as necessary.

DROP WIRES

The simple drop wire is a single pair of twisted copper wire. It connects the distribution cable terminal on the telephone pole, or street junction box, in front of your premises to the network interface device (NID) on the outside of your home or work location.

Since divestiture, the NID has also been called the "customer demarc." Beyond this point, the customer assumes responsibility for all wiring and attached equipment. Telephone company personnel are not allowed onto the customer's premises unless special arrangements have been made or enhanced inside repair service has been purchased.

TYPES OF NETWORKS

We have already discussed several different ways that networks can be classified: by size ((LAN, WAN, MAN), by topology (star, bus, ring), or by direction of data flow (broadcast, multicast, point-to-point), to name a few. Networks may also be classified as either public or private.

Private networks, as their name implies, are owned and managed by an enterprise and are used exclusively by that enterprise. Intranets and LANs are examples of private networks. In contrast, a public network (while owned by a private enterprise) Arents≅ its network to the public. AT&T, Sprint, and MCI WorldCom are public telephone interexchange carriers that rent their services to anyone willing to pay the required access fee. Networks can be further characterized as either switched or dedicated.

SWITCHED NETWORKS

Switched networks are designed to connect many individual users to many other individual users, all at the same time. Switched services rely on the public switched telephone network to connect users to one another for voice, data, or video transmission. Users pay for these services based on the distance, duration, or time of day of the calls.

An individual transmission is sent to a switch, and the switch then determines how to route it. Imagine the alternative—a separate wire going to each person in the world you wanted to communicate with. Not only would that take a lot of wires, but some would be needed for only one call! Switching allows you to communicate with virtually anyone else who is connected to the PSTN. The only dedicated connection in a switched network is from your location to the switch in the central office. From this point, the call or transmission travels over shared transmission paths through a series of switches (if necessary) or routers (for data) to reach its destination.

Switched services allow us to make voice, data, and video calls anytime to anyplace connected to the worldwide public telephone network. An additional advantage is that we pay only for the services that we use. There are some disadvantages, however. Usage charges can add up and become very expensive if you make a lot of calls to the same place each month. Also, the public lines may not be available to you when you need them, or the quality or reliability of the line may not be good enough for critical applications.

In the next chapter, we will discuss variations of switched networks, including circuit-switched, packet-switched, and cell-switched networks.

DEDICATED NETWORKS

Dedicated services, also called private lines or leased lines, are physically and continuously connected, forming a point-to-point circuit for any transmission. Customers may lease point-to-point circuits or even full networks. These services are not switched as the route is predetermined from end to end. Because existing local loops and outside plant are used, the circuits do pass through the telephone company central offices, but they bypass the switches. These circuits or networks are basically hard-wired together in the central office.

There are many advantages associated with dedicated lines. As no one else uses them, these lines are always available, and they are

Public Networks	Circuit Switched	Packet Switched	Cell Switched
Switched	POTS, ISDN	ISDN, X.25	SMDS, ATM
Dedicated [1]	DDS, T1/T3	Frame Relay [2]	SMDS, ATM, SONET [2]
1 dedicated access or point-to-point circuit			
2 access to the network			

Table 10-1

more secure than shared lines. The transmission quality of a dedicated line may be better than a switched line because both the design and implementation are based on specific applications rather than the generic one-size-fits-all nature of the public switched line. Lastly, you pay a flat monthly rate regardless of use. On a heavily used line, this fact could result in substantial overall savings.

Naturally, there are disadvantages to consider as well. If you make fewer calls than the number covered by the flat rate mentioned above, each call is more expensive than it needs to be. Also, if you need to reach many locations, the cost of dedicated lines can really add up. Remember that each dedicated line is a point-to-point line, so interconnecting four locations, for example, would require six dedicated lines.

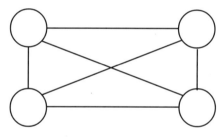

Figure 10-3

SELECTION CRITERIA

Customers should select the appropriate services based on several factors. First, business objectives need to be established; then each one of the factors needs to be evaluated against the business objectives; and, finally, a decision is made based on the needs of the business. The most common selection criteria are listed below.

Cost—At what point does switched service become more expensive than dedicated facilities?

Call setup time—Does the application require a continuous connection because it is used so often? Are occasional dial-up waiting times acceptable?

Volume of data sent—Are large files being transferred all day long? Are just one or two files transferred at night? Are several small files sent during the day?

Frequency of the sessions—Are there only one or two sessions or are there several? What is the idle time of the circuit?

Number of destinations—How many locations must be connected? Three? Eight? Hundreds?

Now that you have an overview of switched and dedicated services, let's look into the various options available.

CIRCUIT-SWITCHED SERVICES

The public switched telephone network service providers offer a variety of circuit-switched services that allow you to make different types of dial-up calls to anyone connected to the network. They include local access, regional toll, and long-distance services (inter-LATA services).

The local loop (POTS and ISDN) is considered the weakest link in the telecommunications networks of the future. The incumbent LECs (ILECs) need to be able to upgrade this link or face severe competition from others, such as cable TV providers, utility companies (gas or electric), or the new crop of competitive LECs (CLECs).

Plain Old Telephone Service (POTS)

The most common service is the analog POTS service provided to residential and small business customers. It works with either rotary dialing or dual tone multifrequency (DTMF) dialing. It usually includes a toll-free calling area, and also provides lifeline (911), directory assistance (411), and calling card services.

When you order your POTS service, you specify how you wish to pay for the calls you make, which provider you want for regional toll service (in states where choice is available), and which provider you want for long-distance service. Customers may also choose additional services that might be available in their calling area. Available features will depend on the type of switch used in the central office and the connection to the signaling network.

Optional services include home intercom, voice mail, additional directory listings, inside installation, maintenance and wiring diagnostics, and temporary phones. Although the customer is now responsible for all communications services within his premises, a service provider will diagnose or repair problems inside the customer premises for a fee.

Switched-based custom calling services are provided by the electronic switching equipment located in the central office. Some of these features include call waiting, three-way calling, call forwarding, and speed calling.

Network-based custom calling services are provided by the Signaling System 7 (SS7) network using out-of-band signaling. These features include automatic recall and callback, distinctive ringing, selective call rejection, calling number delivery (caller ID), and call trace. Local exchange carriers often refer to SS7 as the "advanced intelligent network" (AIN), and we will discuss it further in the next chapter.

CENTREX SERVICES
Up until the time of AT&T's divestiture, the central office was designed to be a network switch dedicated to routing calls only. It offered no helpful features to subscribers, so the PBX was developed to provide those services and features desired by business customers, such as multiline capability, call forwarding, and conferencing. The idea was to include such features on a premises-based switch that interconnected to the public switched telephone network via the central office. Because the LEC owned everything at that time, including the PBX, it could apportion these functions in any way it chose.

However, the PBX was subsequently declared CPE and became the responsibility of the business customer. The local exchange carrier (LEC) could no longer provide PBX services, and PBX manufacturers now had to sell their hardware directly to the end customer. From 1984 through the late 1980s, an alternative to PBXs did not exist, so the LECs were unable to offer a competitive service to business customers.

To remedy this problem, telephone network switch manufacturers initiated a crash program to develop digital central office switches that could provide the same type of services as PBXs. The result was Centrex, a network-based business service that uses the central office switch as a virtual PBX. A portion of the public switch is dedicated to the customer and provides essentially the same services as a PBX.

Every telephone and device in the business location is connected to the switch with its own line, and each telephone is linked directly over twisted-pair copper wires to the LEC's CO switch. In this way, callers are given direct calling capabilities in and out of the company facilities.

Usually the company will pay a one-time installation charge and then a fixed monthly fee on a per-line basis. So, in a sense, business customers are outsourcing their premises communications services to the local exchange carrier.

Advantages of Centrex services include:

- ✓ No large capital investment (you don't have to purchase a PBX)
- ✓ Connection of multiple locations into an area-wide Centrex service (4- or 5-digit dialing)
- ✓ Twenty-four hour maintenance, almost no system failures, and no maintenance expenses
- ✓ Easy expansion for unlimited growth
- ✓ Minimal space requirements
- ✓ No premises power for the switch and no need for uninterruptable power supplies
- ✓ Sophisticated management services
- ✓ Low installation and start-up costs

✓ No charges for unwanted or unused features and
capabilities
✓ Technological obsolescence is avoided

Centrex services also allow the interconnection of LANs, telephones, PCs, and CTI devices through ISDN primary rate interfaces. The main disadvantage of Centrex service is the monthly
service fee per line, which can get expensive for an organization
with many lines.

PBX vs. Centrex

By introducing digital central office switches and Centrex-switched
ISDN services in 1988, the LECs were able to compete with PBX
vendors. In addition, the Telecommunications Act of 1996 gave
LECs the right to sell CPE, including PBXs, through separate
deregulated subsidiaries.

Today, there is very little difference between the features offered
by Centrex service and those available with a PBX. Though Centrex
services were once used only for very large customers, they are
now available for companies with as few as four lines.

Customers should have very specific reasons for choosing a PBX
over Centrex, or Centrex over a PBX. There is no right answer.
Specific communications needs to consider when choosing between a PBX and Centrex are the size and nature of your business,
plus the availability of competitive telecommunications tools.
Additionally, the following considerations should be addressed:

Intra-location calling
If businesses communications needs are mostly within the
same premises, a PBX may be more cost effective.

Incoming calls
Businesses rely on incoming calls, because they can lead
to new or additional business opportunities. It is essential
to have enough facilities and attendants to ensure that incoming calls are promptly answered and efficiently
handled.

Outgoing calls

If the volume of outgoing calls is great, then Centrex may be the better choice. Centrex service provides each telephone with its own dedicated line to the central office, so an outside line is always available. A PBX, on the other hand, may connect 50 telephones to a T1 that provides only 24 voice channels to the central office. If you are the 25th user, you will not be able to get an outside line.

Centrex also aids in controlling telecommunications costs by monitoring outside calls as necessary and routing calls over the most cost-effective facilities, such as a lower-cost long-distance carrier.

SWITCHED 56/64 KBPS SERVICES

Switched 56 or 64 kbps services provide end-to-end digital transmission speeds for individual channels. They are used to transport data, video or multimedia traffic. Switched 64 Kbps service is also referred to as clear channel circuit service.

These services are contracted at discounted subscription rates based on usage-sensitive tariffs. Switched services work well for applications going to many locations.

INTEGRATED SERVICES DIGITAL NETWORK (ISDN)

ISDN is a digital telephone line. The main purpose behind the development of ISDN was to complete the digital network from the backbone, which was already digital, to the end user, which is analog.

Remember, the building block of the digital network is the 64 kbps voice channel. Every transmission speed in the network is a multiple of this number, and ISDN is simply two of these 64 kbps channels. From the standpoint of both technology and cost, it was just as easy to provide two 64 kbps channels as one, so an "integrated" service featuring two channels was developed—one for voice and one for data. As you'll see a little later, another smaller 16 kbps channel was added to the mix for communicating with the Signaling System 7 network.

If ISDN had been deployed as originally intended, all analog POTS lines would eventually have been replaced and the entire PSTN would have been fully digital end to end. Divestiture and the distraction of new competition, among other events, side-railed this deployment, so the local loop remains predominantly analog. ISDN is now considered simply another enhanced service that must be ordered and paid for separately.

Data can be sent much faster over an ISDN than a conventional analog phone line—up to 128 kbps versus the 33.6 or 56 kbps achieved using a modem on an analog line. Plus, a single ISDN line is really three channels, meaning you can have a voice conversation even while your computer is connected to the Internet.

ISDN is based on a series of international standards that allow the simultaneous transmission of voice, data, and video over an individual twisted-pair telephone line. By using only one line to connect to the Internet and talk to your customers at the same time, you save the cost of multiple lines. However, you do need to install special customer premises equipment capable of converting voice, data, or video signals to telephone digital signals for transmission across the PSTN.

Because the telephone company charges by the minute for usage, ISDN is expensive. On the other hand, analog data transmission is a local dial-up call covered by the fixed monthly fee for local telephone service. This difference in cost makes no sense because digital transmission does not tie up the telephone company central office switch as much as the slower analog connection does.

Basic rate interface ISDN (BRI)

When referring to ISDN, most people are talking about basic rate interface (BRI). This is the version of ISDN used for residential, small business, or Centrex service.

BRI, also called 2B+D service, consists of three channels multiplexed onto one transmission circuit. It provides two bearer (B) channels at 64 kbps each and one delta (D) channel at 16 kbps. The B channels are used for circuit-switched voice, data, and video applications or packet-switched data applications, and they may be used separately as two 64 kbps voice (or data) channels or combined into one 128 kbps data channel. The D channel is used for network signaling and for slow-speed 9.6 kbps packet-switched data applications.

Common business applications for BRI ISDN include:

Voice connectivity—High-speed digital connectivity provides all digital features and capabilities.

Internet access —Many ISPs have joined the ISDN fan club, making it possible for a stand-alone PC or small LAN to get to and from the Internet with much better performance than an ordinary analog connection. Normal access speeds reach up to 128 kbps, but new data compression equipment can bump speeds up as high as 512 kbps.

Distance learning—ISDN is used for distance learning applications because it offers sufficient bandwidth to transmit compressed video. Video allows both instructors and students to interact on a one-to-one or group-to-group basis in real time.

Remote LAN access—Voice, data, and video traffic from remote employees is connected to networks at headquarters.

Videoconferencing—Provides conference room and desktop video services.

Primary rate interface ISDN (PRI)

Primary rate interface ISDN is analogous to the T1 digital carrier service discussed below. It is also called 23B+D service. Each one of the 23 bearer (B) channels may be used individually for circuit-switched voice or packet-switched data. Alternatively, the channels may be combined into any multiple of 64 kbps (128, 364, or 768 kbps) for packet-switched data applications.

PRI is often used for dial-up videoconferencing or data backup service. The D channel is also a 64 kbps circuit, so the total capacity of this service is 1.536 Mbps (64 kbps multiplied by 24 channels).

T-CARRIER SERVICES

Businesses needing high-speed data connections often use dedicated high-speed digital trunks. They are expensive, and best-suited for networks with 20 or more users. As T-carrier transmission services are a key part of the PSTN backbone, they will be discussed in detail in the next chapter. However, you should be aware that businesses can lease such high-speed circuits from the local telephone company. T-carrier services may be either switched or dedicated.

With a digital service level 1 (DS-1) speed of 1.5 Mbps, a T1 trunk delivers more than ten times the capacity of an ISDN (BRI) connection. In addition, a T1 trunk can transmit 24 simultaneous voice circuits by using time-division multiplexing. T3 trunks are even faster and can transmit at a digital service level 3 (DS-3) speed of 44.184 Mbps, the equivalent of 28 T1 transmissions. Of course, T3 trunks are considerably more expensive than T1s.

Setting up T1 or T3 connections is best left to professionals. Leased T1 and T3 trunk access services are used by companies for both switched and dedicated access to the PSTN. Customers use these access services to reach the PSTN, public data network (PDN), frame relay network, and ATM networks.

Fractional T1 services

Telephone companies also offer fractional T1 service, charging only for the actual transmission needed. This service is also known as high-speed circuit-switched service and provides transmission speeds from 128 kbps up to 1.5 Mbps.

Fractional T1 service is used when customers require transmission speeds faster than a DS-0, but cannot justify the cost of full T1 carrier service. To support videoconferencing and data backup applications, customers can multiplex the individual channels together with end-to-end digital connectivity and achieve speeds of 128 kbps to 768 kbps.

OPTICAL CARRIER ACCESS SERVICES

Like the T-carrier services described above, optical carrier (OC) services are part of the PSTN backbone and will be discussed fully in the next chapter. Both switched and dedicated OC service can be leased from a LEC or an IXC, and customers use these services

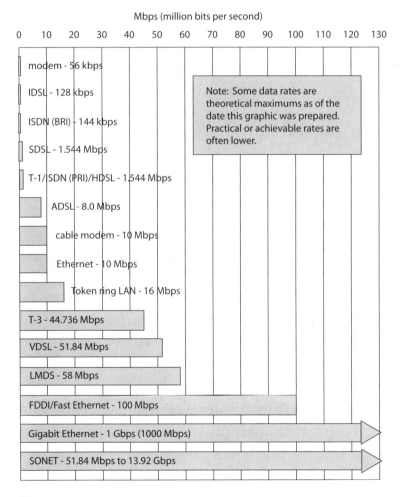

Transmission Rates of Various Data Channels/Transmission Technologies

Figure 10-4

to reach the SONET and ATM networks discussed in the next sections.

At 45 Mbps, optical carrier 1 (OC-1) transmits at approximately the same speed as a T3. OC-3 achieves a transmission speed of 155 Mbps, while OC-12 can reach 622 Mbps. Network service providers are even installing OC-48 services that reach speeds of 2.488 Gbps.

SYNCHRONOUS OPTICAL NETWORK (SONET) ACCESS SERVICES

SONET is also primarily a PSTN backbone technology. Voice, data, and video traffic are transmitted over SONET using a ring topology, and SONET is capable of multiplexing and managing transmission rates ranging from T1/T3 trunk speeds to broadband transmission speeds of 9.9 gigabits per second (Gbps).

Large business or enterprise customers may want to obtain direct access to the local or interexchange carrier's public SONET network. If customers have two or more locations off the public SONET ring, they can take advantage of its redundant nature and high-speed transmission to move voice, data, and video traffic among their own locations.

Sometimes the traffic volume or security needs of a customer will require a separate SONET ring to transmit all traffic among its locations. In these cases, a leased or dedicated SONET ring with separate fiber threads will run side-by-side the public SONET network. Alternatively, a customer may contract with the network service provider to build, install, and maintain a customer-owned SONET ring. In this case, the customer gains complete control of its SONET transport.

METROPOLITAN AREA NETWORKS (MANs)

These public communications networks are furnished by a single service provider, and may also be referred to as intra-LATA service networks.

MANs cover a geographic area the size of a city and its surrounding suburbs, and, usually, there are no long-distance charges associated with MANs. However, some MANs are based on the type of technology used, such as switched multimegabit services (SMDS) or dual queue-dual bus (DQDB).

DEDICATED DIGITAL ACCESS SERVICES

As we have learned, communications networks are systems of interconnected computers, telephones, and communications devices whereby people can communicate with one another and share applications and data. When a more permanent connection is necessary to tie multiple locations together, companies may lease dedicated lines from the telephone service providers. They will also lease lines when building a WAN or an extranet in order to provide a group of affiliated companies with a permanent, always-on connection.

DIGITAL DATA SERVICE (DDS)

Digital data services provide high-quality digital transport for both point-to-point and point-to-multipoint services. DDS is sometimes referred to as digital POTS because transmission rates range only from 2.4 kbps to 64 kbps.

This circuit is dedicated from end to end on a channel-by-channel basis. It is most often used for credit card verification, transaction processing, and point-of-sale services.

DIGITAL T1/T3 POINT-TO-POINT SERVICE

Dedicated T1 and T3 digital trunks are used to provide point-to-point connections between corporate locations for voice, data, and video applications. Customers lease the lines and pay a flat monthly fee for the service.

The data speed for the T1 trunk transmission is 1.544 Mbps (DS-1) and comprises 24 multiplexed voice/data channels at a speed of 64 kbps (DS-0) each. The data speed for the T3 trunk transmission is 44.736 Mbps (DS-3), and it can carry 672 simultaneous voice channels.

Digital Subscriber Line (DSL) Services

DSL is a relatively new form of local loop connectivity. Residential, telecommuter, and small business customers located close to their central office switches use DSL primarily for high-speed Internet and LAN connections. Like ISDN, voice and data applications can be used simultaneously on one line, but unlike the metered charges applied for ISDN use, DSL is charged at a flat monthly rate.

Because some DSL offerings provide a voice channel and a data channel, the circuit is both circuit-switched (voice channel) and dedicated (data channel, usually to an ISP). We have included a discussion of DSL in this section, however, because the main purpose for DSL services is high-speed data transmission.

Depending on which DSL service you use, the cost may be much less than T1 carrier services and the data speeds may be much faster. On the other hand, DSL service is not a mature offering and is unavailable in many parts of the country. Also, a small business customer should have a service level agreement (SLA) to ensure that the bandwidth is guaranteed across the entire network. The major advantage of DSL is its "always-on" access, which is achieved by using packet-switched services over an existing twisted-pair local loop.

Digital subscriber line technology is a new technology that uses special equipment to run over existing telephone lines. DSL dramatically increases bandwidth to the subscriber and utilizes telephone wiring that is in place in virtually every home and business in the world. Telephone companies have billions of dollars invested in existing local loop copper lines, and DSL is a technology that allows them to offer high-speed data services over their already installed infrastructure.

As a packet-oriented technology, DSL is able to provide access to backbone technologies, such as frame relay. This fact allows the creation of a network infrastructure that can meet user demand for non-switched higher-speed access and flat-rate pricing. There are multiple versions of DSL technology, each targeting a different type of customer.

Flavor	Bandwidth	Direction	Distance	Repeatable
ADSL	1.5-8.0 Mbps 16 kbps-1.1 Mbps	downstream upstream	18,000 ft.	no
IDSL	128 kbps	duplex	18, 000 ft.	yes
HDSL	1.54 Mbps (T1)	duplex	12,000 ft.	yes
RADSL	1.5-8.0 Mbps 90 kbps to 1.1 Mbps	downstream upstream	12,000 ft. * note 1	no
SDSL	1.54 Mbps (T1)	duplex	10,000 ft.	yes
VDSL	13-52 Mbps 1.5-2.3 Mbps	downstream upstream	1,000-4,000 ft. * note 1	no
* note 1: depends on speed				

Table 10-2

Asymmetric digital subscriber line (ADSL)

ADSL is primarily a residential service that provides three channels: an analog POTS line, a downstream data line, and an upstream data line. In 1998, there were approximately 63,000 subscribers in North America. The earliest services were priced at $40 to $50 per month for 512 kbps upstream and 1.5 Mbps downstream.

However, this service is capable of transmitting more than 6 Mbps downstream to a subscriber and as much as 640 kbps upstream. Downstream speeds depend on how far the subscriber is from the central office:

Up to 18,000 feet . . . . 1.544 Mbps
Up to 16,000 feet . . . . 2.048 Mbps
Up to 12,000 feet . . . . 6.312 Mbps
Up to 9,000 feet . . . . 8.448 Mbps

Upstream speeds vary from 15 kbps to 640 kbps. The modulation techniques used by ADSL include both carrierless amplitude and phase (CAP) modulation and discrete multitone technology (DMT) modulation.

The major problems associated with ADSL are the distance limitations from the central office (three miles) and slow deployment due to lack of equipment interoperability. Because different equipment companies have a variety of upstream/downstream speed configurations, service providers wishing to offer ADSL will need to standardize their packages and coordinate the proper equipment with the end customers

Universal asymmetric DSL (UADSL)

As I mentioned above, there is a need to standardize ADSL packages. UADSL is one such attempt. The Universal ADSL Working Group, a consortium of Intel Corporation, Microsoft, and Compaq Computer Corporation, has adopted this standard, which is also known as the G.lite standard.

UADSL is projected to have 500,000 new subscribers in 2000 and one million subscribers by 2001. Customers will be able to install the equipment themselves, eliminating the need for carrier technicians. Three common choices for UADSL offer subscribers speed vs. pricing flexibility.

Downstream	Upstream	Price/month
Up to 640 Kbps	Up to 90 Kbps	$ 39.95
Up to 1.6 Mbps	Up to 90 Kbps	59.95
Up to 7.1 Mbps	Up to 680 Kbps	109.95

ISDN symmetric DSL (IDSL)

By using standard ISDN customer equipment with a nailed-up D channel, ISDL can provide 144 kbps. ISDL is very similar to ISDN—it is symmetrical and provides 128 kbps full-duplex service while using existing ISDN hardware.

The difference, however, is that ISDL is a point-to-point (not switched) data service, and it does not support voice. ISDL is basically a form of usage-insensitive ISDN service that provides an always-on connection for a flat monthly fee.

High-bit-rate digital subscriber line (HDSL)

High-bit-rate DSL is used as an alternative to T1 digital carrier service in the local loop area. This service uses less bandwidth than a T1 carrier, and it requires two twisted copper pairs. Depending on line characteristics, HDSL speeds may range from 1.5 Mbps to 2.048 Mbps over distances up to 12,000 feet from the central office. Though HDSL does not require repeaters, they may be used to up the distance to 36,000 feet.

Typical applications include PBX network connections, cellular antenna stations, digital loop carrier systems, IXC point-of-presence connections, Internet access, and access to private data networks, but HDSL does not offer any voice service.

Rate adaptive DSL (RADSL)

Rate adaptive DSL is concerned with various issues in the telecommunications company's physical plant. Based on the makeup of the loop, distance, and noise characteristics, different rates of speed may be achieved.

The technology is evolving and speed improvements are expected in the near future. Currently, RADSL modems achieve 2 Mbps downstream and 1.1 Mbps upstream, but, eventually, the modems should deliver 8 Mbps.

Symmetric DSL (SDSL)

Symmetric (or single line) DSL is suited for the individual telecommuter or small business that might have only one telephone line. Currently, SDSL is geared to business customers needing more than 1.5 Mbps. In 1998, there were about 76,000 subscribers in North America.

Services that provide the same rate of high-speed access for both upstream and downstream transmission are described as symmetric. SDSL has a variable rate infrastructure that transmits from 56 kbps (28 kbps in each direction) up to 1.5 Mbps (768 kbps in each direction) with a loop limitation of 10,000 feet. Typical applications of this service include access to data servers or remote access to corporate LANs.

Very high-data-rate DSL (VDSL)

This service is evolving, but promises to be a true multimedia service at multimegabit rates. Though it will likely offer faster data rates than other services, the connection distances will be shorter. VDSL targets only ATM network architectures.

Up to 4,500 feet . . . 12.96 Mbps
(1/4 Signal Transport 1 [STS-1])

Up to 3,000 feet . . . 25.82 Mbps (1/2 STS-1)

Up to 1,000 feet . . . 51.84 Mbps (STS-1)

DSL MARKET OPPORTUNITIES

The telecommunications market is increasingly competitive. An incumbent LEC's success may very well rely on DSL's ability to satisfy customers with first-to-market solutions for improving efficiency, effectiveness, and entertainment value.

Also, a significant and available opportunity exists for high-speed data access services that enable LANs and PCs to form private networks. Such services would typically include access to corporate LANs, the Internet, multimedia, and video. To acquire rapid market share, using existing network facilities (rather than installing new ones) is imperative. DSL technologies, specifically ADSL products, are well-suited to fulfill these conditions.

Why ADSL?

There are many reasons. ADSL offers sufficient bandwidth to provide high-speed access for the growing number of dial-up PC users, and this service can be offered to the vast majority of the population immediately. ADSL also solves numerous network problems created by the longer-than-average holding times for data users; it provides a migration path to both existing and developing network infrastructures, including ATM networks; and it is compatible with existing data networking equipment.

As fiber is driven further into the distribution infrastructure of the network, ADSL has evolved to provide increased bandwidth that can be implemented as necessary. Also, because no additional development time is needed for ADSL service, established telephone companies have thus gained a time-to-market advantage over their competitors.

All this is accomplished at pricing which is attractive to early users. Recent studies show that consumers are willing to pay between $75 and $100 per month for high-speed access. Users have not embraced other high-bandwidth alternatives, such as ISDN, because they dislike usage-sensitive pricing. ADSL meets the flat-rate pricing preference of most potential users.

The audience for ADSL (and other DSL) services includes the following:

Employees, executives, LAN administrators, and database administrators who **work at home** and want high-speed LAN connections;

Employees needing **remote access** to corporate facilities and databases;

Telestudents attending universities that serve a diversified and geographically dispersed student population;

Online service users migrating to higher-speed **Internet access** (driven by Internet applications); and

Doctors, hospitals, and other medical service providers that share documents (such as records, benefit analyses, X rays, and second opinion reviews) across a widely dispersed patient care provider base—**telemedicine**.

ADSL strengths and weaknesses

As with any other technology, ADSL involves a set of tradeoffs. Telephone companies seem to have gotten the message that customers want flat-rate pricing for high-speed transport services rather than usage-based service, such as ISDN. Also, straightforward installation and setup are notable advantages of ADSL, but its main strengths are high-speed, constant throughput and the fact that the infrastructure is already in place.

Of course, there is the proverbial flip side to the coin. The main disadvantage of ADSL is the limited loop distance. If we add the possibility that rewiring may be required to isolate facilities at either the customer premises or in the local loop, the service begins to show some problems. On top of this, voice service enhancements are limited, and customers may have to forgo some of the advanced features they have come to appreciate.

Many experts view DSL of any flavor as simply a stopgap solution. Naturally, incumbent LECs want to take advantage of their considerable investment in an existing copper infrastructure, but the real end game is fiber to the home or the office. Indeed, competitive carriers currently building out their networks from scratch are using fiber, not copper. With nearly unlimited bandwidth and data speeds, fiber is always the first choice.

VALUE-ADDED NETWORKS (VANs)

Third-party companies lease telephone lines from the public telephone service providers, add additional value to the lines, and then make the same lines available to the public for a fee. These value-added networks, as they are known, provide email, bulletin boards, error detection, public databases, or 900 numbers for special services. Typically, users pay for the services through VAN billing, but sometimes both the telephone company and the VAN are paid separately for their respective parts of the service. Examples of value-added services include:

Messaging systems

These systems allow users to communicate with others through text (electronic mail), voice (voice mail), and written documents (fax mail).

Videoconferencing

Videoconferencing VANs are available for companies that do not want to build their own videoconferencing facilities. Kinko's is a good example. People at various Kinko's locations can engage in sophisticated videoconferences that were once the purview of only large corporations.

Electronic data interexchange (EDI)
Companies can communicate with their vendors or customers by using a computer-to-computer interchange of transactions based on agreed standards. This paperless environment can save money, reduce errors, and improve customer service.

Time-sharing
Early time-sharing applications provided businesses with shared access to computers. Today, however, most businesses have their own computers. In place of computer sharing, VANs now offer time-shared Internet Web-hosting services.

Transaction processing
Common examples of transaction processing systems include automatic teller machine (ATM) networks, point-of-sale (POS) services, and credit card verification services.

Internet Access
Most companies need access to the Internet and the World Wide Web. A host of new companies provide these services for businesses that do not have their own access. Refer to Chapter 12 for a discussion of the public Internet.

ALTERNATIVE ACCESS TO THE PSTN
As a result of the Telecommunications Act of 1996, companies other than telephone service providers are now entering the telephone access business. Both cable TV companies and electric power companies have wire connections into homes. By adding the appropriate equipment to transmit electrical communications signals and by connecting their wiring to telephone company central offices, these companies can provide an alternative to the telephone company's local loop.

Other options include various forms of wireless access from the home or office. Both pricing packages and performance improvements have combined to make cellular phone service an attractive alternative to the LEC's wired POTS service. Some people use cellular phones only, forgoing wired phone service altogether. It is estimated that 17 million lines, over one third of all existing residential phone lines, will be converted to wireless service by the year 2003.

CABLE MODEMS

One of the newest methods for connecting to the Internet is via cable TV coaxial wire. Cable TV Internet connections have many advantages over dial-up telephone Internet connections. With cable modems, the Internet is always available because it is always connected. Cable Internet doesn't tie up your phone line while you are connected to the Internet, nor does it tie up your TV because the Internet and TV use different channels. Also, because the available transmission bandwidth is greater, a cable modem connection is much faster than a telephone dial-up connection. For technical reasons explained later, uploads and downloads of information occur at different speeds.

Residential cable Internet access costs about $30 per month. The ISP's fee as well as the access connection fee is included as the cable provider currently provides both services. On the other hand, dial-up phone service incurs a monthly charge for the telephone line plus a monthly charge for the ISP.

Both cable modems and dial-up modems modulate and demodulate transmission signals, but all similarity between these two modems ends there. Cable modems are more complicated than their telephone counterparts—part modem, part encryption/decryption device, part router, part bridge, part NIC card, part SNMP agent, and part Ethernet hub. Consumers are largely interested in Internet access, but businesses are also interested in the point-to-point Ethernet capabilities of cable modems.

In the past, hybrid fiber/coax (HFC) systems provided only downstream broadcast capability in the 0 MHz to 550/750 MHz band, but, in order to offer Internet access, cable TV service providers upgraded the cable infrastructure to allow two-way transmission. Depending on the direction, cable modems send and receive data in different ways. In the downstream direction, the digital data is first modulated and then placed on a typical 6 MHz television channel located between 43 MHz and 750 MHz. This channel is separate from the TV signals on either side, so the cable television video signals are not disturbed.

The upstream channel, known as the reverse path, is transmitted between 5MHz and 40 MHz. This is a noisy environment with lots of interference from HAM radio, CB radio, and impulse noise from home appliances. Interference may also be the result of loose connectors or poor cabling. Cable TV networks are tree and branch networks, so, as your signals, your neighbor's signals, and environmental noise all travel together upstream, the legitimate data may be degraded. Most manufacturers address this problem by using QPSK (quadrature phase shift keying) or a similar modulation scheme for the upstream direction.

Cable TV systems employ fiber distribution from the head end to the neighborhood fiber node. The head end can be equated to the telephone company central office, and all local cable connections originate from this facility. At the neighborhood node, signals are collected and distributed to multiple coax feeds that cover a given residential area. Fiber nodes are designed to serve 500 to 2000 homes. As mentioned earlier, the upstream bandwidth is shared among the homes passed by the coax cable, and it is limited to the 5–40 MHz frequency band. Performance levels are reduced as the number of users sharing the upstream transmission increases.

Cable modems are not yet widely available, nor do they include basic telephone service. Although cable television was deregulated in March 1999, most areas still have only one service provider. Many private consumers are not satisfied with the level of service provided, but cable access is still an attractive alternative for subscribers to multiple news groups, users of multimedia browsers, school systems, and medical environments.

WIRELESS LOCAL ACCESS

Data applications using wireless radio transmission are generally grouped together into cellular data, paging, and cellular digital packet data (CDPD). Though users have many technology choices that meet the need for specialized niche services, most are priced too high for the consumer market.

The questions mobile professionals must ask are: How extensive are the services I need, and how many features are really necessary? Commercial services include Skytel, packet radio, CDPD, and Global System for Mobile communications (GSM) data services. The simplest service is cellular data transmission, wherein a data adapter connects the user's laptop to a cellular telephone.

The newest growth area is wireless access to the Internet. Business owners can identify those wireless devices, such as smart phones or personal digital assistants (PDAs), that are Internet-accessible by the "mobile media mode" label attached. The mobile media mode also specifies which areas on the Internet are optimized for access through a mobile device.

The screen and keypad capabilities of these devices are limited to Internet messaging. Next generation wireless technologies are being designed that will allow future devices to access the Internet at speeds equivalent to DSL and cable modems. Super-fast Internet access should become available in 2001.

Local multipoint (microwave) distribution systems (LMDS)

Microwave transmission in the 10 GHz band is being used as an alternative to the wired local loop for digital data and video transmission in small regions or cells (up to a six-mile radius). Called "fixed wireless" (because the subscribers are stationary), LMDS offers a high-bandwidth alternative to the local loop.

As I mentioned in an earlier chapter, some competitive LECs are using LMDS to reach customers rather than building out a wired network or leasing lines from the incumbent LEC. This is a viable alternative to high-speed local loop connections, such as DSL. LMDS requires a direct line of sight between the transmitter and the receiver. Atmospheric disturbances, such as snow or rain, can degrade the signal and slow the data rate.

CHOOSING AN INTERNET ACCESS TECHNOLOGY

If you want to connect your PC or your network to the Internet, you can use virtually any of the access service options discussed in this chapter. Your final decision will be based on three factors: bandwidth requirements, cost, and availability.

Many people start out with a slow dial-up connection and quickly upgrade to a higher-speed option. As the Internet assumes more importance in our daily lives, we gradually increase the amount of time we spend online. A slow connection quickly becomes unacceptable and even counterproductive. Soon it becomes obvious that the additional speed of DSL or a cable modem pays off in greater efficiency, more than justifying the extra expense. If you have ever used a 286 computer with 4 megabytes of RAM, you know what I'm talking about! Speed matters.

The following table provides information on current choices for Internet access.

Technology	Bandwidth	Cost	Availability
Voice Modems	56 kbps	low	high
ISDN	128 kbps	high	medium
xDSL	128 kbps-52 Mbps	medium	low
Cable Modems	56 kbps-1.5 Mbps	medium	high
Wireless - satellite	up to 30 Mbps	high	low
Wireless - cellular	2.4-24 kbps	medium	medium

Table 10-3

Chapter 11

Public High-Speed Digital Networks

· ·

SO FAR, WE HAVE DISCUSSED LOCAL NETWORKS and various ways to gain access to the PSTN through the telephone company central office. In this chapter, we will cover what happens beyond that local connection point and within the backbone of the global public network itself.

The present digital transmission infrastructure is founded on technology now over 30 years old. The modern commercial computer is about the same age and the PC appeared in the early 1980s, but both of these devices have since undergone major refinements and redesign. It is hard not to think of the infrastructure technology as something of a technical dinosaur. In spite of its age, though, this technology has served the industry well, providing a cohesive foundation for the modern telecommunications infrastructure.

These early communications technologies were designed to meet modest requirements for voice and relatively slow data transmissions. For example, a T1 link operates at a transfer rate of 1.544 Mbps, and a T3 link operates at approximately 45 Mbps. These transfer rates may seem high, but a T3 transport system supports only 672 simultaneous voice calls. It's obvious that a lot of T3s have to be in operation to support the public telephone network!

Most telephone companies use T1s and T3s as the foundation of their voice network systems, but these T-carriers are now configured for data and video applications as well.

PUBLIC TELECOMMUNICATIONS NETWORKS

The public telecommunications network consists of the public switched telephone network (PSTN) and the public data network (PDN). The PDN is a packet-switched overlay network, developed later than the PSTN, that rides on top of the existing PSTN.

The current public switched telephone network (PSTN) is comprised of both local exchange carriers (LECs) and interexchange carriers (IXCs). There are hundreds of LECs and IXCs, and each owns a piece of the whole interconnected network. Foreign telephone companies, often called PTTs (derived from the generic name of post, telegraph, and telephone), are also part of the global PSTN.

In addition to local loop access, the public telecommunications network provides three key functions: transmission, signaling, and switching. Virtually everything the network does falls into one of these categories, and there are many alternative technologies, services, and standards associated with each function. It is often difficult for newcomers to get a big picture of how the various network technologies and services relate to one another. To help put everything into perspective, I have organized this chapter around these three network functions.

TRANSMISSION

In its first 80 years, the public telephone network infrastructure used analog transmission and switching exclusively. Because optimizing voice transport was the primary goal, switching and transmission technologies were continually refined to increase capacity and improve performance.

The introduction of the digital T-carrier transmission system allowed multiple simultaneous calls to be multiplexed onto existing copper cables, thus substantially increasing the network's capacity. It was also the first system to digitize voice transmission via pulse code modulation (PCM). Later on, the first digital switches were developed to be compatible with the T-carrier systems. The next evolution of the public network infrastructure introduced fiber-optic transmission systems, and they paved the way for broad-band transmission over newly developed systems such as the Synchronous Optical Network (SONET).

Transmission technologies are used to actually move digital bits through the physical pipe, or circuit, whether it is copper or fiber-optic cable. The PSTN backbone infrastructure employs a handful of transmission technologies that include T-carrier, SONET, and wave-division multiplexing (WDM). The fundamental difference between these alternatives is the way in which multiple channels are multiplexed onto the transmission path.

Both the T-carrier systems and SONET are digital transmission systems that use time-division multiplexing (TDM) to cram multiple voice or data channels onto one transmission pipe. Both systems were designed specifically for the circuit-switched voice network to facilitate adding and dropping channels as necessary at each switch. However, SONET is a powerful transmission system that can carry many more channels on one physical cable than a T-carrier can. It uses strictly fiber-optic cable and employs statistical TDM, a more efficient version of TDM.

The point to remember here, though, is that SONET and T-carrier systems are both transmission systems. Their job is to transport digital bits from one point to another, and they remain independent of the switching systems used to route the data once it reaches a network node (whether switch or router).

Lastly, wave-division multiplexing is a type of frequency-division multiplexing deployed over fiber-optic cable. It is suited for long-haul point-to-point applications. Let's take a closer look at each of these transmission systems.

T-Carrier Systems

Introduced in the 1960s, the T-carrier system was the first digital transmission technology used in the PSTN. It evolved in response to increased telephone traffic and the need for a better digital alternative to long-haul analog transmission in the PSTN backbone.

The T-carriers primarily carry interoffice traffic between COs, but they also provide access to the long-distance network through the IXC's point of presence (POP). They use either copper or fiber-optic cables as their transmission media, and they are based entirely on multiples of the 64 kbps digital voice channel. The two most common transmission trunks in the PSTN backbone are the T1 and T3 carriers, which support 24 channels and 672 channels, respectively.

A T1 system multiplexes 24 individual circuits onto a single transmission path. Each group of 24 time slots is called a T1 frame, and each frame consists of 8 bits per time slot to equal a total of 192 bits. An additional bit, the framing bit, marks the end of one frame and the beginning of the next, so the grand total becomes 193 bits per frame.

Because each analog channel is sampled 8000 times per second, the T1 carrier transmits 1,544,000 (193 x 8000) bits per second or 1.544 Mbps. This line rate, called DS-1 (digital signal one), was standardized for digital transmission in the U.S. and in Japan. In Europe, the standards body established 2.048 Mbps as the digital transmission rate, using 32 rather than 24 channels per trunk.

A T3 carrier is the other standard digital transmission line. It is composed of 28 T1 carriers multiplexed together to achieve a transmission rate of 44,736 kbps. AT&T has constructed a digital TDM hierarchy that uses the DS-1 signal as the fundamental building block, but today's actual transmission systems consist primarily of T1 and T3 carriers.

There are several advantages associated with the T-carrier system. Even though T-carriers require the POTS analog signal to be converted to digital for transmission across the network, the overall cost is still less than the analog alternative. Another major advantage of a T-carrier system is its resistance to the impairments that plague analog signals. Regenerative repeaters at intermediate points on the T-carrier recreate the original digital bit stream even if the transmission becomes impaired by attenuation, noise, or other interference. Thus, the transmission is cleaner and more reliable than an analog transmission.

Digital signal (service) levels and T-carrier

Digital signal (DS) levels and T-carriers are often used interchangeably, but that can easily confuse us. It is better to remember that DS levels define the digital bit speeds, while T-carrier defines the actual transmission system used to achieve those speeds. It may be a minor distinction, but it is one that should be understood.

Because the digital backbone of the PSTN was designed specifically for optimizing voice transmission, everything is expressed in the equivalent of multiple voice channels. DS-0 represents one digital voice channel at 64 kbps. This channel is created by using pulse code modulation (PCM) on an analog signal to perform the analog-to-digital conversion. A single DS-0 voice channel has no T-carrier equivalent, but all other levels of DS or T-carrier are simply a multiple of this 64 kbps digital rate.

Digital Signal Level	Number of Voice Channels	Total Capacity (bit rate)	T-Carrier/ Transmission Media
DS0	1	64 kbps	n/a (one voice channel)
DS1	24	1.54 Mbps	T1 paired copper cable
DS1C	48	3.152 Mbps	T1C paired copper cable
DS2	96	6.312 Mbps	T2 paired copper cable
DS3	672	44.736 Mbps	T3 radio microwave or fiber-optic cable
DS4	4,032	274.176 Mbps	T4M coaxial cable

Table 11-1

THE SYNCHRONOUS OPTICAL NETWORK (SONET)

SONET is the U.S. version of the Synchronized Digital Hierarchy (SDH), an international standard for optical transmission. It features high-speed, reliable digital transmission over fiber-optic cables. Although T-carrier transmissions can be carried over either copper or fiber, SONET travels over fiber-optic cables only. SONET has been in use since 1989, so it is a proven transport standard.

Like T-carrier systems, SONET uses time-division multiplexing (TDM). Baseband pulses (light) are interleaved into assigned time slots to create multiple channels over one strand of fiber. SONET has the ability to multiplex and manage transmissions ranging from T1/T3 speeds to 10 Gbps—that's 10 billion bits transmitting through the fiber every second! For the data to make any sense at its destination, the TDM equipment must keep track of both the timing and the assigned time slots—certainly an impressive feat. SONET offers a number of attractive features:

✓ It is an integrated network standard, meaning all vendors can build products upon this standard.

✓ SONET is built on fiber-optic standards that provide for superior performance.

✓ SONET combines and consolidates traffic from different locations through one facility. This concept, known as grooming, eliminates backhauling and other inefficient techniques used in T-carrier transmission.

✓ With its add/drop capabilities, SONET reduces the amount of back-to-back multiplexing that occurs in the T-carrier network.

✓ SONET has improved operations, administration, maintenance, and provisioning (OAM&P) features relative to older technology.

SONET defines a set of networking management protocols that allow the network to be monitored, reconfigured, and maintained centrally. It can accommodate most types of digital signals, such as bursty asynchronous data, high- and low-speed synchronous data, and voice and on-demand services. It also transports ATM cells within the SONET payloads.

SONET topology

User signals are converted, or mapped, into a standard format

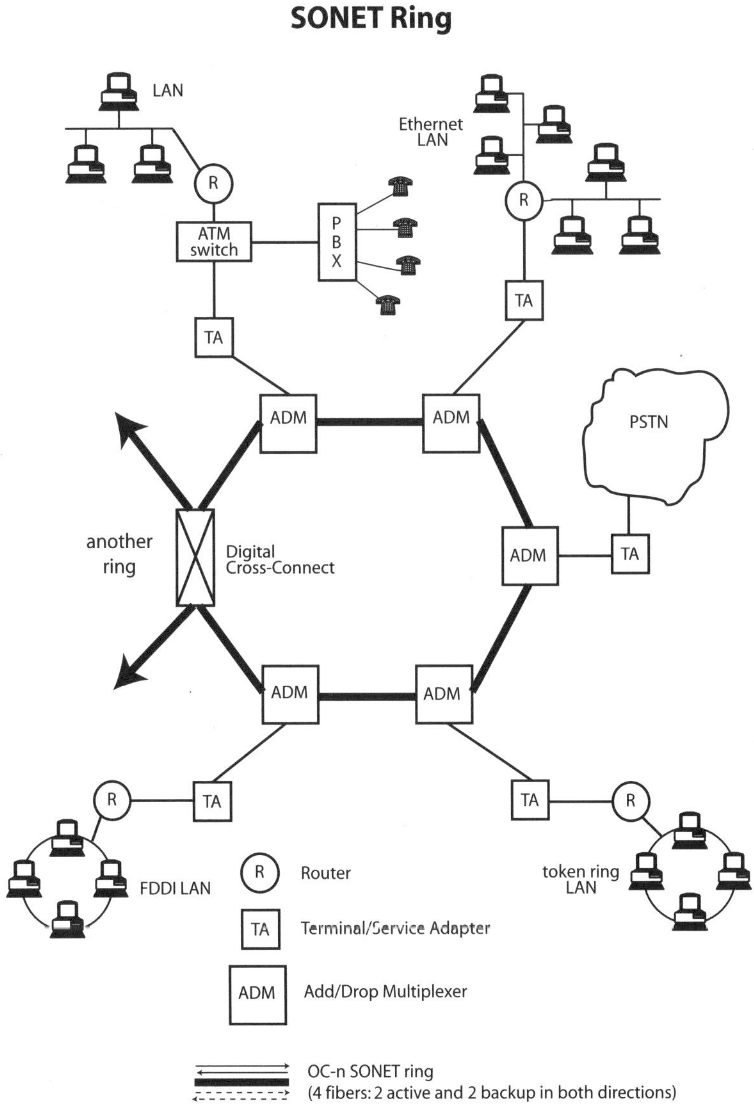

SONET Ring

Figure 11-1

called the synchronous transport signal (STS). Just as DS is the basic channel unit (64 kbps) for T-carrier systems, STS constitutes the basic building block of the SONET multiplexing hierarchy. It defines the digital bit rate, which starts at 51.84 Mbps (STS-1) and increases in multiples of this rate.

The STS signal is an electrical signal. When we see the notation "STS-n," we are being told that the service adapter (described below) can multiplex the STS signal into higher-integer multiples of the base rate.

End user devices operating on LANs and digital transport systems, such as T1s or T3s, are attached to the SONET network through a service adapter. This device is also known as an access node, a terminal, or a terminal multiplexer, and it is responsible for supporting the end user interface by sending and receiving traffic from LANs, T1s, T3s, and so on. It acts as a concentrator and consolidates network traffic into a SONET envelope for transport on the SONET network.

As I just mentioned, a service adapter may be implemented as the end user interface device or it may function as an add/drop multiplexer. The term "add/drop" refers to any device capable of adding payload or dropping payload onto one of two channels. Add/drop multiplexers are used to combine various STS-n input streams into an optical carrier signal. These optical carrier signals are designated as "OC-n," where "n" represents the multiplexing integer, such as OC-3, OC-12, and so forth. OC-n streams are both multiplexed and demultiplexed with the same device.

A digital cross-connect (DCS) acts as a hub in the SONET network. Not only does it add and drop payload, but it also operates with different carrier rates, such as DS-1 or OC-3, and makes two-way cross-connections between SONET rings. A DCS may also consolidate and separate different types of traffic.

Although SONET may be used for point-to-point transmission, SONET topology is usually set up as a ring. In most networks, the ring is a dual ring that operates with one primary fiber thread and one secondary, or backup, fiber thread. The structure of the dual ring permits the network to recover automatically from failures on the channels and in the channel/machine interfaces. This is known as a self-healing ring.

Digital/SONET hierarchy

The synchronous transport signal level 1 (STS-1) forms a base for the optical carrier level 1 signal. In turn, OC-1 is the foundation for the synchronous optical signal hierarchy, and higher levels are derived by multiplexing the lower level signals. Presently, OC-3, OC-12, and OC-48 are the most widely supported applications. Some interexchange carriers are beginning to install OC-192s into their SONET backbones.

Digital/SONET Hierarchy

type	Bit Rate (Mbps)	Voice Channels	T-Carrier	Optical Carrier
DS1	1.544	24	T1	
DS3	44.736	672	T3	
STS-1	51.84	672		OC-1
STS-3	155.52	2016		OC-3
STS-12	622.08	8064		OC-12
STS-48	2488.32	32256		OC-48
STS-192	9953.28	129024		OC-192

Table 11-2

WAVE-DIVISION MULTIPLEXING (WDM)

Also called wavelength-division multiplexing, this is a type of frequency-division multiplexing that uses different wavelengths of laser light to share the same fiber-optic line. By using different colors of light—each corresponding to a different wavelength—for each channel of information, the data streams can be isolated from one another until they reach their destination on the network. There, they are separated by a diffraction grating process that identifies each color.

By using WDM, multiple data bit rates can be transmitted over a single fiber, resulting in a total transmission speed of 100 Gbps or more. That's enough capacity to carry more than one million simultaneous voice conversations. The International Telecommunications Union (ITU) has set the standard wavelength for lightwaves in a WDM system. This wavelength occupies a band between 1500 and 1535 nanometers (a nanometer is a millionth of a millimeter), and the band can be divided into as many as 43 channels. Higher-wavelength WDM systems that operate in the 1550 nanometer band are sometimes called dense wave-division multiplexing (DWDM) systems.

The other dominant multiplexing technique, time-division multiplexing (TDM), does not operate efficiently at speeds higher than 10 Gbps. Unlike WDM, which transmits signals on all channels simultaneously, TDM multiplexes lower-bit-rate channels into a single high-speed bit stream. Each channel travels at this higher bit rate for a short duration of time, after which another channel transmits, again at the higher bit rate. By alternating transmissions between the lower-speed channels, each transmission is ultimately sent at a higher speed. In contrast, different channels multiplexed together via WDM share a common fiber line simultaneously.

To better understand the differences between TDM and WDM (or DWDM), think of a single fiber as a multilane highway. Traditional TDM systems use only a single lane of this highway. To accommodate more traffic, you need to increase the speed of the vehicles in this one lane. On the other hand, WDM uses all the lanes on the highway. In this way, a huge amount of unused fiber capacity is made available. Another benefit of WDM, and optical networking in general, is that the "highway" (fiber) is blind to the traffic it carries—"vehicles" can be ATM, SONET, and/or IP packets.

If you think this sounds complicated, you are right. For example, you can take time-division multiplexed SONET OC-192 streams and put each one onto a separate wavelength. This means that

TDM signals representing up to 129,024 separate voice channels (64 kbps each) are modulated onto multiple analog carrier signals (the light waves)—all inside one thin strand of fiber. You've taken a stream that has already been multiplexed once with TDM, and then you multiplexed it again using an entirely different scheme, WDM. Multiplexing on top of multiplexing. Imagine the complexity of the equipment that can make this happen!

Depending on the kind of fiber used, WDM can multiply bandwidth capacity as much as 40 times. DWDM systems multiplex up to 8, 16, 32 or 40 wavelengths (separate channels), and each signal can be carried at a different rate (OC-3, OC-12, OC-24) and in a different format (such as ATM or SONET). Using a DWDM system, a network operating with SONET signals at OC-48 (2.5 Gbps) can achieve total capacities of 40 Gbps or more. In the future, DWDM systems will carry up to 80 wavelengths of OC-48, a total of 200 Gbps, or 40 wavelengths of OC-192, for a total of 400 Gbps per fiber. This is enough capacity to transmit 90,000 volumes of an encyclopedia in one second over one strand of fiber.

Given the huge bandwidth that WDM offers, it is not surprising that every major telephone carrier and backbone provider is now installing nothing but fiber in their networks, and they are installing a lot of it. The cost of deploying WDM systems has come down in recent years, primarily because lasers can now be built for one-tenth of their original cost. Many people in the telecom industry believe the time is fast approaching when bandwidth will be essentially unlimited.

NETWORK SIGNALING

How the network is controlled and how enhanced services are delivered is the domain of network signaling. We are most familiar with the dialing functions, whether an off-hook signal requesting dial tone or Touch-Tone dialing. Other types of network signaling are transparent to the user, such as testing signals or those that deliver information on circuit availability. These signals are passed back and forth by network switches.

As digital trunks became the norm in the 1970s, attention focused on providing faster call setup procedures. The need for a new common-channel information signaling (CCIS) system became apparent. Both the slow transmission rate (4800 bps) of the existing signaling links and the limited length of the old CCIS signaling message posed a significant bottleneck to flexible signaling. This situation also imposed severe restraints on the increasingly sophisticated uses being projected for the signaling network.

With these factors in mind, the former CCITT (Consultative Committee for International Telegraph and Telephone), which is now the ITU (International Telecommunications Union), convened a study group to address the problem. From 1972 to 1976, this group worked on developing a signaling system that became known as Signaling System 7, or simply SS7. It is a layered signaling protocol that provides flexibility for advanced services and meets the requirement for high-speed call processing through faster signaling links. The most important aspect of SS7 is its capacity to carry more sophisticated information than call control data.

Signaling System 7 is an international, standardized, out-of-band control network. Out-of-band control refers to the fact that the control signaling used to manage telephone calls is carried over channels separate from the calls themselves. SS7 gives us faster call completion and network-based services, such as toll-free calling, caller ID, or distinctive ringing. Much of the intelligence of the network resides in this system, and some LECs call their SS7 network the "advanced intelligent network" (AIN).

Before any part of the message network is established, the called party must answer. Then and only then can the talk path be established. The same rule applies to the service circuits and trunks involved with the call process. The switch must know what service circuits and trunks are available to use and when they have completed their function. Therefore, the primary tasks of the SS7 network include:

✓ Determining the actual talk path required and reserving it until the call is connected

SS7 Out-of-Band Signaling

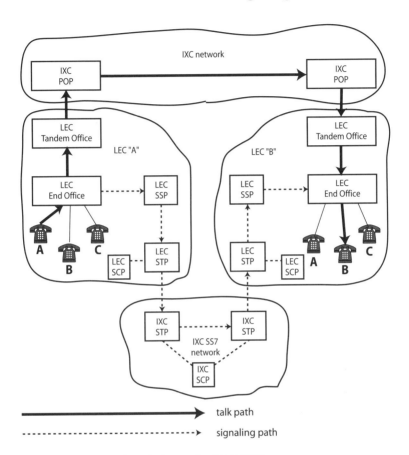

talk path
signaling path

1. Caller A in LEC "A" makes telephone call to B in LEC "B"
2. LEC "A" EO routes call setup to LEC SSP that connects to LEC STP
3. LEC "A" STP routes call setup to IXC SS7 network
4. IXC SS7 routes call setup to LEC "B" STP/SSP
5. LEC "B" STP/SSP routes call setup to LEC "B" EO
6. LEC "B" EO routes call setup to customer B
7. If customer B answers the phone, the LEC/IXC SS7 network establishes the call talk path as shown
8. If customer B does not answer or if the line is busy, no call talk path is established

Figure 11-2

✓ Determining the status of the telephone line of the person you called (such as active, disconnected, idle, busy, etc.)

✓ Establishing the talk path if the other telephone is available and the person you called picks up the phone or has voice mail services that pick up the call

✓ Tearing down the talk path after you or the other person hangs up

The SS7 network is similar to the old CCIS. However, the names of certain components have been changed. The network architecture consists of signaling endpoints, or service-switching points (SSP), and signal transfer points (STP).

The SSP, consisting of hardware and software elements, acts as the entry point from the end central office switch into the signaling network. It understands the signaling communications entities and communicates with both its primary and backup STPs at the same time (all SS7 signals are duplicated to ensure reliability). The signal transfer point (STP) was designed to handle higher channel speeds (56–64 kbps), and it also has sufficient capacity to quickly switch packets.

SS7 enables carriers to offer such services as enhanced 800, virtual private networks (VPNs), and calling number identification (caller ID), and it is the platform that makes ISDN possible. SS7 has also provided a new range of user and system capabilities. For example, look-ahead routing allows calls to be held at the origination point until the actual path is determined. Domino's Pizza is using look-ahead routing for its single, nationwide phone number.

Other popular SS7 services include "follow-me" telephone numbers, which allow mobile users to be reached via one telephone number at a variety of wired or wireless locations, and area-wide Centrex, which allows four- or five-digit dialing to and from Centrex stations spread out over a single metropolitan area.

SWITCHING

We have already discussed how all the digital bits are physically transmitted over the network backbones, but how do they find their proper destination? This is the function of switching.

In Chapter 1, we considered the various ways that networks can be characterized—by size, purpose, or topology—but another way to characterize a network is by how it is switched. The PSTN uses three switching methods to move traffic through the network: circuit switching, packet switching, and cell switching.

The Public Telecommunications Switching Model

Switching:	**Circuit**	**Packet**	**Cell**
Public (switched)	PSTN	PDN (X.25)	SMDS, ATM
Dedicated (nonswitched)	T1, T3, fractional T1, Optical Carrier	T1, T3, fractional T1, Frame Relay	SONET, Optical Carrier

Table 11-3

The networks provided by the telecommunications service providers may be public switched or dedicated connections. Switched services rely on the public switching offices to connect end parties together. Usually, switched services allow you to make a dial-up call to anyone else on the network.

Dedicated services, however, provide connections that are directly wired together from point to point. Although still a part of the public telephone network, these connections bypass the central office switches. They use hard-wired, or "nailed-up," connections in the CO to create a permanent end-to-end connection. The result is unlimited calling at a fixed monthly rate.

Circuit-switched networks use the destination telephone number to identify the end location. They then establish a dedicated path for the duration of the call. Each call you make to the same number may follow a different physical route, but the key point to remember is that it is a dedicated circuit for the duration of the call.

Packet-switched data networks divide the data into packets that are subsequently transmitted over a shared network. Individual channels are not established for each call. The packets of many calls are transmitted at the same time over the same link. If packets are delayed or lost, the sender simply resends the packets. For data traffic, packet networks are more efficient and reliable than circuit-switched networks.

Cell switching is a new broadband form of fast packet switching. It incorporates some circuit-switching features to give us the best of both worlds. Voice, data, or video traffic is first divided into 53-byte cells that are switched into virtual circuits. Then, using various performance criteria, cell switching prioritizes the traffic and transmits it accordingly.

CIRCUIT-SWITCHED NETWORKS

The circuit-switched network routes calls through a series of switches located in the telephone company's central offices. Makes sense. As I mentioned earlier, a circuit-switched call establishes a dedicated circuit for the duration of the call, so the circuit cannot be shared by any other users. Within the digital backbone, this dedicated path is represented by a 64 kbps channel, which may traverse the network through T1s, T3s, SONET channels, or any combination of these.

The earliest switches were manned by an operator, who used a patch panel and jumper cables to manually connect the caller to the called party. As the telephone system grew, electromechanical switching machines were installed in the central office. These systems were considered local exchanges.

Prior to AT&T's divestiture, the network was divided into a hierarchy of five levels. A Class 5 switch referred to the local exchange location, or end office, and the next level, the Class 4 tandem or toll switch, connected multiple end offices together. Class 4 switches were connected to Class 3 primary center switches, and these switches connected to the Class 2 sectional switch. Finally, the sectional switches were connected to one of twelve regional Class 1 switches.

After divestiture, this hierarchy changed. Now the local exchange carriers (LECs) have Class 4 and 5 offices, while the interexchange carriers (IXCs) have the Class 1, 2, and 3 offices. All IXC offices now act as IXC points of presence (POPs), and they connect the LECs to the long-distance network.

Though the end office occupies the lowest level of the class hierarchy, it is considered to be the most important office. This is where the local loop access facilities connect to the public infrastructure for switching, transmission, and signaling. These offices are also known as serving offices or wire centers. There are different levels of central offices based on how they connect to one another, but the switching function is essentially the same in all of them.

Central Office Hierarchy

Class	LEC	IXC
1		Regional Center (RC)
2		Sectional Center (SC)
3		Primary Center (PC)
4	Tandem Office or Toll Center (TC)	
5	End Office (EO)	

Table 11-4

Analog switching

Telephone company central office (CO) switches may be analog or digital. Although a few analog switches are still in use, telephone companies are replacing these older switches with digital equipment when they are retired.

Analog switching uses a space-division concept. This simply means that a call is given a dedicated path, which can be physically identified as belonging to a particular circuit or transmission.

When a caller requests dial tone, the switch connects the user to the dial tone by closing a set of cross points, either mechanically or electronically. The caller enters the digits of the called party, and the switch selects a path for connecting the caller to the appropriate outgoing trunk facility. This is accomplished by dedicating switch components to support the call request. This path is dedicated for the duration of the call and can be traced or identified with that call. When the call is terminated, the switch resources become available for the next call.

Digital switching

A digital switching system is composed of three major components: an interface device, a time-division switch, and the processor. Principal differences among manufacturers' switches include the architecture and proprietary programming.

All information carried within the switch must be in a digital format. In the network, this format is based on T-carrier transmission systems using pulse code modulation (PCM). An interface unit provides access into the digital switch, and it is classified as either on the line (user) side or on the trunk (network) side. These units support both analog and digital input, and they may differ significantly by manufacturer.

Central Office Switch Technology Progression

Generation	Type	Date
1st	Direct connection (no switching)	1876
2nd	Manual switching of mechanical connections	1878
3rd	Electro-mechanical Step-by-step (Strowger)	1919 1921
4th	Solid-state switching	1965
5th	Electronic switching (AESS)	1976
6th	Digital switching	1985
7th	Cell switching	1996

Table 11-5

A device known as a time slot interchanger collects the binary coded input signals and forwards them to time slots on a multiplexed line. The digital switch function is to assign an incoming signal from the receiving interface to an outgoing time slot at the transmitting interface. These functions are under the control of a system processor.

PACKET-SWITCHED NETWORKS

Packet switching was first deployed in the early 1970s to support data networks only. Packet switching networks are the foundation for most data networks, and, initially, they were not intended for voice transmission at all.

The first standardized form of packet switching was based on the x.25 specifications published in 1976. X.25 protocols define the procedures that allow user computers to communicate with network packet switches and transport data to other user computers. These protocols were designed for data systems that operate at what we would consider low speeds today—600 to 900 bits per second. Although the technology is capable of speeds up to 19.2 kbps, most of the embedded x.25 hardware and software operates at much slower speeds.

However, the primary objective of much of today's emerging technology is to move traffic as quickly as possible. This is often referred to as fast packet switching. For example, frame relay and SMDS are part of the family of fast packet protocols. They are meant to take advantage of the digital technology employed in modern networks.

Traditional Data Networks and Protocols

Type	Sponsor	Age	Standard or Proprietary	LAN or WAN
X.25	ITU-T/ISO	25 years	Standard	WAN
OSI	ITU-T/ISO	15 years	Standard	Both
TCP/IP	Internet	15 years	de facto standard	Both
SNA	IBM	25 years	Proprietary	Both
Ethernet	Xerox	17 years	IEEE 802.3 standard	LAN
Netware	Novell	15 years	Proprietary	LAN

Table 11-6

In fast packet networks, the end customer equipment assumes the responsibility of managing congestion and checking for errors. Previously, these functions were performed at every node in the packet network. Data managers accepted the new responsibility as a fair trade-off for increased speeds. If an error occurs or the far end does not receive a packet, the far-end CPE simply asks the originating CPE to resend the packet. The following table compares the two packet services.

Packet and relay hierarchy

Fast packet relay comes in two forms: frame relay and cell relay. Frame relay employs variable-sized protocol data units (PDUs), known as frames, and it is used for data transmission only. It is a private network protocol that operates at speeds of up to 1.544 Mbps.

Comparison of Traditional and Fast Packet Switching

	Traditional (x.25)	Fast Packet Switching
Advantages		
Guaranteed delivery/accuracy	X	
High bandwidth utilization	X	X
Lower overall cost	X	X
Faster transmission		X
Reduced overhead		X
Digital		X
Disadvantages		
Increased network delay	X	
Longer response times	X	
Shared bandwidth	X	

Table 11-7

In contrast to frame relay, cell relay uses a fixed-length PDU, called a cell. The cell consists of a 48-byte payload and a five-byte header. This cell (with slight variations) is being used on both asynchronous transfer mode (ATM) and the IEEE 802.6 standard, more commonly known as the metropolitan area network (MAN.) Cell relay is a public network protocol that operates at speeds of up to 45 Mbps and beyond. It is designed for voice, video, and data applications. Frame and cell relay technologies are compared in the following table.

Fast Packet Comparison

Frame Relay	Cell Relay
Narrowband service	Broadband service
Private network protocol	Public network protocol
Speeds up to 1.544 Mbps	Speeds from 45 Mbps
Variable length data packets (frames)	Fixed length data packets (cells)
Data only	Voice, video, and data

Table 11-8

Cell relay

Cell relay is the technology of choice today, and there are many reasons why this is so. First, though, let's get a better understanding of what cell relay actually is.

In short, cell relay is an integrated approach to networking. It supports the transmission and reception of voice, video, and any form of digital data. Large companies dealing with multiple networks that handle multiple transmission schemes see integrated transmission as a desirable feature. This feature is also appreciated by both local exchange carriers (LECs) and interexchange carriers (IXCs) that support many types of transmission schemes.

In most cell relay systems, the cells are only 53 bytes in length with five bytes devoted to a header and the remaining 48 bytes consisting of user information (the payload). A customer's traffic may be variable in length, but it is segmented into smaller fixed-length cells by the customer premises equipment (CPE) before entering the cell relay system. Unlike many systems today, cell relay does not use a shared medium. Therefore, multipoint lines and shared buses such as an Ethernet are not used. Cell relay uses point-to-point links between all cell relay nodes.

The smaller, fixed-length cell makes cell switching easier to manage and more efficient than packet- and frame-based technologies, resulting in fast, reliable data speeds. The use of fixed-length cells over high-speed virtual connections minimizes the average length of network-introduced delay. They also minimize delay variability and simplify buffer management procedures.

Emerging cell-switching techniques seek to remove as much software as possible from the system. By using ASICs (advanced silicon integrated circuits), switching may be implemented in the hardware to deliver a high rate of cell transfer inexpensively. Cell relay technologies, such as ATM, are designed for simple implementation in silicon.

Evolution of the Public Switched Telephone Network (PSTN)

	Analog	Digital (bit)	Digital (cell)
Transmission	Analog trunks	T-carrier (1968)	SONET (1990)
Switching	Analog switches	5ESS, DMS 100 (1974)	ATM (IXC: 1996; LEC: 1998)
Signaling	In-band CCIS (1978)	Out-of-band SS7 (1992)	B-SS7 (future)
Access services	POTS	ISDN (1978) Dedicated T1, T3 Switched T1, T3	Dedicated ATM (1996) Switched ATM (1999)

Table 11-9

Why is cell relay the technology of choice? To recap, the use of fixed-length cells rather than variable-length frames provides a more predictable performance in the network. Both transmission delay and queuing delay inside the switches are more predictable, and, finally, fixed-link buffers are easier to manage than variable-length buffers.

Cell relay proponents believe that cell relay is easier to implement on VLSI (very large scale integration) chips than is variable-length technology. However, there is concern about the high ratio of over-head (5 bytes) to payload (48 bytes) in cell relay transmission. Also, many people in the industry believe that the constant focus on efficient utilization of raw bandwidth is misguided. They cite the enormous capacity available through fiber optics, along with the continual evolution of faster and faster processors.

Nonetheless, the advantages of the cell relay approach may out-weigh its shortcomings. Users can depend on a superior quality of service (QoS) due to the high input and low delay of cell relay technology.

The future: photonic switching
Advances in switching technology have lagged behind other tech-nological advances. For example, the digital T-carrier transmis-sion facilities were used for about ten years before digital switching was first introduced. Though we could transmit cell relay over SONET at speeds of 622 Mbps, the existing synchronous trans-port mode (STM) switches were only able to switch at approxi-mately 45 Mbps. The new ATM switches solved this problem.

Today, we are able to transmit over fiber-optic networks at speeds in the terabit (Tbps) range, but our switching is now limited to 622 Mbps. This is because the optical signal must be converted back to an electrical digital computer language before being switched by the ATM switches.

Nearly all interoffice and long-distance transmission today is over fiber-optic cable. Most of the local loop also has fiber-optic ca-bling in the feeder portion, and, in near future, the distribution cable to your home will also be converted to fiber optics. So, what is the next generation of switching? Photonic switching.

A switching system that will interconnect a large collection of fiber-optic cables can be assigned to one of three main categories. The first category of switching will feature an optical-to-electrical conversion (o/e), followed by an electronic switch (a fast packet switch), which is then followed by an e/o conversion for transmission over the fiber cable.

The second category is an all-optical switch that will eliminate the need and associated cost for the o/e and e/o conversions. The optical signal will be switched directly without electrical conversion. The control of the network will still be accomplished electronically, but even so, these switches will be able to switch at speeds of gigabits per second.

The last category is similar to the second, except that network control will also be optical. Research in this area is focused on space-, time-, and wavelength-division switching.

VIRTUAL PRIVATE NETWORKS (VPNS)

In the past few years, LANs and WANs have been interconnected by bridges, routers, gateways, and packet-switched networks. These internetworking units are connected to the LANs and WANs via dedicated or leased lines.

As we discussed earlier, the dedicated lines are nailed up end to end through the network directly to the customer premises equipment (CPE) in each business location. A fixed monthly fee is charged for each circuit regardless of how much it's used. Each time your business adds a new location, another dedicated connection is needed. Even though dedicated connection prices are going down, using these lines to interconnect LANs and WANs is still an expensive proposition. Moreover, if you need reliability, individual point-to-point dedicated lines have no backup capability. You must lease a backup line for each primary line.

A better approach would be a LAN/WAN carrier network that provides efficient switching. Users in the network would share access instead of leasing expensive lines. This network would function more like a star network (with a switch in the center) than a fully connected mesh network. Such a network could also provide backup circuits. This concept is known as a virtual network, or a virtual private network (VPN).

Figure 11-3 shows how company A used six dedicated channels to connects its four locations. While effective, this approach is very expensive. It is also unlikely that these lines are being used on a continuous basis. If company B (located in the same area as company A) also has four locations, they must lease six dedicated

Virtual Private Networks (VPNs) vs. Dedicated Lines

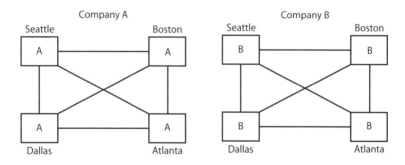

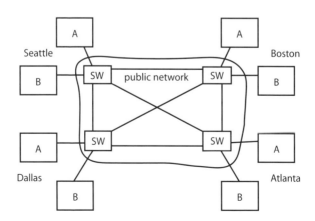

Figure 11-3

lines as well. As a result, the service provider must take twelve lines from the public network to dedicate to customers A and B.

In contrast, the two companies could share the public network's communications facilities through the use of a VPN. The VPN provider may be a LEC or an IXC, depending upon the scope of the network. Customers A and B each lease only one access line from their locations to the nearest VPN switch. This approach allows the traffic to be routed to various endpoints, and it does not require the end user to nail up private leased lines to every possible location. In some installations, companies migrating from a dedicated line network to a VPN have reduced their costs by as much as 30 percent.

The difference between fully meshed leased lines and VPNs is even more dramatic when another location is added to the private network. For example, if company A opens an office in Dallas and needs full connectivity to its other four sites, five additional private lines would be required to connect each location to the new location. With the VPN model, only one dedicated local loop to the most convenient VPN switch would be required.

VPN is a relatively new term in the telecom language, but it describes an old concept. The ideas behind VPN are certainly not new. Public x.25 networks have offered VPN service for years, and switched T1 services also offer VPN-like features. However, we shall see that new technologies, such as ATM, offer much more powerful VPNs than these older technologies.

OVERLAY NETWORKS

The pace of technological evolution really got going in the 1970s, particularly in the area of information technology, which saw the introduction of PCs and local computer networks. Further acceleration occurred in the 1980s, as AT&T's divestiture gave newly competitive telephone companies the opportunity to transport customer data traffic over MANs and WANs.

As the telephone network went digital, telephone companies rushed to develop schemes for transporting data over the existing

PSTN. In addition, the local networks, now interconnected to share resources and exchange data, soon saw the need to upgrade their aging transmission facilities, so telephone companies began installing fiber-optic lines throughout the country. When users got a taste of higher bandwidth possibilities, they embraced these improvements and demanded even more bandwidth.

To meet the increased demand from users, separate overlay networks featuring the newer packet-switching technologies were rushed into deployment. By enhancing the quality and speed of their transmission networks, the telephone companies hoped to encourage customers to stay with their services. However, these new technologies were often developed with proprietary protocols, so the incompatibility problem we have discussed in previous chapters became an issue. Also, the separate overlay networks did not interface with one another.

Everything was evolving so quickly that there simply wasn't enough time to develop the new technology and systems in a manner that would assure standardization and interoperability between all networks and their components. As a result, networks that provided essentially the same services could not be interconnected. The overall infrastructure, which included the PSTN and the separate overlay networks, became an extremely complex and expensive environment.

Although many different types of data networks continue to exist, the industry has developed a variety of devices, such as routers, bridges, and gateways, that perform protocol conversion functions. In this way, different networks are able to pass data back and forth. Nonetheless, this remains a less-than-ideal situation. Every protocol conversion takes time and adds overhead to any given transmission, thus slowing everything down when what we want is speed!

Data traffic carried on the PSTN has been growing at a much faster rate than voice traffic, and this trend is accelerating. Indeed, voice may become only an incidental application on the integrated network of the future. Until then, we will make do with overlay networks that ride on top of the existing PSTN. The ultimate goal, however, is to build one infrastructure that can handle all types of traffic efficiently and reliably.

What do we mean by an overlay network? Basically, the overlay network uses much of the same hardware and transmission facilities as the PSTN. For example, at any given instant, the transmission side of a T1 line with 24 channels might have 12 channels devoted to voice conversations while the other 12 channels are dedicated to data sessions. Everything travels over the same physical wires, but there is a difference in how the digital streams are switched in the central offices. Voice streams are switched through the regular switch, while data streams are diverted to routers or separate data switches.

To create the overlay network, the telephone company installs the necessary equipment in its central offices. The transmission facilities are not affected. T1s, T3s, and SONET channels do not care what kind of bits are moving through them. The key issue is to segregate the traffic and route it correctly through the central offices or other network nodes.

Now let's discuss some of the specific overlay networks involved. Keep in mind that the discussion here relates to methods for *routing* bits through the network, and they are independent of the transmission methods discussed earlier, such as T1, T3 or SONET. Any one or all of these transmission methods can be used to move bits in the networks we will discuss.

The telephone companies have built separate overlay networks to meet the data transmission needs of corporations. These networks include frame relay, switched multimegabit data services (SMDS), and asynchronous transfer mode (ATM). How to characterize these networks can be a big point of confusion. I just used the term networks, while others call them services, protocols, systems, architectures, or technologies. They are all of these things, and each incorporates a different set of protocols and technologies in order to provide data delivery services with a variety of speeds and capabilities.

TRADITIONAL X.25

Traditional x.25 packet switching was developed to transport data across an analog network. The primary advantages associated with this method include guaranteed delivery and accuracy, high bandwidth utilization, and low overall cost. Increased network delay, slow response times, and shared bandwidth are noteworthy disadvantages.

This is an old technology that is rapidly losing ground to the newer high-speed alternatives. Digital networks render many of the traditional x.25 networking functions unnecessary, such as the network-based error checking function, which slows down the data rate throughout the network.

FIBER DISTRIBUTED DATA INTERFACE (FDDI)

FDDI is a LAN technology used in campus settings to provide a backbone ring network. (Refer to our previous discussion in Chapter 9.) Because it is primarily a LAN technology, FDDI permits a fast 100 Mbps shared transmission, and recent enhancements allow it to support multimedia applications as well.

FDDI backbones compete with leased lines, frame relay, ATM, and high-speed private lines. However, this network doesn't offer switching capability.

FRAME RELAY

Frame relay is considered a narrowband fast packet technology. This is because the transmission pipes employed are mostly T1s with a bandwidth limitation of 1.544 Mbps. A frame relay network is often used to connect LANs, or for LAN-to-WAN connections, and it may be implemented on products that currently support packet-switching capabilities. For example, many LAN routers and multiplexers can be modified for frame relay by adding an optional card.

These networks are similar to x.25 networks in that both employ packet-switching technology, but, unlike x.25 networks, frame relay networks can carry packets of varying lengths. Therefore, frame relay networks can accommodate data packets associated with virtually any data protocol. This is an important distinction. For example, an x.25 packet may range in size from 128 bytes to 256 bytes, while an Ethernet frame may be 1,500 bytes—a frame relay network is able to carry both.

Unlike x.25 networks, a frame relay network does not attempt to convert the data protocols of various transmissions to suit an assigned data protocol. Frame relay networks are referred to as protocol independent because they can accept any type of data, then switch it and carry it through the network. On a frame relay network, data protocol conversion is the responsibility of the users transmitting and receiving information. Another contrast to x.25 networks is in how data is checked for errors. Error-checking occurs throughout the x.25's system of network nodes, but data sent on a frame relay network is not checked for errors or lost packets. Any errors must be detected and corrected by the end users. Recall that this is part of the fast packet trade-off for higher speed.

Frame relay's ability to accommodate virtually any data protocol without investing the time or computer energy to convert it to another protocol makes it a less expensive, faster network than other networks available. In a similar fashion, placing the responsibility for error detection and correction on the user results in faster, less expensive transmissions.

Connections in a frame relay network are described as permanent virtual connections (PVCs)—virtual because the customer does not pay for a permanent, dedicated connection. Instead, the customer pays for guaranteed amounts of transmission capacity. Committed information rates (CIR) are used to give the customer guaranteed bandwidth on demand for each PVC. Though frame relay is usually implemented as a private network service, it may be offered as a tariffed public (shared) network service by the telephone company.

Frame relay is most often used by large, corporate customers to interconnect LANs or to connect a LAN to a WAN. Due to the considerable variation in the length of each packet, a frame relay network may be more vulnerable to delays in delivering data. It is especially suited for data traffic that is "bursty," meaning packets are sent in uneven intervals.

Although often referred to as a VPN, frame relay actually has a nailed-up channel for each connection, but this channel is transparent to the end user. The frame relay network consists of network nodes, high-speed digital backbone channels, customer access circuits, data service units/channel service units (DSUs/CSUs), and frame relay assembler/disassemblers (FRADs). In some instances, a router may replace or incorporate the FRAD function.

The customer's equipment can be any device that supports a frame relay interface card. Most manufacturers of networking customer

Frame Relay Network

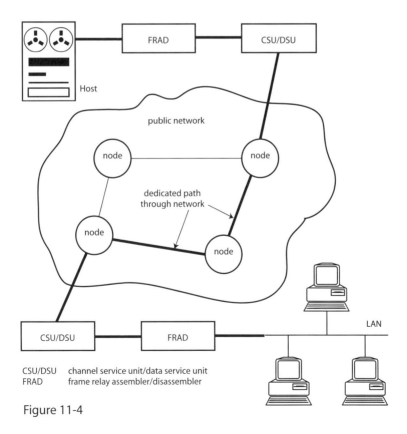

CSU/DSU	channel service unit/data service unit
FRAD	frame relay assembler/disassembler

Figure 11-4

premises equipment (CPE) have modified their product offerings to include this capability. For local area networks, customers most often use routers, although many bridges can be upgraded for frame relay support.

All major brands of multiplexers also provide frame relay interface cards for customers who want to support multiple applications. The link to the network is a dedicated digital private line. This can be provisioned as a single 56–64 kbps link or as a DS-1 data speed link via a T1. The customer is responsible for providing the appropriate DSU/CSU equipment.

SWITCHED MULTIMEGABIT DATA SERVICES (SMDS)

SMDS is a metropolitan area, high-speed data service. It is a connectionless packet-switching service that extends LAN-like performance beyond the subscriber's location. SMDS can span LANs, MANs, and WANs. SMDS is actually a public switched service, and not a technology as such.

Organizations requiring LAN-to-LAN connections among their various locations can eliminate the need for leased private lines by using SMDS. Any SMDS customer can link its LAN to a carrier's public switched network and exchange information with any other SMDS customer. SMDS can be used to create both intranets, for organizations with LANs in remote locations, and extranets, which extend most of the benefits of a LAN over a much greater distance and between separate organizations.

As is the case in other packet-switched networks, SMDS sends each distinct data packet (containing the addresses of both sender and receiver) separately, subject to bandwidth availability. Customers do not need to establish a logical connection in order to exchange data over the network. At any given time, multiple customers may share the SMDS backbone network.

Where LANs are typically limited to 20 Mbps over a distance of several kilometers, SMDS provides much higher speeds over distances of several hundred kilometers. SMDS runs over a T3 (45 Mbps) backbone, and, when connected to SONET, it will run over OC-3 (155 Mbps). Although SMDS runs over a broadband backbone, customers are able to access the network via various classes. The SMDS access classes are 4 Mbps (for compatibility with 4 Mbps token ring LANs), 10 Mbps (for compatibility with Ethernet LANs), 16 Mbps (for compatibility with 16 Mbps token ring LANs), 25 Mbps (for IBM Synchronous Network Architecture [SNA] data interfaces), and 34 Mbps (the maximum effective throughput over a T3 carrier).

SMDS Topology

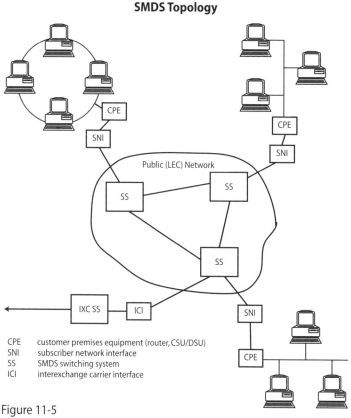

CPE	customer premises equipment (router, CSU/DSU)
SNI	subscriber network interface
SS	SMDS switching system
ICI	interexchange carrier interface

Figure 11-5

Customer equipment may be any device that supports an SMDS interface card, and most manufacturers of networking CPE have modified their products to include this capability. LAN customers often use routers, but many bridges can be upgraded for SMDS support, too. Customers wanting to support multiple applications can purchase SMDS interface cards from the major multiplexer vendors.

SMDS is linked to the PSTN via a dedicated digital private line—whether a single T1 facility, multiple T1 facilities, or a T3 link. As with frame relay, the customer is responsible for providing the appropriate channel service unit/data service unit (CSU/DSU) capability. SMDS services compete with leased lines, x.25 packet networks, frame relay, and ATM, but not all telephone service providers are able to offer SMDS.

BROADBAND ISDN

Enterprise customers, the government, and Internet service providers continue to demand flexible, high-speed network services to support information-intensive applications and internetworking. In 1984, The International Telecommunications Union-Telephony (ITU-T) published the broadband ISDN standard in anticipation of this demand for new networks.

The ITU defined broadband services as having transmission speeds greater than 45 Mbps. Some might consider a T3 digital carrier or FDDI as broadband services, but the ITU further defined this future network as broadband ISDN (B-ISDN). B-ISDN is a version of narrowband ISDN capable of supporting multiple services, such as voice, data, and video. This network uses standardized hardware and software interface definitions. B-ISDN basic rate interface (BRI) is 155.52 Mbps over OC-3 facilities, while B-ISDN primary rate interface (PRI) is 622.08 Mbps over OC-12 facilities.

The network of the future had been envisioned by the ITU planners as a single network using cell relay technology over fiber rings. Before B-ISDN could be implemented, copper transmission facilities had to be upgraded to fiber optics, circuit switching had to be upgraded to cell relay, and end-to-end application standards had to be completed. The time for that future network is now, but you won't hear anything about B-ISDN. That is a standards body term that nobody uses. The B-ISDN networks are actually composed of ATM cell switching over SONET fiber rings.

Today, a multigigabit transmission infrastructure has been constructed in the interfacility network. The major network service providers (both LECs and IXCs) have begun deploying cell relay switching, and some networks, such as Sprint's ION (integrated on-demand network), are 100 percent cell relay. Eventually, a set of broadband signaling and service definitions will need to be installed as a framework for broadband services.

The combination of asynchronous transfer mode (ATM) and SONET meets the B-ISDN specifications. Though this standard was published long before the public Internet, cable modems, and Internet service providers existed, it is still adequate for any of these applications. Amazing, isn't it?

Those clairvoyant network planners of 1984 also anticipated other future needs and classified B-ISDN services as either interactive or distribution. Interactive services imply an ongoing dialogue between users, or between users and service providers. Distribution services also deal with a dialogue, but from one service provider to many users.

Interactive services are further classified as conversational, messaging, and retrieval services. Conversational services are interactive dialogues with real-time operations. The simplest example is a real-time telephone call between two people. Other types of conversational services are interactive teleshopping, LAN-to-LAN communications, and building-surveillance services. Messaging services include user-to-user communications, such as video mail service or electronic mail service, which can be performed on a conversational basis. Retrieval services are store-and-forward applications that permit a user to obtain information stored for public use, such as catalogs or train schedules.

Distribution services *without* user control include conventional broadcast services, such as television and radio. These service provide continuous flows of information, and users are granted unlimited access to the information. Distribution services *with* user control allow a central source to distribute information to either a large or small number of users based on some type of cyclical repetition. Some types of video- or television-on-demand fall into this category.

ASYNCHRONOUS TRANSPORT MODE (ATM)

Asynchronous transfer mode is a high-speed, fast packet-switching technology based on fixed-size 53-byte cells that incorporates the best features of both circuit switching and packet switching. ATM brings switched dedicated bandwidth directly to the desktop over existing twisted-pair copper or fiber-optic cabling at transfer rates ranging from 51Mbps to 1.2Gbps.

ATM is also a connection-oriented transport technology. It uses ATM-logical connections, known as virtual paths (VPs) and virtual circuits (VCs), to provide an end-to-end connection. Each VC connection requires the end user and the transport network to negotiate the quality of service for handling applications traffic. By using a switching approach, each user receives a guaranteed bandwidth for data transfer. Contrast this with the shared medium approaches common in premises networking that use traditional packet-switching methods. The cell relay approach, using small, fixed-length units of data, ensures that traffic flow and buffer allocation will be closely regulated.

What does asynchronous mean?

Because ATM supports synchronous traffic, such as voice and video applications, newcomers may very well wonder why ATM has the term "asynchronous" as part of its name. The reason is that traffic is not necessarily assigned to fixed slots (cells) on the transmission channel as it is in a conventional time-division multiplexing (TDM) system. Therefore, the cells from one sender are not always in a fixed position in the channel.

ATM requires each individual cell being transported by itself through the network to have a header attached to it that will identify it in the cell stream traffic. This scheme permits either synchronous or asynchronous allocation of the cells. Even synchronous traffic, such as voice, can be placed into an ATM network in an asynchronous (bursty) fashion, as long as the receiving machine smooths the bursty cell flow to a TDM-type presentation.

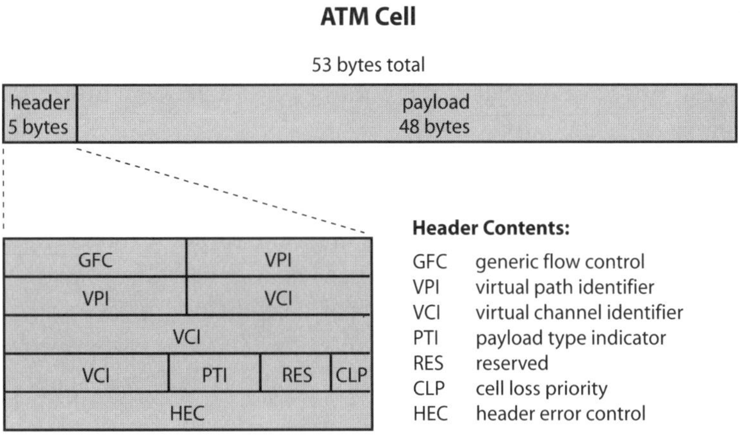

ATM Cell

53 bytes total

header 5 bytes	payload 48 bytes

Header Contents:

GFC	VPI
VPI	VCI
VCI	
VCI	PTI	RES	CLP
HEC	

GFC generic flow control
VPI virtual path identifier
VCI virtual channel identifier
PTI payload type indicator
RES reserved
CLP cell loss priority
HEC header error control

Figure 11-5a

What is ATM?

ATM standards have been developed primarily by the ITU-T, but an industry group, the ATM Forum, has also been instrumental in standardizing ATM technology to the point where it is today.

Today's ATM is a high-throughput, low-latency statistical switching technique that is based on cell relay. In cell relay, cells are switched through the network statistically over connections that display latency characteristics matching the latency requirements of the applications. This technique is efficient and cost effective, and, due to the speeds at which cells are passed through the network, it is able to emulate circuit-switched environments.

ATM interfaces

Multiple protocols are required to support full ATM operations. The number of protocols required will depend on where the user traffic is being transported. The most important protocol is the user network interface (UNI). It defines the procedures for the interworking between user equipment and the ATM node.

Two forms of UNI are supported: the private (customer premises) UNI and the public (telephone network) UNI. The major difference between these interfaces involves the physical communications links between the machines. A private UNI will likely have a link such as a private fiber-optic or twisted-pair line. A public UNI will likely consist of SONET or T3. Also, a private UNI might not have the elaborate monitoring and policing procedures that exist at the public UNI.

ATM topology and service

The ATM topology is usually a star, point-to-point topology, but it could also have other shapes. ATM is designed to support multiple applications. Its convergence functions permit the relaying of voice, video, and data traffic through the same switching fabric. The interconnection of LANs using different protocols can also be supported by ATM technology.

A wide area network (WAN) is the public network offered by telephone companies. The ATM nodes of a WAN use a public UNI to connect to the ATM nodes of the customer premises equipment. In turn, the ATM nodes on the CPE use private UNIs to connect to LANs and PBXs.

ATM allows multiple users to share a line at the UNI through subscription agreements with each ATM customer. These agreements define the amount of traffic that the network must support, as well as several QoS features, such as delay and throughput. The agreements also place restrictions on how much traffic the customer can submit to the network during a given measured period.

ATM backbones can be seamlessly integrated into wide area networks to provide data and video to the desktop. If you believe the tremendous hype ATM has received throughout the industry, it may seem like the ultimate solution to all networking needs. However, it is really nothing more than a fast media access control (MAC) layer transport.

Implementing ATM may not be for everyone; only specific networks will realize benefits from its adoption. In its purest form, ATM is designed to carry information at high speeds from one point to another, transparently. It doesn't matter whether the information is voice, video, or data. Due to the small cell structure

ATM Topology & Services

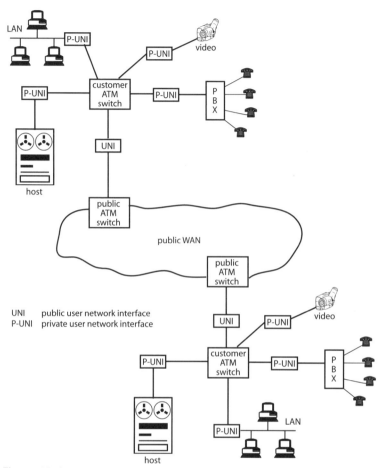

Figure 11-6

used in ATM networks, virtually any type of digital information can be transported over any type of medium.

ATM connection identifiers

As I mentioned at the beginning of this discussion on ATM, the virtual channel (VC) and the virtual path (VP) are two multiplexing hierarchies used by ATM. The virtual path is a node-to-node connection, much like a trunk between switches in the PSTN. A transmission can travel over many virtual paths on its end-to-end journey, depending on how many ATM switches it passes through.

A virtual channel is the end-to-end channel. Each transmission has only one virtual channel. However, any given virtual path can contain multiple virtual channels in the same way that the PSTN's T1 trunk can carry multiple phone calls.

The virtual path identifier (VPI) and the virtual channel identifier (VCI) are found in the ATM cell header. A VPI identifies the physical VP that the transmission will take to get to the next node. There may be multiple VPs between ATM nodes, but the VPI identifies which one will be used. At each node, the ATM cell acquires a new VPI in its header for identifying the next VP to the next node. The VCI, on the other hand, remains the same because it identifies only the end-to-end channel.

In the telephone network, a good parallel to the VCI would be the two telephone numbers involved in a phone call: the originating number and the called number. The two numbers define both ends of the transmission, and they do not change for the duration of that call. The VPI simply identifies the various trunks used between switches, which may be different for each separate call between the same two parties.

This approach allows VCs to be nailed up end to end in order to provide semipermanent connections for the support of a large number of user sessions. A virtual channel identifier (VCI) is used to identify a unidirectional facility for the transfer of the ATM traffic and is assigned at the time a VC session is activated in the ATM network. VPIs and VCIs can also be established on demand.

Routing can occur in an ATM network at the VC level. If VCIs are used in the network, the ATM switch must translate the incoming VCI values into outgoing VCI links. The VC links must be concatenated to form a full virtual channel connection (VCC). VCCs are used for user-to-user, user-to-network, or network traffic transfers.

If the VCI is nailed up end to end as a permanent, nonswitched connection, it is called a permanent virtual circuit (PVC). If it is switched, meaning that the actual physical route is established

ATM Virtual Channels & Virtual Paths

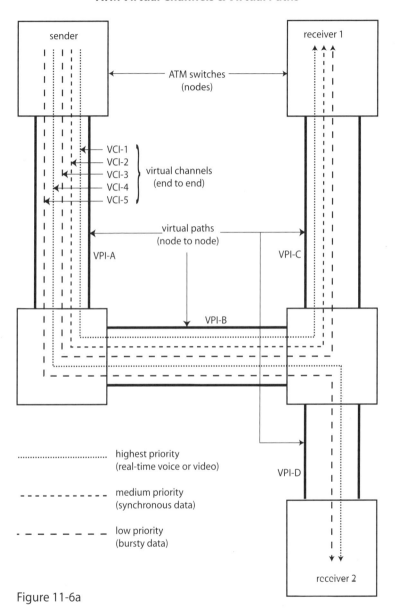

Figure 11-6a

each time the call is made, it is called a switched virtual circuit (SVC).

THE INTERNET

The Internet is the granddaddy of overlay networks. It not only overlays the PSTN, but it also consists of independent private networks and dedicated backbone pipes. It's a huge network of networks. Given its size and importance, the Internet will be discussed fully in its own chapter following this one.

OVERLAY NETWORK COMPARISONS

The applications requiring new technologies are shown in Table 11-11. As you can see, many technologies can handle different types of applications. The ultimate goal, however, is to construct one network infrastructure. With so many choices, it can be very difficult for customers to decide which technology to use for which applications. The following tables summarize these comparisons.

Figure 11-7 represents the bandwidth and distance capabilities of the major technologies. As the figure suggests, Ethernet and token ring technologies are distance limited to a few hundred meters, and their maximum capacity is restricted to 16 Mbps. FDDI provides a higher capacity than the other LANs and also supports greater geographical distances. However, all these technologies are restricted in relation to their transmission capacity and their ability to span large geographical areas.

The metropolitan area network (MAN), implemented as SMDS, offers an interesting combination of distance and capacity. It can operate in the multimegabit range and can span a large geographical area in conventional LANs. There is no technical reason that precludes SMDS from spanning an even larger geographical area, but this network was designed for a reasonably constrained geographical area, such as a city. It is interesting to note that since the deployment of ATM, new MANs are not being implemented. They were merely an interim solution.

Frame relay is not constrained by distance, and it is designed for metropolitan and wide area networks. However, the physical layer is implemented solely over T1 transmission pipes, so standard frame relay implementations are not able to operate above 1.544 Mbps. On the other hand, proprietary frame relay systems that offer

Comparing Emerging Technologies

	SMDS	Frame Relay	ATM
Technology	MAN	MAN/WAN	LAN/MAN/WAN
Application	High-speed data	Bursty data	Multimedia: data, voice, video
Competes with	Frame relay	X.25, SMDS	X.25, SMDS
Packet type	"Slot"	Frame	Cell
Connection management	Carrier level	Yes, PVC	Yes, PVC
Payload integrity	None	None	Yes
Bandwidth on demand	Yes	CIR	Yes, with agreement
Data rates	Fast (4-34 Mbps)	Slow (1.544 Mbps)	Very fast (45+ Mbps)

Table 11-10

Targeted Applications for Network Technologies

	Wireless	FDDI	Frame Relay	SMDS	ATM
Low-speed data	x		x	x	
High-speed LANs		x			x
Seamless LAN/WANs			x	x	x
LAN interconnections			x	x	x
Graphics, photos			x	x	x
X-rays			x	x	x
Large database transfers			x	x	x
CAD/CAM			x	x	x
Medium quality video				x	x
Connectionless data transfer				x	x
Connection oriented data			x		x
Voice	x				x

Table 11-11

greater transmission speeds are being deployed, but users will be locked into the vendor's proprietary equipment.

ATM technology is not constrained to any particular line speed, and the standard does not require any specific physical layer solution. Moreover, there are no distance limitations. It can be viewed as a switching and backbone solution for both wide area and local area networks. It is shown at the top of the bandwidth because it is intended to operate on top of high-speed fiber optics and SONET.

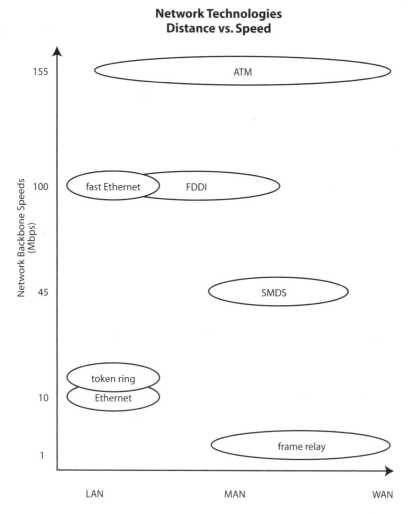

Figure 11-7

Chapter

12

An Exploding Internet

PICK UP ANY MAGAZINE OR NEWSPAPER, and you will find an article on the Internet. What is generally referred to as the Internet, or what I will call "the public Internet," is really more than 30 different Internet backbones with thousands of smaller networks interconnected through the backbones. This allows users on one network to communicate with any user on any other network. Most users are connected to the Internet through an Internet service provider (ISP) or a commercial online service provider, such as America Online or Prodigy.

Businesses may also create their own private intranets for employees by using Internet-like protocols. When companies allow their customers or vendors to use their private intranets on a limited basis, these expanded intranets are called extranets.

The Internet keeps growing, and no one knows exactly how big it is. In 1997, Network Wizards surveyed the Internet and found at least 1,301,000 separate computer networks and more than 19 million host computers.

Today's Internet has millions of destinations that anyone can access. They include online bookstores, magazines, record stores, florists, real estate listings, job information, libraries, and databases, to name only a few. Some companies no longer print catalogs. All their product information is published on the Internet, often in an interactive format that offers a lot of useful information to the consumer. Researchers have access to huge databases of technical information and recreational users can send email, chat with friends, play games, or download music. The Internet has created a whole new way of communicating.

There are three ways to connect to the Internet. The most common way is to establish a dial-up connection by using a modem that is connected to your computer or installed inside of it. Your modem dials a local telephone number to reach your ISP, and, in turn, your ISP provides entry to the worldwide network. The second way is via a cable modem, where the cable provider is also the ISP. A cable modem provides "always-on" access, meaning you do not have to dial up to establish a connection. The third way is through an organization's network (LAN) and its dedicated leased line. This line is usually a high-speed digital line, such as a T1.

As I mentioned briefly in the last chapter, the Internet is an overlay packet-switched network that rides on top of the PSTN. But it's even bigger than that. It also rides on top of thousands of private data networks, so it interconnects virtually every communications network on earth. In fact, the various overlay networks we discussed earlier, such as frame relay, SMDS, and ATM, can and do carry Internet traffic. The Internet essentially overlays all of them, too.

All computer networks operate under a system of protocols, which, as we know, is a set of rules used by computers to communicate. The Internet is no exception. The official language of the Internet is TCP/IP, which stands for Transmission Control Protocol/Internet Protocol. The Internet uses TCP/IP to divide the data you are transmitting into packets. Each packet contains both data payload information and addressing for its destination. Computers on the network examine the address information and pass the packet along from site to site until it reaches its destination. Each packet is independent, and packets in the same message may travel over many different routes.

HISTORY OF THE INTERNET

The Internet traces its beginnings to a small network built in 1969 by the Department of Defense. It purpose was to link defense installations, and it was called ARPANET (Advanced Research

Project Agency Network). Military, government, and academic researchers used this network to connect to large supercomputers via dedicated phone lines. During the 1970s, ARPANET expanded to include even more universities and research centers, and, by the late 1970s, it began to move away from its military and research roots. ARPANET was eventually split into two networks: MILNET, for military purposes, and ARPANET for non-military purposes. The two networks were connected by using Internet protocol (IP), which allowed communications between them. Even at this stage, IP developers visualized the eventual connection of thousands of networks.

Before ARPANET, communications networks were point-to-point networks. Each node was dependent on the link before it, and if one point in the network was cut, the entire network would become disabled. However, a new kind of mesh communications network was developed that featured multiple links to each node. Now, information could find its way through the network even if a section was out of service. This network eventually grew into the Internet—a network of networks with millions of nodes.

By the mid-1980s, ARPANET had reached the limits of what it could do. The National Science Foundation (NSF) furthered the migration from ARPANET to the Internet by setting up an extensive network to connect all the huge supercomputers together. These computers were being used for complex mathematical calculations and scientific research, and the resulting network was called NSFNET.

NSFNET replaced ARPANET as the backbone of the Internet. Initially, commercial network traffic was banned from the NSFNET, but, eventually corporations were allowed to use the Net. Then, as PCs became increasingly popular, the Net was opened up to individuals as well. Because of the extensive internetworking of PCs that ensued, people began referring to the Net as the "Internet." The name stuck.

The NSF lifted its restrictions on commercial use of the Internet in 1991. By doing so, it cleared the way for the age of electronic commerce. In the same year, a team from the University of Minnesota developed "Gopher," the first point-and-click navigation tool of the Internet.

In 1992, the Internet Society was formed as a private sector effort to help promote the evolution of the Internet. It is a professional society composed of individual members, but the bulk of its initial financial support came from industry contributions. Also in 1992, the Internet Architecture Board became part of the Internet Society. Its decision-making responsibilities on Internet standards were delegated to the leaders of the Internet Engineering Task Force (IETF).

TODAY'S INTERNET

Although the Internet was originally developed as a tool to link university researchers, its uses are manifold today. The most common use of the Internet is for communications and access to information. Entertainment is a growing use, and e-commerce promises to be a huge application that will change our society in much the same way the automobile transformed society in the last century.

New applications that simplify the Internet use are constantly being introduced. Imaginative entrepreneurs are inventing new applications we could not have imagined a few years ago. Some describe the Internet as the global "information superhighway." That may now be an understatement. It connects millions of people around the world, and it continues to grow exponentially. Its importance and its ultimate impact on society transcend words.

The Internet is not owned by public telephone service providers or regulated by governments. It is a perfectly democratic organism under the control of no one, and it operates through the cooperative effort of many individual networks and organizations. It is probably ungovernable, and it will likely evolve in ways we cannot now foresee.

THE PUBLIC INTERNET

The Internet began to explode when businesses started using it in earnest. Nearly every business desktop now has a PC and Internet access. What was unknown five years ago is commonplace today. Workers routinely exchange millions of email messages over the Net through a variety of commercial services. World news is also distributed instantly over the Internet. There are international bulletin boards, chat rooms, and electronic discussion groups. Today, most companies and organizations also have their own Web pages.

The Internet can be characterized as an hierarchy, similar to the PSTN. At the lowest level are devices used for network access, such as a modem and telephone line for individual users, or a router and dedicated line for corporate users. Individuals connect to the public Internet through ISPs, the second level of the Internet hierarchy. Large corporations sometimes connect directly via high-speed access to the regional networks, and regional networks interconnect with each other through the backbone NAPs (network access points). Some NAPs are colocated inside IXC switching offices, where the Internet overlaps the PSTN.

THE BACKBONE

As I stated earlier, the Internet is actually made up of multiple backbone networks and thousands of private networks. Each component of the Internet is vital in bringing end users data when they request it. The backbones are the fastest and most direct routes for transmitting Internet data, and they carry most Internet traffic. Originally, there was one NSFNET backbone consisting of 56 kbps paths. When commercial companies began using the NSFNET, the government transferred the backbone network to two privately funded and competing Internet carriers, UUNET Technologies and Performance Systems International (PSI).

At first, the private backbones consisted of T1 trunks that connected the major metropolitan areas. Since 1995, separate backbones have been built, and they are maintained and managed by large interexchange carriers, such as MCI WorldCom, Sprint, and Cable and Wireless USA. These companies, referred to as tier one ISPs, sell backbone access to the smaller regional ISPs, which in turn sell access to even smaller local ISPs. Eventually, the end user contracts with the local ISP for service, which is really nothing more than access.

Today, there are thousands of miles of fiber-optic cable in the backbone networks, and networks are constantly being upgraded for the purpose of acquiring more bandwidth from the fiber transmission. The fastest backbones today use OC-12 fiber trunks, which transmit data at 622 Mbps, but even that is not fast enough for the enormous growth of the Internet and the new applications expected. For example, Sprint is upgrading its backbone to OC-48 trunks that deliver data transmission speeds of 2.5 gigabits per second. These speeds are great for data traffic, such as email and file transfer, but what about real-time voice conversations and video transmissions?

Data packets move through the network over the best available route, and packets from the same message often travel different routes and arrive at the end at different times. The packets are reassembled in the right order before being delivered to the recipient, but this process may take varying amounts of time. Such delays don't affect data traffic, but they would definitely not work for real-time voice or live video. You might hear later parts of a conversation before you hear the first part!

To avoid this problem, voice and video transmissions are limited to the number of "hops" they make over the network. This means that there is a maximum number of switches or routers that the packets can go through on their entire trip. Typical Internet traffic averages 10 to 12 hops, which is fine for data. For real-time voice and video traffic, however, the acceptable maximum is three hops.

Therefore, it becomes obvious that voice and video traffic must assume a higher priority than data on the network. Asynchronous transfer mode (ATM) is a technology that allows voice and live video to move efficiently over a packet network, and we discussed how ATM excels at moving bits quickly and efficiently in the Chapter 11. Because the ATM cells are transmitted in a virtual circuit, they can be prioritized.

The TCP/IP data packets that travel over the Internet are OSI Layer 3 and 4 protocols, which means that they can travel over any lower layer protocol, such as frame relay or ATM, both at Layer 2. For this reason, tier one Internet carriers are now installing ATM equipment on their fiber lines so that transmission quality is guaranteed from end to end.

NETWORK ACCESS POINTS (NAPs)

NAPs are public Internet exchange points where the major Internet backbone networks intersect. The Internet backbones of various network service providers (UUNET, Sprint, AT&T, or GTE) and hundreds of local and regional Internet access providers all meet at these exchange points to pass Internet transmissions from one network to another. At these NAPs, enormous amounts of data are sent to and from each connected network. NAPs are the points where data is transferred onto or off the Internet through ISPs, or where it gets routed through different networks. NAPs are like massive freeway interchanges with scores of on- and off-ramps.

NAPs are also where peering takes place. Peering refers to an agreement established between two or more ISPs. Rather than using the standard Internet backbone, the ISPs forward each other's packets directly across a special link created between them. For example, suppose a client of ISP A wants to access a Web site hosted by ISP B. If A and B have a peering relationship, the data packets will travel directly between the two ISPs. In general, this provides faster access because there are fewer hops. Also, it is an economical arrangement for the ISPs because it eliminates the fees charged by a third-party network service provider.

If more than two ISPs are involved, all traffic destined for any of these ISPs is first routed to a central exchange, called a peering point, and then forwarded to the final destination. Peering points are similar to the network access points (NAPs) managed by the major backbone providers, but on a smaller scale. Both public NAPs and private peering points are major intersections of the Internet, where large amounts of data traffic converge and where most of the congestion takes place.

INTERNET ADDRESSES

Computers, routers, and other intelligent devices on the Internet are assigned a kind of address so that IP data packets traveling over the network can find them. For networks using the TCP/IP protocol, messages are routed by the IP address of the destination computer. Your PC may not have its own IP address if you use dial-up access, so the IP address of your ISP's mail server will be used instead. This is how your email messages get to you.

IP addresses are written as four numbers separated by periods. They are actually 32-bit (4-byte) numeric addresses. You may recall that one 8-bit byte yields 256 possible combinations of 0s and 1s, so each number of the address will be between 0 and 255. For example, 208.216.182.15 is the IP address for Amazon.com's Web site. Don't get this numbering scheme confused with ASCII code, which includes letters and punctuation in its 256-character scheme. The bytes in IP addresses represent numbers only, because a totally different coding system is used.

Within an isolated network, IP addresses are assigned at random as long as each one is unique. However, connecting a private network to the Internet requires the use of registered IP addresses (called Internet addresses) to avoid duplication. Every host and router on the Internet has an IP address, and each combination is unique—no two machines have the same IP address. All IP addresses are 32 bits long, and they are used in both the source and destination address fields of IP packets.

IP addresses are administered by the Internet Network Information Center, also known as the InterNIC or just plain NIC. NIC is funded by the National Science Foundation, and it is chartered to provide Internet information services and to supervise the registration of addresses and domain names.

Each IP address consists of two parts—a network portion and a host portion. Both parts are dependent on the class of the network, and there are three classes of IP addresses. Class A supports 16 million hosts on each of 127 networks; Class B supports 65,000 hosts on each of 16,000 networks; and Class C supports 254 hosts on each of 2 million networks. The first group of digits in an IP address identifies the class of that address.

Class	Number
Class A	1-126
Reserved	127
Class B	128-191
Class C	192-223
Reserved	224-254

Class A addresses devote the first byte (number group) to the network address, and the remaining three bytes are assigned to hosts (computers). These addresses are suitable for a small number of big networks with lots of computers on each network. Class B addresses devote the first two bytes to the network address and the second two bytes to hosts. Class C addresses devote the first three bytes to network addresses and the last byte to hosts. These addresses can identify many networks, but only 254 possible hosts. Therefore, Class C addresses are appropriate for LANs.

If you look at the numbers carefully, you will notice that they don't always add up. This is due to the fact that some of the bits in the first byte are fixed, resulting in fewer than 256 possible numbers in that position. Also, some addresses are reserved or otherwise unavailable. In principle, over 2 billion addresses exist, but the practice of organizing address space by classes wastes millions of them. In fact, we are rapidly running out of IP addresses.

This looming disaster has sparked a great deal of controversy within the Internet community on what to do. Because all of the Class A addresses have been used and there are very few Class Bs left, new addressing schemes are required for networks consisting of more than 254 hosts. Classless inter-domain routing (CIDR) may be one temporary solution.

The basic idea of CIDR is to allocate Class C addresses in contiguous blocks. For example, if a site needs 2000 addresses, it is assigned a block of eight contiguous Class C addresses rather than one Class B address. In addition, the world is divided into four zones, and each zone receives a portion of the remaining Class C space.

Europe . . . . 194.0.0.0 to 195.255.255.255
North America . . . . 198.0.0.0 to 199.255.255.255
Central and South America . . . 200.0.0.0 to 201.255.255.255
Asia and the Pacific . . . . 202.0.0.0 to 302.255.255.255

In this way, each region now has about 32 million addresses to allocate, and another 320 million addresses are left in reserve (204.0.0.0 through 223.255.255.255).

Domain Name System (DNS)

Remembering IP addresses is difficult. Humans do much better with names. People don't address one another by their telephone numbers. If they did, a conversion might begin: "Hi, 989-555-1234, how's it going?" Instead, we use names like Ralph and Trixie.

Computers, on the other hand, like numbers. In fact, that's all they really understand. The purpose of the domain name system (DNS) is to reconcile this difference between humans and computers. In the early days of the Internet, a file of all the IP addresses was updated nightly and distributed to every host computer. As the Internet grew, that approach was no longer possible. So an hierarchical domain-based naming system was invented, and a distributed database was set up to support it.

Domain name servers maintain the DNS database and correlate the IP numerical addresses with ASCII character strings, or letters, in the form of names and words. Managing a large and constantly changing set of names is not trivial, but by using hierarchical addressing, there is less confusion. Each name server sends queries that it cannot resolve to the IP address of a name server higher in the hierarchy.

Full DNS names are composed of two parts: a host name and a top level domain name. An example of a full DNS name is *amazon.com*. In this example, "amazon" is the name of the host

(IP address: 208.216.181.15), and ".com" is the top level domain name for commercial sites. The top level domain names currently in use include:

Commercial organizations	.com
Educational institutions	.edu
Government organizations	.gov
International organizations	.int
Internet access providers (ISPs)	.net
Nonprofit organizations	.org
U.S.-based military	.mil

UNIFORM RESOURCE LOCATORS (URLS)

IP addresses and the DNS system are sufficient to take you to a host computer, but URLs, which incorporate IP/DNS addresses, take you one step further to a specific file or Web page on that host computer. URLs make it possible for both people and software applications to access the huge bank of information available from a number of different Internet protocols.

Most commonly, you will run into URLs on the World Wide Web (WWW) as that medium uses URLs to link Web pages together. In your Web browser's "location" box, the item that generally starts with "http:" is a URL. Files available over protocols besides HTTP, such as FTP and Gopher, are also referenced by URLs. When you want to access a specific resource, you use the URL name to search for it on the Net.

The URL is made up of three parts. The first part refers to the type of application used, such as Gopher, Telnet, or HTTP (the protocol used by the Web to move information). The identifier is always followed by a colon. The second part always begins with a double slash (//) followed by a string of information necessary for finding and accessing the host where the resource can be found. This is the IP address in the form of the DNS name. On most Web browsers, you can also type in the IP address number if you know it. The third part, usually preceded by a single slash (/), describes the path to the specific file or Web page you want.

The whole URL will look something like this:

scheme://machine.domain/full-path-of-file

As an exercise, let's look at the URL for the book you are now reading on Amazon.com's Web site:

http://www.amazon.com/exec/obidos/ASIN/1890154156/
102-7423541-4812041

The scheme for this URL is "http" for HyperText Transfer Protocol. The Internet address of the machine is www.amazon.com, and the path to the file is "exec/obidos/ASIN/1890154156/ 102-7423541-4812041." This Web site is huge with millions of books and other product listings, so the file name is long. Nonetheless, most URLs will appear very similar to the overall structure of this one.

THE WORLD WIDE WEB

With thousands of computer sites and so much information available on the Internet, how do you find what you want? Several search and navigation techniques have been developed to help users steer their way through this enormous sea of information. These systems present information in a user-friendly, menu-based graphical environment, and they also establish links between themselves and other services so that information can be cross-referenced and made more readily available.

Early systems included Gopher, Archie, and Veronica, but the most popular one today is the World Wide Web (WWW, or the Web). The Web is growing faster than any other protocol on the Internet, and many consider the Web to *be* the Internet. Technically, though, this is not correct.

The Web is responsible for the recent unprecedented growth of the Internet. The "real" Internet is a text-based environment where users navigate by keystrokes and commands—an environment only techies and engineers can love. The introduction of the Web's easy-to-navigate graphical user interface (GUI) was a hit with non-technical users, and the result was explosive growth.

The Web is nothing but millions of Web sites. Individuals, businesses, governments, and other organizations have Web sites. These sites are stored on the hard drive of a server computer that is connected to the Internet. A Web site consists of an organization's entire collection of Web pages, whether a one-page presence or thousands of pages. The so-called home page is simply a virtual page that serves as a doorway to the collection of information at that particular site.

BROWSER PROGRAMS

The best way to access the Web is through a browser program. These programs display the Web as a graphical environment, using icons, links, and pointers to make your navigation painless. Popular browser programs include Netscape Navigator/Communicator (http://www.netwscape.com), and Microsoft Internet Explorer (http://www.microsoft.com). By clicking on underlined text or a highlighted graphic, the browser will take you to a hyperlinked page on the same site or anywhere else on the Internet.

Some value-added online service providers, such as America Online or Prodigy, provide their own browser software as part of their front-end service. The two browsers mentioned in the preceding paragraph also include additional features beyond simple Web browsing. To simplify everything and facilitate administration and troubleshooting, you should standardize your entire network by adopting one browser.

Hypertext Transfer Protocol (HTTP) is the primary language protocol of the Web, and it permits the transfer of Web pages, graphics, and other types of media used on the Web. When your Web browser connects to a Web server, HTTP is the language is uses to request Web pages.

Hypertext Markup Language (HTML) is the internal format used for Web pages. It a set of commands embedded inside the Web pages that control the appearance and layout of the pages. HTML specifies the format of the document, where links go, and how images and sound are presented, and it also allows links to other pages.

Browser Features

	Internet Explorer	Netscape Navigator
Email program	Outlook Express	Netscape Messenger
News group program	Outlook Express	Netscape Collabra
Web page creation	Microsoft FrontPage	Netscaper Composer
Online meetings	NetMeeting	Netscape Conference
News group subscription		Netscape Netcaster
Chat programs	Microsoft Chat	

Table 12-1

THE PRIVATE INTERNET: INTRANETS AND EXTRANETS

The main difference between an intranet and the Internet is that only the computers in your own company are interconnected. Companies discovered early on that the Internet was a valuable means for distributing information within the company as well as between companies. However, to keep outsiders from getting access to sensitive materials, something more private was needed.

An intranet uses the same tools and protocols as the Internet, but it's private. It is really a small, local version of the World Wide Web. An intranet is accessed through an Internet browser, but it does not require a dial-up connection or an ISP. An extranet is simply an intranet that has been expanded to include one or more outside organizations, such as suppliers, vendors, or customers. In all other ways, it is identical to an intranet.

Intranets can distribute just about any type of company information. All the information accessed is stored on the company's own server computers. The two most basic applications of an intranet are publishing and transactions.

Publishing applications post information in the form of pages that can be viewed from any computer that has access to the intranet. This type of intranet application is commonly used for company newsletters, policy manuals, price lists, catalogs, and so on.

Transaction applications typically gather information from various users of the intranet. In some applications, this information is then assembled, packaged, and displayed in a manner that is helpful to everyone else on the intranet. Examples include filing online expense reports, sales statistics, or inventory levels.

There is a key difference between these two types of applications. Publishing applications flow information in one direction: from the intranet to the user. The user requests information and the intranet delivers it. In a transaction application, the information flows in both directions. This means the intranet can request information from the user, and vice versa. Publishing applications are simple to install, but transaction applications are more complicated.

Intranets are fairly simple to set up. Here's what you will need:

A LAN
An intranet doesn't require its own cabling. It can operate on an existing Ethernet LAN that uses twisted-pair copper wiring.

A server computer and software
The server computer must be connected to the intranet, and it requires at least 16 MB of RAM and 2 GB of disk space. The more users you have on the intranet, the more RAM and disk space you will need.

Operating system
The server computer should run either Windows NT server or a UNIX operating system.

Web page creation tools

To create Web pages, you will need programs that you can create yourself (by learning HTML) or by using special software. The process is actually rather simple, and there are dozens of good books available that will show you how.

End users

Each client PC or computer accessing the intranet will need a 486 or better processor, at least 8 MB of RAM, 20 MB or more of free disk space, and a connection to the LAN.

Web browser

A Web browser, such as Netscape Navigator/Communicator or Internet Explorer, must be installed on each client computer.

INTERNET PROTOCOL (IP) TECHNOLOGY

Typically, several levels of interfaces and protocols are required to support an end-user application across a network. Remember the OSI model? Network protocols are layered on top of one another. Each layer provides additional capabilities and uses the layer below. For the following discussion, it may be helpful to refer back to the OSI description in Chapter 6.

The glue that holds the Internet together is not the physical structure, but rather a Network Layer protocol known as Internet Protocol (IP). Unlike most of the older Layer 3 protocols, IP was designed from the beginning with internetworking in mind. The job of the Network Layer is to provide a "best-effort" way to transport packets from source to destination. It disregards whether or not machines are on the same network or whether other networks are in between.

In addition, IP uses the datagram approach, meaning that there is no guarantee the packets will arrive in any particular order or that they will arrive at all. With this approach, errors in transmission simply require the sender to retransmit. An IP datagram consists of a header part and a text part. The header has a 20-byte fixed part and a variable-length optional part.

Communications on the Internet begin at the Transport Layer. Here, data streams are broken up into datagrams for transport through the network. In theory, datagrams may be up to 64 kilobytes in length. In reality, however, they are usually about 1500 bytes and may even be fragmented into smaller units by other network protocols, such as ATM. When all the pieces arrive at their destination, they are reassembled by the Network Layer into the original data stream. This stream is then handed to the Transport Layer, where it is inserted into the receiving input stream.

INTERNET TRANSPORT PROTOCOLS

The Internet mainly uses two Transport Layer protocols: Transmission Control Protocol (TCP) and User Datagram Protocol (UDP). TCP is connection-oriented and provides end-to-end reliable service. UDP provides a connectionless service and is considered unreliable.

As I stated earlier, IP gives no guarantee that datagrams will be delivered properly, so it is up to the transport service to retransmit when necessary. When the order of arriving datagrams is scrambled, TCP reassembles them in their proper sequence. In short, TCP makes up for IP's shortcomings. Where reliability is critical for important data transmissions, it makes sense to use TCP.

UDP is used in many client-server applications that require only one request or response. UDP provides a way to send raw IP datagrams without having to establish a connection. Because reliability isn't an issue, the UDP header format is short and uncomplicated. UDP works fine for applications that require speed more than reliability, such as audio and video transmissions over the Internet.

TCP vs. OSI

TCP/IP and OSI seek to accomplish the same objective of supporting interoperability among heterogeneous networks. However, they were created in different contexts and represent contrasting philosophies.

OSI standards were developed in an international context. There are over one hundred members in the ITU-T, and when standards are up for ratification, each member gets only one vote. Therefore, for any standard to be finalized, it has to be agreeable to a large group of users who represent a diversity of technological theories and approaches.

While the Internet was still a private academic network, TCP/IP was developed to facilitate its operation and management. TCP/IP became increasingly popular because it was easy to implement and inexpensive—how do you beat free? By the time the OSI standards were published, TCP/IP had a proven track record and most of its bugs had been worked out. In contrast, OSI had competing protocol stacks to contend with.

Meanwhile, PCs and local area networks were introduced and adopted. Like TCP/IP, neither were concerned with international

OSI Model Compared to TCP/IP Protocol Stack

OSI Layer	TCP/IP			
Application	File Transfer	Email	Terminal Emulation	Network Management
Presentation	File Transfer Protocol (FTP)	Simple Mail Transfer Protocol (SMTP)	TELNET Protocol	Simple Network Management protocol (SNMP)
Session				
Transport	Transmission Control Protocol (TCP)		User Datagram Protocol (UDP)	
Network	Internet Protocol (IP)			
Data Link	Ethernet, token ring, frame relay, ATM, etc.			
Physical	UTP copper, coax, fiber, T1, SONET, etc.			

Table 12-2

standards. As a result, TCP/IP protocols have gained worldwide acceptance, while the OSI has not. The OSI Model has been relegated to the status of a benchmark model. Table 12-2 illustrates the relative position of the TCP/IP protocol stack in relation to the OSI Model.

ATM vs. IP Protocol

ATM has been touted as the solution for true integration between voice and data services over a single network. Why, then, is IP taking off? And why are some people calling for pure IP networks?

Networks that employ only IP are very simple and easy to manage. It's important to remember, however, that IP and ATM are not mutually exclusive. ATM operates at the Data Link Layer, Layer 2. Thus, it is a lower-level protocol concerned with transmitting and switching whatever type of data may come along, whether voice streams, frame relay, SMDS, or IP packets.

Because IP is a Layer 3 addressing protocol, it can ride over any Layer 2 protocol, such as ATM. The advantages and disadvantages of ATM and IP are contrasted in Table 12-3.

	IP	ATM
Advantages	Widely used	Guaranteed QoS
	Widely understood	
	Embedded	
Disadvantages	QoS (latency)	Equipment costs

Table 12-3

VOICE OVER IP (VoIP)

When digitized voice is transmitted over Internet Protocol (IP) data networks, it bypasses the public switched telephone network (PSTN) for part or all of the transmission path. The Internet is the most common data network used for this purpose, so the term "Internet telephony" is used to refer to this type of transmission.

Three forms of Internet telephony currently exist: (1) computer to computer, (2) computer to telephone, and (3) telephone to telephone. If an analog telephone is utilized at one or both ends of these transmissions, an Internet telephony service provider (ITSP) must act as the gateway between the PSTN and the data network (usually the Internet).

Some organizations are now using IP telephony over their WANs, thus saving money on long-distance and international calls. This is the purest form of IP telephony because the PSTN is totally bypassed. The caller's voice is first digitized using pulse code modulation (PCM), which the telephone instrument performs itself, and then packetized according to Internet Protocol. The telephone plugs directly into the LAN via an RJ-45 jack. As there is never an analog component to the transmission, the voice quality is theoretically superior to that of a PSTN call. Also, once the necessary equipment is bought and installed, these calls are basically free because the voice traffic rides on an existing data network.

If only five percent of the voice traffic in the United States moved to Internet telephony, the traffic on the current Internet backbone would triple. Higher-speed access services, such as ADSL and cable modems, would create bottlenecks. To pay for the increased load on the network and the increased bandwidth needed to handle it, Internet service providers (ISPs) are exploring different pricing models. They are currently considering tiered pricing, higher flat-rate pricing, advertising fees, and transaction fees.

QUALITY OF SERVICE (QoS)

One of the drawbacks of Internet telephony is the quality of service. Though there are many factors affecting the quality of a voice conversation, latency (or delay) is the biggest challenge. Callers are willing to tolerate a slight delay, or even reduced quality, for lower cost—especially over very long distances such as international calls.

The degree of latency experienced depends on the connection speed of each party, the number of hops involved, plus the amount of Internet traffic at the time of the call. The maximum acceptable delay is considered to be 400 milliseconds, but 300 milliseconds can be attained by better-quality systems. Satellite systems experience a 200 millisecond delay that is still noticeable. Delay is also introduced by the PC. Voice quality can become distorted if the software interpolates too many packets or if the compression schemes are too complex. Callers may sound as if they are speaking under water.

The solution to latency appears to center on providing a higher priority for real-time voice packets over the Internet. Using ATM to achieve a more circuit-switched type of packet network is one scheme being considered.

PSTN	Internet
Distance sensitive	Bandwidth sensitive
Time sensitive	Flat fee - unlimited usage
Charged for distance and length of call	Charged for bandwidth (faster connections cost more)

Table 12-4

STANDARDS

Internet Telephony has its own set of standards that apply equally to both voice calls placed over the public Internet and those placed over a private network (using Internet protocols).

H.323 was originally the ITU standard for audio/videoconferencing over LANs. Version 2 of this set of protocols allows IP gateways from different vendors to communicate. Gatekeepers perform intelligent routing, billing, and security functions in IP telephony networks. Version 2 also allows the gateway to forward and transfer IP calls to telephones on the public switched telephone network.

G.723.1 is part of the H.323 standard. It is the code standard for Internet telephony and operates in low-bandwidth environments.

T.120 is the data conferencing standard for real-time, multiuser collaboration. It defines a data conference session, including network interfaces, wire formats, and data transmission facilities.

Real-time Protocol (RTP) and **Real-time Control Protocol (RTCP)** manage both audio and video signal transmission and synchronization. RTCP also provides feedback on network conditions to the Internet telephony software so that compression schemes may be invoked where necessary.

Session Integrated Protocol (SIP) is an alternative to H.323, but it is less complex and also less accepted.

Lightweight Directory Access Protocol (LDAP) is emerging as the standard for Internet telephony directories. It ensures interoperability between the Internet and the public switched telephone network.

INTERNET TELEPHONY ISSUES

The FCC has taken a hands-off approach to the Internet, and it is also maintaining a wait-and-see attitude toward Internet telephony. As the FCC requires traditional public telephone companies to pay universal service fees, there are questions whether Internet telephony providers will be required to do the same. After all, they are providing telephone service.

However, it is difficult to monitor and control Internet calling. How do you differentiate a voice packet from any other packet? Once it's on the Internet, it's all data. In some foreign countries, there are bans or blocks on Internet calling to protect the interests of the government-owned telephone companies. Because it is difficult to detect an incoming Internet call, the bans really affect only calls originating from those countries

It is anticipated that Internet calling will take off in the next three to five years. In order to improve their position in the marketplace, Internet telephony service providers will offer packages that include Internet access, long distance, fax, and voice mail options. Capital expenditures for the expansion and upgrading of the Internet backbone will need to keep pace with the demand for services and applications.

Lower-cost long-distance calling, especially for international calling, will drive the advancement of Internet telephony usage and applications. Because private IP networks have predictable bandwidth, they can provide high QoS for voice over IP. They will continue to utilize their existing IP router networks and simply add voice gateways.

Internet telephony is also driving the convergence of voice and data networks employing multimedia applications. Web-enhanced call centers will one day allow consumers to reach a sales or service agent by clicking on an icon rather than placing a separate voice call for assistance. As consumers become familiar with Internet calling through these types of services, they will likely expand their calling patterns.

SECURITY

As businesses become more and more dependent on computer technology, they must address the increasingly significant problem of data security. Companies storing valuable or sensitive information in their computers must acknowledge how easy it is for competitors or thieves to raid their databases by simply dialing in through a modem. Even firms that don't share their databases are subject to security breaches.

In the mid-1990s, U.S. corporations spent more than $6 billion each year on network security. Even so, over 40 percent of 400 companies surveyed reported security break-ins, and the estimated annual cost of computer crime is as high as $10 billion. The entire U.S. electronic infrastructure, which includes banks, financial markets, transportation systems, power grids, and telecommunications systems, could be vulnerable to attack. In a recent case, Russian hackers broke into Citibank's network and electronically stole $10 million.

The typical computer hacker is 13 to14 years old, and, according to experts, these kids see hacking as a challenge. However, computer crimes are also committed by disgruntled employees or by organizations seeking trade secrets. The FBI reports that more than $24 billion in proprietary information is being taken every year from companies such as General Motors, Intel, and Hughes.

The Economic Espionage Act of 1996 imposes fines of up to $10 million and prison sentences of up to 15 years in computer theft cases that involve espionage, but, thanks to the computer's ability to store information electronically, spies can steal information without physically taking anything. There is no trace of the theft. Business enterprises must still take strong precautions to protect themselves.

NASTY INVADERS

Computer viruses present another critical security challenge. Some perverse hackers take pleasure in creating programs designed to corrupt or destroy the data on computer systems. These viruses are initially hidden in ordinary programs, but they then work their way into the computer system to erase or corrupt data and other programs. For example, computers at National City Corporation, a mortgage lending firm, contracted a virus that shut down 3,000 of the company's servers and more than 8,000 workstations.

Computer viruses behave much like human viruses; they attach themselves invisibly to any computer data or programs that that they come into contact with. Viruses can be spread by diskettes, electronic bulletin boards, or computer networks, including the Internet. Some of these nasties are described below.

Viruses

These programs attach themselves to executable files (files ending in .exe, .bat, .com), and they require some action to be activated. Once activated, the programs multiply exponentially and interrupt the flow of data. A virus can attack immediately, or it may wait for a specific action to trigger it, such as a warm boot or a specific date. Viruses cannot run by themselves. They need another program to infect.

Worms

These programs *can* run without other programs. In addition, they can duplicate themselves in other machines. For example, a worm may be set up to penetrate a database and forward information to unauthorized individuals. Worms are particularly insidious because they are virtually untraceable across the network.

Trojan horse

Trojan horses disguise themselves as something harmless, such as a dialog box requesting a log-on. When the secret password is entered, it is transferred to another location.

There is no way to entirely stop the spread of computer viruses as new ones are being created all the time. However, a number of excellent anti-virus programs exist. These programs search your system for viruses and destroy any that they find. They also prevent new viruses from infecting your computer system. Recommendations for keeping your system virus-free include:

❏ Use anti-virus programs and update them
   frequently
❏ Back up files regularly
❏ Avoid downloading "freebies" from the Internet
❏ Do not open attached email files from strangers
❏ Establish a firewall between your network and
   the Internet

PHYSICAL SECURITY

The most obvious security need is often overlooked—physical security. It is important to control access to the most sensitive components in your computer network, such as the network administration terminals or the computer room. Even without evil intent, an untrained user may accidentally grant unauthorized access or override certain protective configurations.

PASSWORDS

Although passwords are a common form of security, there are a number of ways a password can be compromised. Unauthorized users wanting to access a system can "listen" while an authorized user gains access over a public network. Authorized users may also lend their password to a coworker or inadvertently leave a list of system passwords in a nonsecured location.

Fortunately, there are password technologies and tools to help increase your network security. For example, password aging requires users to create new passwords every so often. Good password policy dictates that passwords must be a minimum number of characters and a mix of letters and numbers (alphanumeric).

Many enterprise computer networks require users to have different passwords to use different parts of the system. As users acquire more passwords, they write them down or create easy-to-remember passwords. A better method is the single sign-on system, where a centralized access control list determines who is authorized to access different areas of the computer. Users need only one password to sign onto the system.

Security server

Smart cards provide a higher level of secure password protection. Unique passwords, based on a challenge/response scheme, are encoded on a small device the size of a credit card. When the password is entered as part of the log-on process, it is validated against a password server, which maintains logs of all access to the system. These systems can be expensive to implement, but they do provide more secure network access, particularly in remote log-on environments.

FIREWALLS

Unwanted traffic can be prevented from traversing an organization's internal network by using a firewall. These barriers allow certain applications, such as email, FTP, and remote log-in, to take place, but bar other types of access to the internal network. Firewalls are also deployed within an internal network for the purpose of controlling access to different servers and networks.

Firewall systems employ an authorization mechanism that assures only specific users or applications can breach the firewall. Also, firewalls typically supply a logging and alerting feature. It tracks designated usage and provides alerts when necessary, based on specified events. These systems also offer address translation, a technique that masks the actual name and address of any machine communicating through the firewall. Unfortunately, all firewall systems have some performance issues. Let's take a look at the three main categories of firewalls.

Network address translation (NAT)

NAT is really a method for providing Internet access to multiple PCs within an enterprise LAN. It does this by dynamically assigning an IP address on a temporary basis. The IP addresses are allocated to computers using Dynamic Host Configuration Protocol (DHCP). The firewall or router remaps each private address to a dynamic address, thus hiding the real address.

Proxy firewalls

Requests from both the internal network and the Internet are taken by a proxy firewall program, which then logs them and sends a duplicate request to the appropriate side. Proxy firewalls also provide opaqueness because all requests emanate from a single IP address.

Packet filtering

To identify alien traffic, these firewalls track the ongoing dialog between computers and compare these connections to a rule-based algorithm. Although these algorithms are very complex and introduce some amount of delay, packet filtering is considered the firewall of choice.

ENCRYPTION

Encryption is the process of coding data, whether through an algorithm or a translation table, into seemingly unintelligible data. It can be used on both stored data and data transmitted though a network. Virtual private networks (VPNs) use encryption to provide secure transmissions over public networks.

Encryption mechanisms use passwords as keys. The longer the password, the more difficult the encryption is to break. The Data

Encryption Standard (DES), endorsed by the National Institute of Standards and Technology (NIST), relies on a 56-bit key length. Some mechanisms have keys that are hundreds of bits long. Private-key encryption uses the same key to encode and decode the data. Public-key encryption uses one key to encode the data and another key to decode the data.

The DES is the most readily available encryption standard, but another emerging encryption mechanism is PGP (pretty good privacy). It allows users to encrypt information stored on their system in addition to sending and receiving encrypted email. PGP also provides tools and utilities for creating, certifying, and managing keys.

SECURE PAYMENT PROTOCOLS

One of the biggest barriers to the acceptance of e-commerce has been payment security. People have heard horror stories involving unscrupulous operators who obtain credit card numbers or bank account information for their own use. Fortunately, different types of secure payment protocols exist that address these concerns.

Internet Keyed Payment Protocol (iKP)

This family of secure payment protocols are used to implement credit card transactions between the customer and the merchant. The iKP protocols have been designed to serve as a starting point for developing standards on secure electronic payment.

Secure Socket Layer (SSL)

SSL is an open protocol designed by Netscape Communications, and it is used to protect credit card transactions over the Internet. SSL also supports authentication and confidentiality for Web browsing sessions over HTTP, FTP, and Telnet protocols.

Secure Electronic Transmission (SET)

This protocol is an emerging standard for credit card transactions conducted over the Internet. VISA and MasterCard are pushing the development of SET. Eventually, it will most likely replace SSL once it achieves wide-scale implementation.

Secure Hypertext Transfer Protocol (S-HTTP)

Secure HTTP is an extension of HTTP. It provides security services for transactions, such as confidentiality, authenticity, and integrity. Original HTTP authorization mechanisms allowed the client to attempt access and be denied before the security mechanism was employed. In contrast, S-HTTP supports end-to-end secure transactions.

Message protection via key management

Message protection may be provided via signature, authentication, encryption, or any combination of these (including no protection). Multiple key management mechanisms are employed, including password-style manually shared secrets, public-key key exchange, and Kerberos ticket distribution.

ELECTRONIC MONEY

To make purchases over the Web, customers can use smart cards, electronic checks, digital IDs, or cybercash. These are just a few of the latest advances that have made shopping online safe for consumers. As a result, Internet commerce is expected to skyrocket over the next several years.

Smart cards are the next generation of debit cards. Money and information, such as your credit card number or frequent flyer account numbers, are loaded onto a small computer chip embedded in the card. When the loaded money is used up, you reload more onto the microchip=s memory.

E-cash refers to money stored on a smart card's embedded micro chip or loaded into your computer for online purchases. By linking to your bank account, e-cash can be downloaded and debited directly from your account balance. When you make a purchase, that amount is deducted from your e-cash balance. E-cash can be loaded onto your smart card or into your computer at any time by using an ATM, a specially equipped telephone, or even the Internet.

Chapter

13

Putting It All Together

. . . .

WE HAVE COVERED A LOT OF GROUND in this book. Though the concept of networks is pretty simple, the actual technologies and implementation are quite complex. Many of the technologies involved are new and not yet well established, let alone proven, and it's likely that newer technologies and protocols will be developed to replace those covered in this book. That's the nature of progress.

Just keep in mind that the primary objective is to move digital bits through the network quickly, efficiently, and reliably. Whichever technology does this best will be the eventual "winner." Underlying technologies, such as pulse code modulation, modulating signals onto carrier frequencies, or time- and wave-division multiplexing, do not change and are common to each of the networking technologies. However, protocols and technologies built on top of these underlying technologies—SONET, ATM, SMDS, Ethernet, TCP/IP, and the like—*will* change and improve.

A DAY IN THE LIFE OF A DATA PACKET

I thought that a good way to summarize what we have learned would be to follow the progress of an individual data packet through a typical network, all the way from the sender to the recipient. We would be able to see how the signal gets modified, packaged, converted, and transmitted as it travels from device to device and from network to network on its journey.

There's actually a simple way to accomplish this through the Internet, so I have decided to trace the actual data path from my editor's office in Newport, Rhode Island to Amazon.com's Web site in Seattle, Washington. We'll start at his office PC, which has a 56 kbps dial-up modem connection, and travel through his ISP and over the Internet to Seattle.

TRACING A ROUTE

A "trace route" is a utility that traces a packet from your computer to an Internet host. It shows how many hops from router to router the packet requires to reach the host and how long each hop takes. If you're visiting a Web site and pages are appearing slowly, you can use a trace route to figure out where the longest delays are occurring.

The original trace route is a UNIX utility, but nearly all platforms have something similar. Windows includes a utility called "tracert." In Windows 95/98, you can run this utility by first selecting Start>Run and then entering "tracert" followed by a space and the domain name of the host. For example: tracert www.amazon.com.

Trace route utilities work by sending packets with low time-to-live (TTL) fields. The TTL value specifies how many hops the packet is allowed before it is returned. When a packet can't reach its destination because the TTL value is too low, the last host returns the packet and identifies itself. By sending a series of packets and incrementing the TTL value with each successive packet (starting with one), a trace route finds out who all the intermediary hosts are.

This is very simple, and you may want to try it yourself. First of all, make sure you're online. In Windows 95/98, go to the Start>Run dialog box and enter the following:

tracert amazon.com

Then click "OK," and you'll see the progress of the data packet as it travels across the country to Seattle. You can also do this from the DOS prompt, typing in the exact same thing. Here's what we got from my editor's PC:

Tracing route to www.amazon.com [208.202.218.15] over a maximum of 30 hops:

1	150 ms	143 ms	147 ms	connect-tnt-1.efortress.com	[205.181.169.1]
2	148 ms	145 ms	143 ms	CONNECT-RTR.efortress.com	[38.150.212.1]
3	144 ms	144 ms	141 ms	s6-0-11.bstnma1-cr1.bbnplanet.net	[4.24.80.137]
4	141 ms	146 ms	128 ms	p5-0.bstnma1-ba1.bbnplanet.net	[4.24.4.209]
5	148 ms	140 ms	135 ms	p7-0.bstnma1-br1.bbnplanet.net	[4.24.7.117]
6	145 ms	145 ms	139 ms	p2-0.bstnma1-br2.bbnplanet.net	[4.24.7.114]
7	165 ms	156 ms	139 ms	p4-0.washdc3-br1.bbnplanet.net	[4.0.1.245]
8	154 ms	153 ma	147 ms	p3-0.washdc3-br2.bbnplanet.net	[4.24.4.146]
9	220 ma	222 ms	215 ms	p3-0.lsanca1-br2.bbnplanet.net	[4.24.5.134]
10	215 ms	216 ms	217 ms	p2-0.lsanca1-br1.bbnplanet.net	[4.24.4.13]
11	239 ms	247 ms	248 ms	p4-0.evrtwa1-ba1.bbnplanet.net	[4.0.6.38]
12	253 ms	237 ms	246 ms	p1-0.evrtwa1-cr1.bbnplanet.net	[4.24.5.102]
13	257 ms	254 ms	255 ms	h2-1-0.internap13.bbnplanet.net	[4.24.125.2]
14	253 ms	254 ms	241 ms	border15s.fe1-1-0-fenet2.sea.pnap.net	[206.253.192.214]

Table 13-1

This is an exact reprint of the results. Each stop in this path is a
"router hop," and the corresponding number at the end of each
line is the IP address of the router. This path does not show the
other devices the data packet goes through, such as CSU/DSUs,
modems, or multiplexers. Because those devices are lower on the
protocol stack, the IP packet doesn't really care about them. Routers, on the other hand, are quite important because they direct
the data packet to its destination. This tracing function can be
performed from your PC to any host computer on the Internet.

A trace route tells us several important things. Here's how to interpret the columns:

Column 1: This number is the hop count (TTL value for
returning the packet). The last number in the column tells
you how many "router hops" your packet took to get where
it's going.

Columns 2, 3, and 4: These numbers measure the round-
trip times (in milliseconds) to that specific router or host.
The three different measurements give you a range of times.
Don't get confused if the round-trip time is shorter for a

router further downstream. It just means that those specific packets went through the network faster than the earlier ones. The three time measurements for the last router or host indicate the total round-trip time to your destination.

Column 5: This column identifies the router or host. In the above example, both the geographic location and the network of the host/router is identified.

Column 6: In this column, the IP address of the host/router is specified.

Because most of the trip was over a network named "bbnplanet," we visited the bbnplanet Web site and discovered that it is now part of GTE's Internet backbone network. We then downloaded the GTE backbone map, which shows all the transmission links and their speeds. Now we have a pretty good idea of the exact path the data took, filling in some of the blanks with educated guesses as necessary.

A DATAGRAM'S ROUTE

To make this exercise a little more meaningful, let's assume Bob (my editor) sent an email message to Amazon.com inquiring about the status of a recent order.

To: customer_service@amazon.com
From: editor@aegisbooks.com
Subject: Order Status

We have not yet received the book we ordered two weeks ago. The title is *How to Make Millions of Dollars Publishing Books About Data Networking.* Please explain the delay.

This message has a total of 217 characters (both letters and punctuation), plus another 38 spaces and carriage returns, for a total of 255 characters, all of which must be encoded. We know that the computer only understands bits, so each key stroke is translated to 8-bit ASCII codes in the upper layers of the communications protocol stack. The total number of bits needed to transmit the text of this message is:

255 characters multiplied by 8 bits per character to equal 2040 bits (255 bytes)

We can use Table 6-2 (in Chapter 6 of this book) to translate the text into ASCII code, the universal language for text communications. Translating the entire message could take us awhile, so, for our exercise, let's translate just one word: **explain**.

e	=	01010011
x	=	00001111
p	=	00000111
l	=	00011011
a	=	01000011
i	=	01001011
n	=	00111011

An email software program, such as Eudora or Microsoft Outlook, then puts the message into the correct SMTP (Simple Mail Transfer Protocol) protocol. Next, the message goes to the TCP/IP stack (already built into the Windows operating system), where it is translated into an IP datagram, or packet. As we mentioned earlier, IP datagrams are variable in length, but they usually average 1500 bytes. As our message is only 255 bytes, the whole thing will fit into one datagram easily. However, we need to add several more bytes for the addressing information included in the datagram's header, so the grand total will be about 271 bytes.

After composing the message, Bob dials up his ISP (efortress) by using a local telephone number over a regular POTS line. Because all local loops lead back to the telephone company central office, this local call is always the first step in any dial-up connection. At this point, the modem in Bob's PC has modulated the digital bits onto the analog carrier by using quadrature amplitude modulation (QAM), one of the modulation techniques discussed in Chapter 7.

The local POTS line, a two-conductor twisted-pair copper wire, now carries the signal to the central office located in Newport. Upon arriving in the Newport central office, the signal passes through the main distribution frame (MDF) and immediately undergoes analog-to-digital conversion.

The existing analog signal, still consisting of the analog carrier signal modulated by QAM, now passes through the pulse code modulation (PCM) process, just like all the other incoming voice signals on adjacent POTS lines. (These incoming signals would be analog voice modulated onto the analog carrier.) PCM doesn't care about what it modulates; it simply samples the modulated analog signal 8000 times per second and assigns an 8-bit value to each sample for a total of 64,000 bps. Remember, the entire backbone of the PSTN is digital, so all incoming calls over POTS lines (voice or data) must be converted to digital signals.

Datagram Route Through the PSTN & Internet

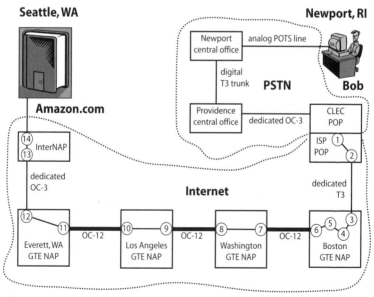

(n) traceroute hop

Figure 13-1

It is important to emphasize that the analog POTS signal is not demodulated by another modem in the CO at the other end of the POTS line. Analog-to-digital conversion takes the already modulated signal "as is" and digitizes it using PCM. While traveling through the PSTN, the Signaling System 7 network routes the bit stream to the destination phone number. The PSTN will never read the address header in the underlying datagram—it uses only telephone numbers to direct digital bits to their destination. Transmission takes place at the fast, lower levels of the OSI Model (Layers 1 and 2), and the only function of the equipment at these levels is to move bits through the telephone company switches and transmission facilities. Whether IP packets or voice, the bits are simply directed to the right telephone number.

As the bit stream passes through the digital switch, it is routed in the direction of the T3 trunk line that connects to Bell Atlantic's central office in Providence, Rhode Island. The reason the bits get directed to Providence is that Bob's ISP has arranged for a foreign exchange (FX) service. This type of service basically treats calls from Newport to Providence as local calls and transparently forwards them from the Newport CO to the Providence CO.

The Providence central office is located across the street from the ISP's POP in the same complex of buildings, which is a common situation. Prior to transmission over the T3 from Newport to Providence, the bit stream passes through a time-division multiplexer. A total of 672 voice or data streams (including Bob's) undergo an electrical-to-optical conversion and are then multiplexed onto one strand of fiber. At any given time, the 672 channels may be broken down into various combinations of voice and data channels. As many as half of the channels may be carrying data traffic, and many of them would be from dial-up Internet users just like Bob.

At the Providence central office, the signal undergoes an optical-to-electrical conversion and is then demultiplexed off the T3 trunk. It is next routed through the CO switch and directed to a dedicated OC-3 link that transfers it across the street to Connect, a CLEC, that terminates calls to this exchange on behalf of Bell

Atlantic. CLECs terminating these types of calls are compensated by Bell Atlantic for the service.

Bob's ISP is located in the same building as the CLEC, and they have a business arrangement where the CLEC delivers all the appropriate PSTN dial-up modem traffic to the ISP. In fact, virtually all of the local ISPs are located in this same building. Our signal now passes through the CLEC's switch and is directed to the ISP's POP.

Upon entering the ISP's POP (right next door to the CLEC in the same building), the signal is demodulated. Demodulation takes place in two stages because there are two layers of modulation that must be reversed. First, the pulse code modulation process (PCM) that originated at the Newport CO is reversed, and the QAM-modulated analog signal is rebuilt. This first step is known as digital-to-analog conversion. Up to this point, the bit stream has been a telephone-company-specified PCM/64 kbps signal that uses telephone numbers to find its way through the PSTN. Having reached its telephone number destination, it is now converted to an Internet signal so that the IP addressing will be understood.

Take a moment to refer to the first line on the trace route. The "tnt" noted on this line can be thought of as a modem bank (205.181.169.2), where all incoming bit streams are demodulated. In fact, it is basically a computer that does the job of 300 individual modems. In order to read the original digital bits sent from Bob's computer, the analog signal must be demodulated and reconstituted. Remember, a modem is always needed at either end of an analog line: one to modulate and the other to demodulate.

It is important to understand that the analog signal was converted to a digital signal between Newport and Providence for the sole purpose of efficient transport through the network. Now the QAM process is reversed, and the original datagram is stripped off the analog carrier. All modulation, both QAM and PCM, is removed, and Bob's datagram, which began its journey via Bob's modem and the POTS line in Newport, is returned to its original form, complete with IP protocol and address in its header.

We are now at a pivotal point in the transmission process. Here we make the transition from telephone company signaling, switching, and transmission to the TCP/IP protocols of the Internet. The building block of the voice telephone network—the 64 kbps channel that carries PCM voice traffic—is no longer needed. We have now entered the packet-switched world. From here on, routers will read the IP address contained in the datagram's header to send it on its way.

Our datagram now passes through the ISP's Cisco 4700 router (38.150.212.1). For local transport within the ISP's POP, the bit stream is enveloped into an Ethernet protocol frame, which is a handy way to move the data within the ISP's facility. This is how it works. The IP datagram is placed into an Ethernet frame, which can accommodate a "payload" ranging from 46 to 1500 bytes. Think of the Ethernet frame as nothing more than a local delivery truck. It doesn't care about what it is carrying—it simply transports its cargo, our datagram, to the appropriate local stop.

Next our datagram is sent through a time-division multiplexer (TDM), where it is multiplexed onto the ISP's dedicated T3 link to GTE's NAP (network access point) in Boston, Massachusetts. GTE contracts with efortress to carry its Providence-originated Internet traffic. At this point, we are no longer concerned with dividing the T3 into multiple 64 kbps, voice-based channels. There is no voice over this T3 link—only TCP/IP Internet traffic. The T3's entire bandwidth of 45 Mbps is dedicated to packet-switched Internet traffic.

Once on the Internet, we use routers rather than telephone company switches. However, we do use other elements of the PSTN. Many Internet nodes share space and facilities with PSTN switching offices. Although the Internet and PSTN signals might not share the same strand of fiber, they may indeed share the same multiple-fiber cable. In fact, the GTE NAPs that make up GTE's Internet backbone network are also GTE switching offices. (See Figure 13-1 above.) The traffic is handled differently within the facility. Internet traffic is directed through routers, while PSTN traffic passes through digital switches.

While in Boston, the datagram passes through four routers on GTE's network (lines 3, 4, 5, and 6 of our trace route). This is essentially a consolidation process within GTE's POP. The datagram arrives from Providence over a T3, and is then passed through a TDM to be demultiplexed. From here, it travels around within the GTE POP via an Ethernet frame in the same manner as it did in the ISP's POP. After leaving the TDM, it hits a "leaf" router, which feeds it to another bigger router that handles traffic from numerous New England locations. Finally, it reaches a "core" router that will direct it to an OC-12 SONET link for transport to Washington, DC. Before making this transfer, however, our datagram must undergo an electrical-to-optical conversion. Then it is multiplexed onto the fiber-optic OC-12 link.

From Boston to Everett, Washington, the datagram travels along GTE's Internet backbone network, made up entirely of OC-12 links. At each NAP, the incoming OC-12 bit stream is sent through an optical-to-electrical conversion and demultiplexed before being sent to the inbound router. This is because routers are not yet capable of routing optical signals. The inbound router reads the IP address in the datagram header and sends it to the right outbound router. Then the bit stream is multiplexed once more, converted from electrical to optical signals onto another OC-12 link, and the whole process is repeated until it reaches Everett.

In Everett, the datagram is transferred to InterNAP's private Seattle NAP. InterNAP, an Internet bandwidth provider, affords big bandwidth pipes to major e-commerce sites, such as Amazon.com. These pipes provide dedicated, high-bandwidth links directly to all the major Internet backbone service providers, thereby avoiding the congestion of public NAPs on the Internet backbone. This is an obvious advantage for a big site like Amazon.com's.

When our datagram arrives at the Amazon.com email server, its journey is completed. Here, Bob's message will be retrieved by someone in the customer service department, and a reply will follow a similar path in reverse. There are dozens of alternative routes, however. The exact route will depend on which backbone network InterNAP chooses to carry the traffic.

PROTOCOL HIERARCHY

When studying networks, understanding how the various protocols relate to one another is often a big source of confusion. Which
protocols can "ride" on top of which? Which protocols are mutually exclusive?

Figure 13-2 is intended to show the relationship among various
common network protocols. Where the protocols are joined together (Ethernet/token ring or frame relay/SMDS) indicates that
they are mutually exclusive and that they basically do the same
things in different ways. You can't use both protocols at the same
time, nor does one ride on top of the other.

Protocol Hierarchy

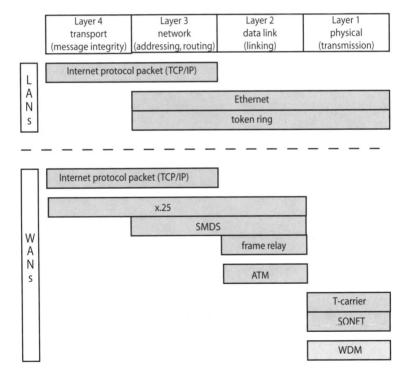

Figure 13-2

When the figure shows a separation between protocols, it means that a data packet can travel from one protocol to the next. For example, a TCP/IP packet can be placed into a frame relay frame, which is next placed into an ATM cell, which is then transmitted in a T-carrier frame from one point to another in the network.

A TCP/IP packet does not have to travel through each protocol. It can skip one or more middle protocols and go directly onto a T-carrier or a SONET frame. This may be the case for a dedicated link that doesn't travel through any public networks. However, protocol conversion must take place in the order shown. In other words, frame relay can ride on top of ATM, but ATM cannot ride over frame relay. The layers must be respected vertically.

LAN protocols are much simpler than WAN protocols because their task is easier—moving data a short distance to a nearby computer or node. For this reason, we find that LAN protocols span multiple layers of the protocol stack. On the other hand, WANs often consist of numerous networks using different protocols, so the layered design is more important. It allows for protocol conversions as the data moves from one network to another.

Older WAN protocols, such as x.25, span all four layers of the protocol stack. They were designed to do everything from end to end with proprietary equipment and standards, but the newer, faster protocols have much narrower roles. These protocols are specialists rather than generalists. As such, they are much better at moving bits quickly and efficiently.

Today's computers possess a great deal of raw processing power, so it makes sense to let these devices perform the software-based functions of the higher layers, such as error correction and message integrity. This trend explains why fast packet technologies, such as frame relay and ATM, span only a single layer of the protocol stack, Layer 2. The role and function of the network have been simplified.

This trend has encouraged multiple vendors to design equipment that will interoperate in a layered network, thus freeing us from depending on proprietary equipment end to end. Nowadays, we can mix and match the devices that make up our networks with the confidence that they will operate with one another.

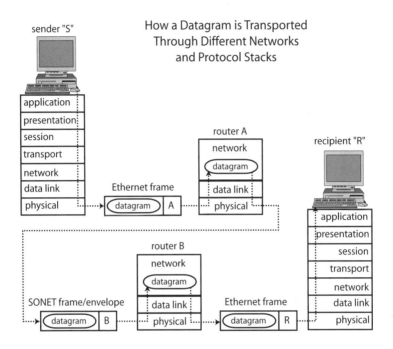

Figure 13-3

FRAMES VS. PACKETS

The terms "frame" and "packet" are often used interchangeably, but we need to know how they differ. Frames are usually associated with lower-level, local transport. Ethernet frames, T-carrier frames, and SONET frames can all be thought of as local or point-to-point delivery vehicles. They're not very smart, but they're quite good at doing a specialized job well. They will carry just about anything, including TCP/IP packets or digital voice. Frames are a Layer 1 element, while packets are a Layer 3 element.

Packets ride in frames. Earlier in this chapter, we traced Bob's datagram, which is another name for a TCP/IP packet, from Newport, Rhode Island to Seattle, Washington. Along the way, it rode in dozens of different frames as it went from place to place. Frames can provide either local delivery (Ethernet LAN) or one point-to-point delivery (Boston to Washington via OC-12), but they don't do anything else.

Figure 13-3 summarizes this concept. An email message travels down through the protocol stack, and, at Layer 3, the datagram is built. It is then encapsulated into an Ethernet frame at Layer 1, where address "A" goes into the frame's address header, and is subsequently delivered to router A. At router A, the datagram is unloaded from the Ethernet frame and moves back up to Layer 3 where the destination address can be read.

Now the router checks its routing tables and knows to send the datagram to router B. Because the link between routers A and B is SONET, the datagram is loaded into a SONET frame/envelope for transport to router B. (Address "B" is now in the frame's address header, and the datagram has been multiplexed and converted from electrical to optical form). At router B, the datagram is unloaded from the SONET frame/envelope (after being demultiplexed and converted back to electrical) and travels up through the router's protocol stack to Layer 3.

Here, router B reads the address, determines that the datagram has reached the right LAN, reloads it into an Ethernet frame for local delivery, and assigns address "R" to the frame's address header. When the datagram reaches the right computer, it travels all the way up through the protocol stack and is converted into a message that the recipient can read. In our earlier datagram example, this process took place many times as the datagram passed through several NAPs and routers. Though the various frames, or transport vehicles, changed many times, the datagram never changed at all.

WHAT'S NEXT?

Many data networking books cover only LANs and LAN protocols. Internet books discuss TCP/IP and associated Internet protocols, and telecommunications books cover the PSTN. However, I decided to cover all these subjects in this book for one important

How Equipment Stacks Up in OSI Layers

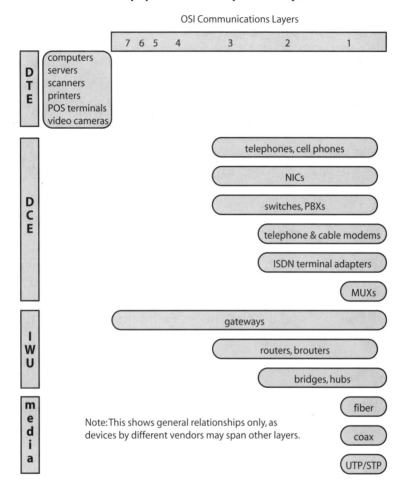

Figure 13-4

reason: these networks are converging, and you cannot limit your understanding to only one.

Writers in the telecommunications field also come from different perspectives. So-called "Netheads" are the data/Internet information technology (IT) folks, and "Bellheads" are the telephone company people. They have different backgrounds and divergent ideas about what an integrated network should look like.

Bellheads are used to controlling the operation of the network and are concerned with quality of service (QoS) issues. After all, they have been delivering voice service with 99.999% ("five nines") reliability for many years. Because the processing power of today's computers is enormous, some Netheads advocate a "stupid" network, where the intelligence resides in these peripheral computers. Bellheads like the idea of ATM all the way to the desktop as a means of delivering QoS for voice and video. Netheads like the simplicity of using IP throughout the network and doing away with all the protocol conversions. Bellheads want to push ATM to the edges of the network, while the Netheads want to push IP from the edges out to the backbone.

Which side is right? I have no idea. Although I admit to being a Bellhead by background, I can see the merits of both arguments. I was recently asked if I would rather purchase 100 shares of Cisco (a Nethead company) or 100 shares of Lucent (a Bellhead company). I would purchase both, because a lot of smart people in each camp are working on solutions to the challenges facing this industry.

One thing I believe completely, however. There will be no decisive winner between Bellhead and Nethead, because the integrated network of the future will feature the best of both approaches.

Index

Other Books From Aegis Publishing Group

Available in bookstores or by calling 800-828-6961
(bulk purchases: 401-849-4200)

Winning Communications Strategies
*How Small Businesses Master Cutting-Edge Technology to Stay Competitive,
Provide Better Service and Make More Money,* by Jeffrey Kagan
$14.95, ISBN: 0-9632790-8-4, paper, 219 pages, 5-1/2" x 8-1/2"

Find out how even the smallest companies are leveraging technology by
using powerful tools–such as fax-on-demand, voice mail, interactive voice
response, intranets, videoconferencing, and computer-telephony
integration–to stay ahead of their largest rivals.

Telecom Made Easy
*Money-Saving, Profit-Building Solutions for Home Businesses, Telecommuters
and Small Organizations,* by June Langhoff
$19.95, ISBN: 1-890154-14-8, paper, 400 pages, 5-1/2" x 8-1/2"

More than 100,000 copies in print! The best basic telecom guide in print.
Find out how to benefit from the latest technology, from basic wiring
options and answering devices to ISDN and going online. Used by
telephone companies for training their own nontechnical sales and customer
service people, and as a premium for their business customers.

Telecom Business Opportunities
*The Entrepreneur's Guide to Making Money in the Telecommunications
Revolution,* by Steve Rosenbush
$24.95, ISBN: 1-890154-04-0, paper, 320 pages, 5-1/2" x 8-1/2"

This first-of-its-kind guide by *USA Today* telecom reporter Steve Rosenbush
shows where the money is to be made in the evolving, deregulated
telecommunications industry. Includes 20 fascinating profiles of the
entrepreneurs who are reshaping this enormous $750 billion global industry.

The Business Traveler's Survival Guide
How to Get Work Done While on the Road, by June Langhoff
$9.95, ISBN: 1-890154-03-2, paper, 128 pages, 5-1/2" x 8-1/2"

This handy guide covers the technology of how to stay connected on the road, including remote working, data security, groupware, teleconferencing, what to pack in the road warrior's tool kit, and international modem connections. Pack it on every business trip for ready reference.

1-800-Courtesy
Connecting With a Winning Telephone Image, by Terry Wildemann
$9.95, ISBN: 1-890154-07-5, paper, 144 pages, 5-1/2" x 8-1/2"

Much more than a book about telephone manners, *1-800-Courtesy* offers a unique and effective method for winning friends and influencing people over the telephone. Learn to identify verbal cues, project a positive attitude, and provide superior service.

The Telecommuter's Advisor
Real World Solutions for Remote Workers, 2nd edition, by June Langhoff
$14.95, ISBN: 1-890154-10-5, paper, 251 pages, 5-1/2" x 8-1/2"

Over 100,000 copies sold. The bible for remote workers who need help putting the latest technology to use in getting their work done while away from the office. Ideal for organization-wide telecommuting training and support programs.

900 KNOW-HOW
How to Succeed With Your Own 900 Number Business, 3rd edition, by Robert Mastin
$19.95, ISBN: 0-9632790-3-3, paper, 350 pages, 5-1/2" x 8-1/2"

Become a toll collector on the information highway. Learn the secrets to success in one of the most exciting new businesses spawned by the exploding information age. Launch a 900 number business and make money by the minute selling information 24 hours a day.

Telecom & Networking Glossary
Understanding Communications Technology, by Aegis Publishing Group
$9.95, ISBN: 1-890154-09-1, paper, 144 pages, 5-1/2" x 8-1/2"

Ever wonder what *asynchronous transfer mode* really means? Or how *ISDN* or
ADSL can help your business? Or what *packet switching* is all about? This
glossary of telecom and data networking terms will demystify the arcane
language of telecommunications so that nontechnical end users will
understand what it all means and how to put it to use to solve everyday
business challenges.

Data Networking Made Easy
The Small Business Guide to Getting Wired for Success, by Karen Patten
$19.95, ISBN: 1-890154-15-6, paper, 344 pages, 5-1/2" x 8-1/2"

The smallest organizations will prosper by taking advantage of the latest
networking technology. Electronic commerce and the Internet are the
future, and even mom-and-pop businesses are using LANs and WANs to
conduct business more efficiently. This book tells you how to get connected
properly.

The Telecommunication Relay Service (TRS) Handbook
Empowering the Hearing and Speech Impaired, by Franklin H. Silverman,
Ph.D.
$9.95, ISBN: 1-890154-08-3, paper, 128 pages, 5-1/2" x 8-1/2"

Telecommunication Relay Services (TRS) allow those who are hearing or
speech impaired to communicate with anyone in the world. They can order
a pizza, make a doctor's appointment, chat with a friend or discuss business
with a client–common interactions the nonimpaired take for granted every
day. This easy-to-read handbook will help both impaired and nonimpaired
people communicate with one another for their mutual benefit.

Phone Company Services
Working Smarter with the Right Telecom Tools, by June Langhoff
$9.95, ISBN: 1-890154-01-6, paper, 102 pages, 5-1/2" x 8-1/2"

From Call Forwarding to Caller ID to 500 Service to ISDN to Centrex, this book describes phone company services in detail, and how to put them to their best use in real-life applications. This book clarifies the features and benefits of the myriad services available from phone companies, a subject that is getting more complex as the line between local and long-distance companies blurs.

The Cell Phone Handbook
Everything You Wanted to Know About Wireless Telephony (But Didn't Know Who or What to Ask), by Penelope Stetz
$14.95, ISBN: 1-890154-12-1, paper, 336 pages, 5-1/2" x 8-1/2"

Cellular phones have gone from a *gee whiz* curiosity to an indispensable communications link for more than 70 million U.S. subscribers. Despite cell phones' enormous popularity, it has been difficult to get reliable, objective information on which to base purchases and maximize performance. Until now. This book gives you a solid understanding of wireless technologies so you can make an informed purchase decision the next time you buy wireless equipment or services.

How to Buy the Best Phone System
Getting Maximum Value Without Spending a Fortune, Sondra Liburd Jordan
$9.95, ISBN: 1-890154-06-7, paper, 136 pages, 5-1/2" x 8-1/2"

Small businesses are faced with a confusing array of choices in purchasing the company's most vitally important business tool: the communications system that interacts with the outside world and gives that all-important first impression to callers. A phone system can either facilitate or impede smooth communications, and the difference can make or break a small business. This straightforward book will help the busy, nontechnical manager make the right choice.

Getting the Most From Your Yellow Pages Advertising
Maximum Profits at Minimum Cost, 2nd edition, by Barry Maher
$19.95, ISBN: 1-890154-05-9, paper, 304 pages, 5-1/2" x 8-1/2"

The perennial bible on the subject. Learn how to get the most mileage out of your advertising dollars, increasing sales as cost-effectively as possible. Learn what kinds of ads pull the best response, and how to avoid common money-wasting mistakes. Invest your advertising dollars as wisely as possible and watch your sales soar.

Digital Convergence
How the Merging of Computers, Communications, and Multimedia Is Transforming Our Lives, by Andy Covell
$14.95, ISBN: 1-890154-16-4, paper, 240 pages, 5-1/2" x 8-1/2"

The tools of human interaction–images, video, sound, and text–can now be defined and represented digitally. This common digital format–where virtually everything is represented by 1s and 0s–allows information to be transmitted, stored, combined, and manipulated in ingenious ways that are still being discovered and perfected. The World Wide Web, videoconferencing, e-mail, groupware, Internet telephony, and digital television are only the earliest examples of new technologies spawned by digital convergence.

Strategic Marketing in Telecommunications
How to Win Customers, Eliminate Churn, and Increase Profits in the Telecom Marketplace, by Maureen Rhemann
$39.95, ISBN: 1-890154-17-2, paper, 320 pages, 5-1/2" x 8-1/2"

The telecommunications industry is undergoing unprecedented upheaval as the world deregulates and monopolies break apart. This book offers telecom professionals up-to-the-minute guidance on how to tackle the tough marketing issues that face them. They will learn what is working and not working for other companies in the industry, and they will find solutions to the unique challenges of the telecom industry.